THE YALE LIBRARY OF MILITARY HISTORY

Donald Kagan and Dennis Showalter, *Series Editors*

THE
BATTLE OF
MARATHON

Peter Krentz

Foreword by Donald Kagan and Dennis Showalter

Yale

UNIVERSITY PRESS

NEW HAVEN AND LONDON

Published with assistance from the Kingsley Trust Association Publication Fund
established by the Scroll and Key Society of Yale College, and from the foundation established in
memory of Calvin Chapin of the Class of 1788, Yale College.

Designed by James J. Johnson
Set in Minion type by Achorn International, Inc.
Printed in the United States of America.

Library of Congress Cataloging-in-Publication Data
Krentz, Peter.
The battle of Marathon / Peter Krentz ; foreword by Donald Kagan and Dennis Showalter.
    p.   cm. — (The Yale library of military history)
Includes bibliographical references and index.
ISBN 978-0-300-12085-1 (alk. paper)
1. Marathon, Battle of, Greece, 490 B.C.   I. Title.
DF225.4.K74 2010
938'.03—dc22   2010007096

A catalogue record for this book is available from the British Library.

This paper meets the requirements of ANSI/NISO Z39.48–1992 (Permanence of Paper).

10 9 8 7 6 5 4 3 2 1

Age shakes Athena's tower, but spares gray Marathon.
The sun, the soil, but not the slave, the same;
Unchanged in all except its foreign lord—
Preserves alike its bounds and boundless fame.
The Battle-field, where Persia's victim horde
First bow'd beneath the brunt of Hellas' sword,
As on the morn to distant Glory dear,
When Marathon became a magic word;
Which utter'd, to the hearer's eye appear
The camp, the host, the fight, the conqueror's career,
The flying Mede, his shaftless broken bow;
The fiery Greek, his red pursuing spear;
Mountains above, Earth's, Ocean's plain below;
Death in the front, Destruction in the rear!

—Lord Byron, *Childe Harold's Pilgrimage*

Contents

Foreword

War has been a subject of intense interest across the ages. Very early literary works like Homer's *Iliad* and the Rigvedic hymns of ancient India talk of war. Few can fail to be stirred by such questions: How and why do wars come about? How and why do they end? Why did the winners win and the losers lose? How do leaders make life-and-death decisions? Why do combatants follow orders that put their lives at risk? How do individuals and societies behave in war, and how are they affected by it? Recent events have raised the study of war from one of intellectual interest to a matter of vital importance to America and the world. Ordinary citizens must understand war in order to choose their leaders wisely, and leaders must understand it if they are to prevent wars where possible and win them when necessary.

This series, therefore, seeks to present the keenest analyses of war in its different aspects, the sharpest evaluations of political and military decision making, and descriptive accounts of military activity that illuminate its human elements. It will do so drawing on the full range of military history from ancient times to the present and in every part of the globe in order to make available to the general public readable and accurate scholarly accounts of this most fascinating and dangerous of human activities.

More than any other battle of classical antiquity, even Thermopylae, Marathon holds iconic status. Sir Edward Creasy describes the future of Western civilization as having rested on its outcome. The Athenians were no less certain of its implications. From Marathon's immediate aftermath they honored their dead and memorialized their victory. Monuments and festivals celebrated liberation not merely from tyranny, but from fear: fear of a universal military empire that bestrode the world like a colossus—until the free men of Greece showed its feet of clay.

The myth endured, revitalized in the nineteenth century by a synergy of classical education, liberal thought, and democratic politics. It survived a revisionist backlash arguing that Marathon settled nothing and encouraged Athenian imperialism. But what is the face of that battle in the light of contemporary developments in archaeology and anthropology? What is Marathon's place in the context of a surge in Achaemenid studies that has fundamentally altered our understanding of the Persian Empire? Above all, where does Marathon stand in the changing matrices structuring approaches to the interaction, military and otherwise, of "the West and the Rest"?

Peter Krentz begins by contextualizing Marathon. He describes the Athenians' deposition of the last of their tyrants, and the new democracy's successful search for a Persian alliance to counter what seemed an overwhelming threat from a Spartan-led coalition of rival city-states. He argues convincingly that the alliance was enough to destabilize the coalition even without direct Persian involvement. And he describes the "flight forward" in which Athens, refusing to accept the submission required of a Persian connection, instead supported a rebellion of the Greek city-states of Asia Minor against their Persian overlords.

After six years of seesaw fighting, the revolt was defeated and the rebels tamed. Persia looked across the Hellespont. Great King Darius, ruler of 70 million people, dispatched an expedition. Its commander was charged with bringing Athens to submission. The price of failure was his head.

The rest is history—or is it? Krentz effectively establishes the site of the battle despite significant changes to the geography of the coastal plain. He convincingly reconstructs the Greeks' decision to fight. And he successfully restores in general terms the often-challenged credibility of the account Herodotus gave. His major contribution, however, is a consequence of addressing one of Marathon's major anomalies: the eight-stadia run.

Eight stadia equals about nine-tenths of a mile. Herodotus insists that the Athenians charged that distance at a run. Military historians since Hans Delbrück have dismissed this as hyperbole: a physical impossibility for fully equipped men without collapsing from exhaustion or falling into disorder. Krentz begins by establishing the maneuver's necessity. The Athenians, he shows, had to reach the Persian infantry before their cavalry, a devastatingly effective force built around horse archers, could deploy in the plain and shoot the vaunted hoplite phalanx to pieces. At close quarters the Greeks could fight on equal terms. And the charge succeeded because the hoplite phalanx as generally understood did not exist.

Contemporary scholars like Victor Davis Hanson hold that a Greek hoplite carried about 70 pounds of armor and weapons: almost half his body weight. They deployed in close formation, with about three feet of space per man, advanced to contact, and pushed forward like "a rugby scrum on steroids." Light-armed men, archers and slingers, played peripheral roles compared with the panoplied citizens.

Krentz makes a contradictory argument. He points out that Greeks were tough: physically active, used to hard work and systematic exercise. He then carefully reconstructs the weight carried by a hoplite, reducing it to a maximum of about fifty pounds. He goes further, arguing that not every hoplite was fully equipped, that from choice or necessity many carried no more than helmet, shield, and spear. The phalanx in the era of Marathon might have included archers and slingers, who sought targets of opportunity under cover of the hoplites. It might even have included dismounted horsemen.

The broken nature of Greek terrain meant that any charge at any pace was likely to scatter or bunch—more like the cavalry charges in an old Western than the clockwork movements of eighteenth-century regiments. The Greeks attacked not in close order, but together. The "push" (*othismos*) was not literal, but a description of hand-to-hand combat resulting in step-by-step retreat.

That is what happened at Marathon. According to Krentz's reconstruction, the Athenians broke camp, fell into line of battle, and marched forward until they were less than a mile from the Persians, who believed they had plenty of time. No Greek army had ever charged a Persian one, and the Athenians seemed to have neither cavalry nor archers in support. Then Miltiades shouted, "Rush them!" The rush, actually more of a jog, took ten or twelve minutes to reach the Persian line through a hail of arrows. In heavy close-quarters fighting the Persians broke through the Athenian center, but the Greeks prevailed on the flanks, then closed in the center as temporarily victorious Persians tried to escape the suddenly formed pocket. As they fought toward the ships, the rest of the now-defeated army had time to board. Approximately 6,400 Persians fell in the battle. The Athenian dead, carefully numbered, totaled 192.

Krentz's case for his scenario and its surrounding context is sufficiently plausible that the hoplite origins of the "Western way of war" will benefit from reexamination. What this work validates is a wider truth: that Marathon challenged and broke the aura of invincibility that enveloped the Persian army and the Persian Empire. To build on Krentz's words, the confidence born on that day in 490 BC made Salamis conceivable, made Plataea possible, and foreshadowed the victories of Alexander the Great.

Donald Kagan and Dennis Showalter

Illustrations

Acknowledgments

I first visited Marathon in 1975, while participating in an American School of Classical Studies at Athens summer session led by Steve Tracy. Like many other visitors, I remember the thrill of standing on the Athenian burial mound. It is only one of many good memories of that summer, which began a long affiliation with the American School. I have always found it a welcoming home away from home. I did much of the groundwork for this book in 2000–2001, when I was a visiting professor at the American School and taught a seminar on ancient Greek warfare.

I am grateful to Donald Kagan for inviting me to contribute to Yale University Press's series in military history. Richard Dunn generously shared with me his work on the geological history of the Marathon plain, which he has presented at a conference and hopes to publish soon. He patiently answered many questions and allowed me to use his sketch map of the plain, on which Figure 30 is based. The University of Chicago Press granted me permission to quote from Richmond Lattimore's translations of Homer, *The Iliad* (copyright 1951 by the University of Chicago) and *Greek Lyrics* (copyright 1949, 1955, and 1960 by Richmond Lattimore). Carcanet Press Limited gave me permission to quote Robert Graves' "Persian Version" from *The Complete Poems in One Volume,* edited by Beryl Graves and Dunstan Ward (Manchester, 2000). I have used Andrea L. Purvis' translation of Herodotus in *The Landmark Herodotus: The*

Histories, edited by Robert B. Strassler (New York: Pantheon, 2007). I have followed this edition's spelling of names.

I would also like to thank Joe Gutekanst, master of the interlibrary loan universe, for getting me more books than I can recall; Malcolm Wagstaff, who is writing a biography of Colonel William Leake, for answering several Leake-related questions; Jim Wright, for finding photographs in the Bryn Mawr archives; Margaret Miller and Lâtife Summerer for generously sharing drawings they had commissioned; and Kelly Sandefer of Beehive Mapping for preparing the maps.

An anonymous reader for Yale University Press, my good friend Charles Reed, a lot of Krentzes—my mother Marion, my father Edgar, my brother Christopher, my wife Jeri, and my son Tyler—and Phillip King, my editor at the press, read various drafts of the manuscript and offered many good suggestions from their different perspectives.

Finally, I want to express my gratitude to Davidson College for a sabbatical leave and to the National Endowment for the Humanities for a fellowship that gave me the time to write this book.

Chronology

All three-figure dates are BC unless otherwise indicated. Many dates go back to a list of Athenian officials whose annual terms began in the summer, resulting in dates such as 511/10, meaning the second half of 511 and the first half of 510. See Appendix B for the date of the battle.

522	Darius (522–486) becomes king of the Persian Empire
c. 513	Darius invades Scythia
510	Spartans expel Hippias from Athens
508/7	Kleisthenes institutes democracy in Athens
507/6	Athenians give earth and water to Persians
506	Spartan invasion of Attica aborts Athenians defeat Thebans and Chalcidians
505?	Thebes allies with Aegina "Undeclared war" begins between Athens and Aegina
499	Persians besiege Naxos Ionian Revolt begins
498?	Greeks attack and burn Sardis
495	Battle of Lade
494	Persians take Miletus and recapture Caria
493/2	Artaphrenes' settlement in Ionia Darius' heralds visit Greece
492	Mardonios' settlement in Ionia and campaign in Europe

492/1	Darius sends ultimatum to Thasos and orders shipbuilding	
491/0	Datis and Artaphrenes appointed to command	
490	March	Persian army and fleet gather in the Aleian Plain
	April	Persians advance to Rhodes, Samos, Icaria
	May	Persians take Naxos, Paros, Delos
	June	Persians take other Aegean islands
	July	Persians take Karystos and Eretria
	August/	
	September	Battle of Marathon
480		Battles of Thermopylae, Artemision, and Salamis
479		Battles of Plataea and Mycale

Introduction

Miltiades squinted as he walked directly toward the Persians. The morning sun was rising behind them as they deployed. Miltiades had served with the Persians in the past and knew what to expect: row upon row of infantry archers who specialized in raining arrows down on their enemies, and mounted archers, riding sturdy Iranian horses, who threatened to disrupt the Athenian charge. If the Greeks broke and ran for their lives, the Persian cavalry would ride them down and shoot them at little risk to themselves. After all, every Persian learned to ride, to shoot a bow, and to tell the truth. The mounted archers knew their business.

Miltiades walked among his relatives and neighbors. As one of ten generals elected by the Athenian assembly, he led one of ten Athenian tribes. Each one comprised fathers and sons, brothers and cousins, neighbors and drinking buddies. They did not march in step wearing government-issue uniforms. Rather, each man supplied his own battle rattle: one or two spears, a short sword, a bronze helmet (perhaps one inherited from his grandfather), a round wooden shield, a corslet made of linen and leather to protect his chest, shin guards, and sandals. Some had all of these items; others were more lightly equipped. They walked with determination, most of them, and not a little trepidation.

After a week of watching the Persians ravaging and burning the fertile plain of Marathon, Miltiades had decided that he would fight today.

It was a bold decision. Aside from a contingent from Plataea, the Athenians had no allies present. Though the Spartans had promised to help, they had not arrived. The Athenians had no archers or horsemen capable of matching the Persians, who had chosen to land at Marathon partly because it was good ground for horses.

Miltiades had a plan. When he saw what he was looking for, he raised his arm, pointed at the Persians, and shouted *Hormate kat' auton* (Rush at them). The trumpet blew and the Greeks started to run. Before reaching the Persians they had to cover eight lengths of a Greek stadium, a total of 0.9 miles.[1]

The Persians heard them advancing like Homer's Trojans, who

came on with clamour and shouting, like wildfowl,
as when the clamour of cranes goes high to the heavens,
when the cranes escape the winter time and the rains unceasing
and clamorously wing their way to the streaming Ocean,
bringing to the Pygmaian men bloodshed and destruction.

Astonished to see the Greeks charging without archers or cavalry, the Persians thought they were crazy.[2]

The Significance of the Battle

The outcome of that charge at Marathon on a late summer day in 490 shocked most everyone who heard about it. Over the previous two generations, through one brutal conquest after another, the dynamic Achaemenid dynasty had built the first world empire, extending from Ionia in the west to India in the east (Figure 1). The Great King Darius ruled some 70 million people. When he put Datis the Mede in command of a new expedition to add the Aegean islands to his empire, he told the general to bring the Athenians back in chains, if he wanted to keep his head.

I doubt that Datis worried much. No reason to. After suppressing the Asian Greeks' revolt in the 490s, the Persians controlled the sea. No Greek ships would oppose their fleet of 300 or more triremes, the biggest and best warships of the day, so expensive that the Athenians had only a handful of them. No Greek force had ever defeated a Persian land army.

Though Athens was large by Greek standards, it had only 30,000 adult male citizens. Given the competitive, quarrelsome nature of the fiercely independent Greek city-states, Athens was not likely to have many allies.

Moreover, Datis had right on his side. The Athenians had reneged on their initial submission to Darius, sent ships to support the Greek revolt, and participated in a surprise attack on Sardis, the wealthy capital of the Persian province in Asia Minor. They had burned the temple of Kybele, god the mother, whose indigenous ancient cult the Persians had not disturbed. The gods would surely be with the Persians, who respected the religious traditions of all their loyal subjects.

Datis had achieved all of his objectives but one. He had taken the Cycladic islands with little difficulty. He faced resistance at Eretria, the largest city on the island of Euboea, for barely a week. He had every expectation that he would take Athens too. The former tyrant (dictator) of Athens, Hippias, accompanied him and assured him that his friends would rally to the Persians' side. The chains were ready.

Then came Marathon. In one of the great upsets in world history, the Athenians killed 6,400 Persians while losing only 192 of their own men. They even managed to board and capture seven Persian ships before they could escape to deep water. Datis sailed back to Asia with empty chains.

Almost immediately, the Athenians heroized their dead and monumentalized their victory. The fallen were cremated on the battlefield. Over their ashes the Athenians erected the burial mound known today as the Soros (heap). Gravestones listed the warriors who died; duplicate gravestones were erected in the public cemetery just outside the Dipylon Gate at Athens. An Ionic column went up on the Acropolis with an inscription honoring Kallimachos, the titular commander of the army who died in the battle. Another Ionic column marked the battle's turning point. On the plain, the Athenians erected a separate monument to Miltiades, the general credited with the victory. Appropriate offerings went to Olympia and Delphi, the major panhellenic sanctuaries of Zeus and Apollo, where such dedications would impress the visitors who came to watch the Olympic games or to consult the Delphic oracle. New sanctuaries were created for Pan and Artemis in Athens, honoring them for their help in the battle.

1. Map of the Persian Empire under Darius

Aral
Sea

Jaxartes R.

Sacae

Oxus R.

Baktrians

HINDU KUSH

Indus R.

E M P I R E

INDIA

atana

ZAGROS MTNS.

sians

Pasargadae

Persepolis

PERSIA

Persian Gulf

Arabian
Sea

Festivals kept alive what scholars call "collective memory." The Athenians competed in new or enlarged athletic games at the sanctuary of Herakles at Marathon, where the Athenians camped before the battle. They held an annual torch race in honor of the god Pan, who had appeared to the messenger Philippides and offered his help (Figure 2). Every year they sacrificed 500 goats to Artemis to repay a vow made the morning of the battle. Every year young Athenian men visited the Soros, where they "honored with wreaths and funerary sacrifices those killed in the fight for freedom." Artists commemorated the battle for decades afterward. Before he died in 489, Miltiades erected a statue of Pan in his new sanctuary. Thirty years later, Myron painted the battle on a wall of the Stoa Poikile (Painted Stoa) on the north side of the Athenian Agora, while the sculptor Pheidias made a colossal bronze statue of Athena Promachos (Front-line fighter or Defender) that stood on the Acropolis. Sixty years after the battle, Agorakritos made a statue of Nemesis from the block of Parian marble that the Persians had intended for a monument celebrating their anticipated conquest.[3]

"The monuments, the trophies, the votive offerings, the processions, the pictures and sculptures, the songs, and the panegyric harangues that celebrated the victory," wrote Bishop Connop Thirlwall in 1845, "not only proved, but, in part, made its importance." Within a generation of the battle, Marathon had become a powerful myth, the justification for Athens' claim to primacy among the Greeks. Though their public prayers asked the gods to bless the Athenians and the Plataeans, at other times the Athenians tended to forget the Plataeans who had fought by their side at Marathon, much as the Spartans failed to remember the Thespians who died with the 300 at the battle of Thermopylae in 480. At Marathon, the Athenians said, they had stood alone against the barbarians and won. The philosopher Plato maintained that Marathon began "the salvation of Greece" that the battle of Plataea completed in 479. Only those two battles, he felt, made the Greeks better. The naval battles of Artemision and Salamis, which most Greeks and barbarians credited with saving Greece, made the people worse. A tourist who came through Athens more than 600 years after the battle wrote that the Athenians were prouder of Marathon than of any other victory. As evidence, he cited the epitaph that

2. Interior of an Athenian black-figure cup, c. 490, showing a torch race in honor of Pan (Martin von Wagner Museum, Würzburg, XXXX44630; courtesy Martin von Wagner Museum der Universität Würzburg [Photo: K. Öhrlein])

Aeschylus (c. 525–456/5 BC) composed for himself. The great tragic playwright did not mention his distinguished literary career. He wrote only these lines about what he regarded as the greatest day of his life:

> The dead Aeschylus, son of Euphorion, the Athenian
> this tomb covers in wheat-bearing Gela;
> the grove of Marathon can attest his famed valor,
> and the long-haired Mede who knew it well.[4]

In modern times, classically trained Europeans found Marathon equally meaningful, especially once they visited the evocative site (Figure 3). To Samuel Johnson (1709–1784), the literary critic known for

3. Detail of a sketch of the Marathon plain drawn by Giovanni Battista Lusieri in
1801 (Published in the quarto edition of Edward D. Clarke, *Travels in Various
Countries of Europe, Asia, and Africa* [London: Cadell and Davies, 1810], opposite
p. 14 in volume 4)

his snappy one-liners, Marathon was *the* example of a place renowned for
bravery. "Far from me and from my friends," he wrote, "be such frigid
philosophy as may conduct us indifferent and unmoved over any ground
which has been dignified by wisdom, bravery, or virtue. That man is little
to be envied, whose patriotism would not gain force upon the plain of
Marathon." Born just four years after Johnson died, the sixth baron Byron visited Marathon during the Ottoman occupation and found himself
thinking of freedom:

> The mountains look on Marathon—
> And Marathon looks on the sea;
> And musing there an hour alone,
> I dream'd that Greece might still be free.
> For standing on the Persians' grave,
> I could not deem myself a slave.

Byron actually joined the War of Independence in Greece, where he
caught a fever and died in 1824, before seeing his dream come true.[5]

The early years of the nineteenth century saw many travelers in
Greece: Rev. Edward D. Clarke, Colonel William Leake, the artist Edward

Dodwell, Sir William Gell, to mention only some who wrote books about their trips, including excursions to Marathon. Their reports fired the imaginations of British children. At age 12 or 13 Elizabeth Barrett, future wife of Robert Browning, wrote a 1,462-line poem called "The Battle of Marathon" that her proud papa had published in 1820 (50 copies). She later described it as "simply Pope's Homer done over again, or rather undone." But the fact that a young girl could conceive of writing such a poem reveals the penetrating power of the Marathon myth.[6]

In nineteenth-century England, the notes sounded by the Greek historian Herodotus (c. 484–c. 425) rang loud and clear: Athens' military success followed her liberation from tyranny; the Athenians at Marathon were the first Greeks to look at the Persians without paralyzing fear. British writers revered Marathon as a critical turning point in human history. "There is no battle in ancient or modern times more deserving of applause for its military conduct," proclaimed historian George Finlay in 1839, "none more worthy of admiration for its immediate results on society, or more beneficial in its permanent influence on the fate of mankind." John Stuart Mill asserted that "the Battle of Marathon, even as an event in English history, is more important than the Battle of Hastings. If the issue of that day had been different, the Britons and the Saxons might still have been wandering in the woods." For florid prose, few could match Edward Bulwer-Lytton, the leading historical novelist of his day:

> And still, throughout the civilized world (civilized how much by the arts and lore of Athens!), men of every clime, of every political persuasion, feel as Greeks at the name of Marathon. Later fields have presented the spectacle of an equal valour, and almost the same disparities of slaughter; but never, in the annals of earth, were united so closely in our applause, admiration for the heroism of the victors, and sympathy for the holiness of their cause. It was the first great victory of OPINION! And its fruits were reaped, not by Athens only, but by all Greece then, as by all time thereafter, in a mighty and imperishable harvest,—the invisible not less than the actual force of despotism was broken. Nor was it only that the dread which had hung upon the Median name was dispelled—not that free states were taught their pre-eminence over the unwieldy empires which the Persian conquerors had destroyed,—a greater lesson was taught to Greece, when she discovered that the monarch of Asia could

not force upon a petty state the fashion of its government, or the selection of its rulers. The defeat of Hippias was of no less value than that of Darius; and the same blow which struck down the foreign invader smote also the hopes of domestic tyrants.

In 1851 Sir Edward Shepherd Creasy solidified Marathon's position as a battle of the first importance by leading off with it in his *15 Decisive Battles of the World,* on the grounds that "the whole future progress of human civilization" rested on it.[7]

Perhaps nothing has shaped the modern impression of Marathon more than Robert Browning's "Pheidippides," published in 1879. The poem reaches this climax:

> So, when Persia was dust, all cried, "To Acropolis!
> Run, Pheidippides, one race more! the meed is thy due!
> 'Athens is saved, thank Pan,' go shout!" He flung down his shield
> Ran like fire once more: and the space 'twixt the fennel-field
> And Athens was stubble again, a field which a fire runs through,
> Till in he broke: "Rejoice, we conquer!" Like wine through clay,
> Joy in his blood bursting his heart, he died—the bliss!

For Browning, Pheidippides died at his peak, with cheers ringing in his ears, knowing he had saved the city he fought to save. The ancient Athenian sage Solon would have understood.[8]

The twentieth century saw a backlash against such exaltation. After the Great War of 1914–1918, what the historian G. B. Grundy had earlier titled *The Great Persian War* did not seem so great after all, nor did European civilization, given the horrific loss of life it had inflicted on itself. If Marathon was "the birth-cry of Europe," as Major General J. F. C. Fuller called it, what sort of child did it produce? Universal historian Arnold J. Toynbee pointed out that the Greeks failed to learn the potential of a united people from the Persian Empire. The Athenian victory at Marathon launched an era of great energy in Athens, but that energy frightened other Greeks and prevented them from uniting. Except for the brief moment in 480–479 when 31—only 31—city-states allied against Xerxes' invasion, "chronic fratricidal warfare" characterized the history of the Greek people, who were so brilliant in art, drama, history, and philosophy.[9]

Revisionists also emphasize that Marathon settled nothing. Darius' son Xerxes invaded ten years later with 5,283,220 men, according to Herodotus' calculations. Historians of the battles in 480–479 suggest that they mattered more than Marathon. Paul Cartledge dubs the attempt to stop Xerxes at Thermopylae—a Greek defeat that slowed the Persian advance for less than a week—"the battle that changed the world." Barry S. Strauss proclaims the battle of Salamis "the naval encounter that saved Greece—and western civilization." Ultimately Greece's fate rested on the battle of Plataea, the largest land battle of the Persian Wars.[10]

The poet Robert Graves even questioned whether Marathon was much of a win. Here's his poem "The Persian Version," a clever riff on Herodotus' statement that Persians were taught to ride, to shoot a bow, and to tell the truth:

> Truth-loving Persians do not dwell upon
> The trivial skirmish fought near Marathon.
> As for the Greek theatrical tradition
> Which represents that summer's expedition
> Not as a mere reconnaissance in force
> By three brigades of foot and one of horse
> (Their left flank covered by some obsolete
> Light craft detached from the main Persian fleet)
> But as a grandiose, ill-starred attempt
> To conquer Greece—they treat it with contempt;
> And only incidentally refute
> Major Greek claims, by stressing what repute
> The Persian monarch and the Persian nation
> Won by this salutary demonstration:
> Despite a strong defence and adverse weather
> All arms combined magnificently together.

For military historians, Marathon retains its fascination. Although it does not make every list of decisive battles, it fares pretty well. It is included in Richard A. Gabriel and Donald W. Boose, Jr., *Great Battles of Antiquity* (1994), and Paul K. Davis, *100 Decisive Battles* (1999). Michael Lee Lanning ranked it number 28 in *The Battle 100* (2003), and William Weir ranked it number 1 in *50 Battles that Changed the World* (2001), on the grounds that democracy depended on it.

Marathon is the first battle in Western military history that we can even hope to reconstruct, thanks to the wonderfully engaging narrative of Herodotus, whom the Roman orator Cicero called the "Father of History." Born on the east coast of the Aegean Sea, Herodotus wrote the earliest extant account of the battle. It is not contemporary, but Herodotus did visit Athens, where he gave public readings of his work. No doubt he talked to many veterans. It's unlikely that he talked to any of the generals, but he could have spoken with their sons. Still, the fourth-century historian Theopompos of Chios complained that "the battle of Marathon did not happen as everyone celebrates it, nor did any of the other things that the city of the Athenians brags about and uses to deceive the Greeks." Can we trust Herodotus? What methodology is appropriate, given the nature of the evidence?[11]

On the Possibility of Reconstructing Marathon

I tell my students who are interested in Marathon to read Herodotus and then find a paper by Noah Whatley, originally read in Oxford in 1920 but not published until 1964. (I would love to know what the reaction to the original presentation was, for a number of the scholars whom Whatley skewered were sitting in the audience.) In "On the Possibility of Reconstructing Marathon and Other Ancient Battles," Whatley identified five "Aids," as he termed them, for interpreting ancient writers such as Herodotus.

First, the study of geography and topography. Whatley described this study as essential, but providing better negative results than positive ones. Unless we know precisely the formations the Greeks and Persians adopted, he says, "it is hopeless to try and trace on the ground the exact movements of troops." Nevertheless, understanding of the geography and the topography of the Marathon plain has progressed (chapter 6. It is critical for reconstructing what happened, even if the reconstruction cannot be exact.[12]

Second, the use of deductions from modern works on strategy and analogies from modern battles. Such deductions and analogies can widen the historian's sense of the possibilities, but Whatley rightly stressed that ancient battle was altogether simpler than modern warfare. Ancient Greek officers did not attend a West Point or a War College. Outside Sparta ancient Greek warriors had little, if any, formal training before they departed on a campaign. I generally avoid citing modern parallels or theoretical discussions.

Third, *Sachkritik,* or the attempt to reconstruct in accordance with *die Realität der Dinge* (the reality of things), the German military historian Hans Delbrück's mantra. This principle seems to me unobjectionable as long as we keep in mind that our understanding of the reality of ancient things is not fixed. A good case in point for Marathon is the feasibility of the running charge. Delbrück's vigorous denial that it could be done—and the scientific tests Walter Donlan and James Thompson conducted to prove him right—rested on faulty assumptions about the weight Greek hoplites carried (chapters 2 and 7).

Fourth, the study of the armies, their strategy and tactics, their equipment and how they used it. Whatley suggested that this Aid had been underutilized. On the Persian side, that is unfortunately still true. Despite the surge in Achaemenid studies in the past several decades, a scholarly monograph on the Persian military, making full use of the archaeological evidence, has yet to appear. Greek warfare, on the other hand, has been the subject of vigorous debate in the past three decades. Scholars disagree about how Greeks fought in the Archaic period (chapter 2). I first conceived this book as a way of increasing awareness of this debate.

Whatley's last Aid, which he called the Sherlock Holmes method, combines the other Aids with selected statements from later authors in order to improve on Herodotus. "The modern method," he wrote, "is so often to accept as sound any element in the later stuff which suits a particular theory . . . and to reject the rest as valueless." This one is not really an Aid in the same sense the other four are. Instead, it cuts to the heart of a fundamental methodological issue. What is the proper use of the literary sources themselves? Can the later sources supplement or even correct Herodotus?[13]

The use of this method stems from an overall dissatisfaction with Herodotus' account. I will not waste time on the hypercritics who think Herodotus is the Father of Lies rather than the Father of History. Most historians today take him at his word that he wrote down what he heard people say, though those people were more likely ordinary people he met on his travels than truly learned individuals.

But even critics who take a more charitable attitude toward Herodotus find fault with his account of Marathon. A. W. Gomme, best known for his commentary on Thucydides, began his article on the battle by stating flatly, "Everyone knows that Herodotus' narrative of Marathon will not do." Herodotus' great commentator, R. W. Macan, found six major cruces or problems in Herodotus' account:

- The major role of the supernatural: two visions (Philippides, Epizelos), two dreams (Hippias, Datis), and one divine coincidence (the Athenians twice camping at a sanctuary of Herakles).
- The exaggerated claim that the Athenians were the first Greeks to charge the enemy at a run (for almost a mile, no less) and to endure the sight of Median dress and the men wearing it (that is, Persian soldiers); previously even the name of the Medes caused fear.
- The anachronistic portrayal of the *polemarchos* (war leader) Kallimachos, in saying that he was chosen by a lottery and that he voted with the generals, rather than being the supreme commander.
- The inconsequential role of Miltiades and therefore an inadequate explanation of why the battle occurred when and where it did.
- The absence of the Persian cavalry, despite the fact that Herodotus says the Persians landed at Marathon because it was good cavalry country.
- The unsatisfactory tale of the shield signal (something Herodotus himself admits).[14]

I propose to apply two principles when interpreting Herodotus. First, adapting Aristarchos of Samothrace, the Hellenistic textual critic of Homeric poetry: *Herodoton ex Herodotou saphenizein*, "clarify Herodotus by way of Herodotus." So, for example, when considering whether to believe Herodotus' statement that Datis had a fleet of 600 ships, we should look at the numbers Herodotus gives for other Persian fleets. Herodotus should not be forced into a precision he did not intend.

Second, adapting Martin Luther, whose explanation of the eighth commandment ends with "put the best construction on everything," we ought to put the best construction on what Herodotus says. For instance, instead of objecting to Herodotus' two-fold explanation for the Persian landing at Marathon on the grounds that neither half is true—Marathon is neither the closest landing point in Attica to Eretria nor the most suitable land in Attica for cavalry—we should take the point that Marathon best combines these two qualities. There is no closer landing point that is any good for cavalry, and no better cavalry country anywhere near Eretria.

If we follow these two principles, the six major difficulties identified by Macan turn out not to be such big hurdles after all. I will take up each of them in its place. Here I will only note that in comparison to later writers, Herodotus is restrained. The stories of Epizelos and Kynegeiros, for example, grew in the telling (see chapter 7), as did the size of the Persian expedition (chapter 4). Herodotus says nothing about the best-known Marathon tale, the messenger Philippides' run to Athens and announcement of the victory before he died (chapter 8).

It is most certainly true that Herodotus did not write the sort of battle narrative that a modern military historian would. He does not give the exact date, the numbers of combatants, or the names of all the commanders. He does not explain the topography of the plain, or where on it the fighting took place. He does not say why the Athenians fought when they did, or why they ran for almost a mile.

We would like to know all these things. To what extent are we justified in using the later sources? And I do mean later, for aside from ten lines in Aristophanes' comedy *Wasps* (produced in 422) and bits from the fourth-century writers Ktesias, Plato, and Xenophon, the other sources all come from the time of the Roman emperor Augustus or later, 500 or more years after the battle. (See the list of sources in Appendix A.)

One of these late sources, Pausanias (second century AD), deserves particular attention because he describes both the topography and the great painting of the battle in the Stoa Poikile, an original work of the 460s. This painting would be our earliest source for the battle, had it survived. (A nineteenth-century reconstruction of it appears in Figure 4.) There is no reason to doubt that Pausanias saw what he says he saw, though the painting may have deteriorated so that, for instance, the color of the sea turned into a color Pausanias interpreted as a marsh. Or it may have been restored and "improved" before Pausanias saw it.

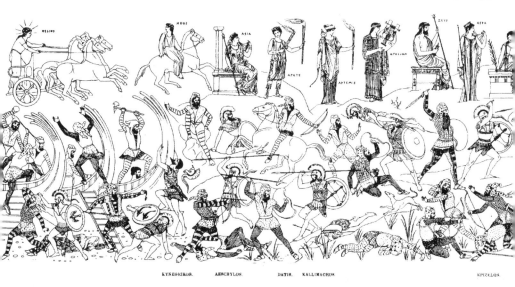

4. Reconstruction of the painting in the Stoa Poikile (Painted Stoa), drawn by
Hermann Schenck to accompany Carl Robert, *Die Marathonschlacht in der Poikile
und weiteres über Polygnot* (Halle: Niemeyer, 1895)

    For the rest, I take the approach my former teacher, Donald Kagan,
likes to call the "higher naïveté": Believe anything an ancient writer adds
to Herodotus unless it is "demonstrably self-contradictory, absurd, or
false." Herodotus always trumps a later writer. I do not doubt that there
is a detail somewhere on which Herodotus is wrong and a late source
right, but I do not see any methodological principle by which historians
could distinguish that kernel from the chaff. When we reject Herodotus,
as J. F. Lazenby remarked, "we are cutting off the branch on which we
sit." We may decide that the branch is not very firm, or whittle away parts
of it, but we should not fool ourselves into thinking that later writers provide anything sturdier to sit on.[15]

An Outline of What Follows

My goal is to reconstruct the battle of Marathon, taking full account of
the ancient evidence, accounts of early travelers who saw the plain in a
much less developed state than it is in today, archaeological discoveries,

and modern interpretations. I confess that one of the pleasures of study-
ing Marathon, for me, lies in exploring all the clever ideas that scholars
have produced, sometimes with what seems like willful disregard of the
evidence. I do not shy away from proposing my own solution to what I
consider the biggest challenge posed by Herodotus' account: *Why* did the
Athenians run so far at the beginning of the battle?

I begin with the threat that drove the Athenians to approach the Persians for an alliance in 507. I also try here to give the reader a sense of the
Persian Empire and the way its soldiers fought, not only to make clear
why the Athenians looked east for help, but also to set up the battle to
come.

Chapter 2 suggests that Athens' alliance with Persia successfully de-
terred a Peloponnesian army from advancing farther into Attica. It then
describes how, after the Peloponnesians went home, the Athenians won
battles against cities to the north that had invaded simultaneously with
the Peloponnesians. Here I discuss the Greek way of war, including the
weight of Greek military equipment. Currently accepted estimates are

much too high. The correct, lower weight has important consequences for Archaic warfare generally and Marathon specifically, as will become clear in chapter 7. The chapter ends with the Athenians' fateful decision to renege on their submission to Persia.

Chapter 3 tells the story of the Ionian Revolt, an unsuccessful attempt by the Greeks of Asia to liberate themselves from Persian rule. The Athenians and Eretrians sent ships and men to aid the rebels, which provided the Great King a reason to campaign against them in 490. In this chapter I digress on ancient ships and naval warfare, for though there was no fighting at sea in 490, Datis sailed from island to island until he reached Attica.

Chapter 4 describes events in mainland Greece after the Ionian Revolt. It tells the stories of the Persian expedition to northern Greece by land in 492 and of the first part of Datis' island-hopping campaign in 490, ending with his arrival at Marathon.

Chapter 5 looks at the situation from the Athenians' point of view, assesses their options, and describes their arrival at Marathon, including an estimate of their numbers and the number of Plataeans who came to help.

Chapter 6 reviews the geography and topography of the plain, locating as best I can the positions of the Persian camp, the Greek camp, and the site of the clash. I regard this chapter as absolutely essential to the battle's reconstruction, but readers who are not interested in such matters may prefer to read the summary at the chapter's end. Read at least that before chapter 7.

The story climaxes in chapter 7. Any attempt to understand Marathon involves a certain amount of historical conjecture. I base my reconstruction on the topographical conclusions in chapter 6. I defend the accuracy of Herodotus' account as far as it goes, including the long running charge that he emphasizes. I try to show how that charge determined the battle's outcome.

Chapter 8 treats what happened after the fighting stopped. I analyze the infamous shield signal, Philippides' fatal run to Athens, the Persians' next moves, and the burial of the Greek war dead.

Chapter 9 indulges in speculation: What if Miltiades' plan had not worked?

CHAPTER 1

Athens' Alliance with Darius

A Desperate Situation

irect relations between the Athenians and the Persians began
when the Athenians, finding themselves isolated and vulnerable
in Greece, approached the closest Persian satrap (governor) for
help. Here's what happened. In 510 BC, the Spartans had expelled the
Athenian tyrant Hippias. The son of the popular tyrant Peisistratos, Hippias had become more repressive after the assassination of his brother.
He had exiled the wealthy Alkmeonid family, among others. They had
tried to return by force, building a fort in Attica to attract like-minded
individuals, but Hippias had defeated them. So they plotted to bring in
allies who wouldn't lose. With extravagant gifts, they persuaded the Delphic oracle to support their cause. Every time a Spartan came to consult
the oracle, Herodotus says, he heard, "Liberate Athens."[1]

The advice fell on willing ears. Probably well-informed ears, too,
for though no source says so, it seems likely that Kleisthenes, the leading Alkmeonid, had spoken directly with influential Spartans such as
Kleomenes, one of Sparta's two kings. Kleomenes had already pulled off
one diplomatic coup by getting residents of Plataea, just beyond the border of northwest Attica, to ask the Athenians for help against their powerful neighbors to the north, the Thebans. The Athenians had agreed to

help the underdog. The bitter feelings that resulted between Athenians and Thebans did not surprise Kleomenes. They would prevent the two cities from combining against Sparta. Kleomenes probably saw an opportunity to create a wedge between Athens and Argos, the home of one of Peisistratos' wives and a traditional enemy of Sparta. Liberating Athens by removing Hippias and restoring the exiles would leave the Athenians feeling grateful to Sparta and perhaps willing to break off their tie to Argos. Intervening in Athens would fit Sparta's traditional policy of expelling tyrants and supporting conservative aristocracies.

It took two tries—Hippias managed to drive off the first invasion that came by sea—but Spartan soldiers under the leadership of Kleomenes penned up the Peisistratids on the Acropolis, caught their children trying to sneak out of Attica, and forced them all to agree to leave Attica in order to get back their children unharmed. Hippias went to an Athenian colony ruled by his half-brother on the Asian side of the entrance to the Hellespont.

The Spartans' attempt at regime change did not turn out as they anticipated. Things went well enough at first. The exiles returned, and the Athenians resumed the jockeying for power typical of elites in Greek cities during the Archaic period (eighth–sixth centuries). The two most prominent men were Kleisthenes and Isagoras. When Isagoras won the election for archon, the highest political office in Athens, Herodotus says, Kleisthenes "added the commons [the *demos*] to his supporters" and began the democratic reforms for which he is still celebrated. He abolished the four traditional Athenian tribes and then reassigned all citizens, based on where they lived, to one of ten new Athenian tribes. He established a new Council of 500, 50 citizens from each tribe chosen by lot. The councilors served for a single year, during which they met daily to supervise state officials and prepare motions for the assembly. All free adult male citizens could speak and vote in the assembly. These changes, the philosopher Aristotle thought, made Athens "much more democratic than it had been in the time of Solon" (before the tyranny of Peisistratos).[2]

Whether that was Kleisthenes' intent, at least at first, is not clear. He has always remained a rather shadowy figure. His father had been a major player in his day, prominent enough to marry the daughter of the tyrant of Sicyon, after whom Kleisthenes was named. Kleisthenes' sister married Peisistratos, though the marriage did not last. Kleisthenes himself held the archonship in 525/4, before going into exile.

His was not the first exile for the Alkmeonid family. More than a century earlier, the Alkmeonids tangled with an Olympic champion named Kylon who had married the daughter of the tyrant of Megara. With soldiers borrowed from his father-in-law, Kylon seized the Acropolis in an attempt to make himself tyrant of Athens. Besieged by angry Athenians, he and his brother managed to escape, while his supporters took refuge at the altar. When they were on the point of starving to death, the Athenians on guard promised them their lives, brought them out of the Acropolis, and killed them. The Athenians held the Alkmeonid who was serving as archon responsible for this sacrilege. Considering his family polluted and accursed, the Athenians drove the Alkmeonids into exile. By the middle of the sixth century they were back. The experience of exile and return must have dominated many dinner conversations at their houses. After returning from his own exile, Kleisthenes did not want to emerge the loser again. He may have appealed to the people in the hope of becoming tyrant himself.

Neither a democracy nor a new tyranny in Athens was what the interventionist Spartan king had in mind. Kleomenes wanted a nice conservative government he could count on to support Spartan policies. When Isagoras asked him to intervene again, the Spartan king agreed. Their friendship was recent. Isagoras had hosted Kleomenes when he came to Athens to overthrow Hippias, so they now considered themselves guest-friends. (Rumor added that Kleomenes had enjoyed Isagoras' wife.) Kleomenes sent a herald to tell the Athenians to banish Kleisthenes and all his relatives on the grounds of the old family curse. Bowing to the inevitable, Kleisthenes left town before Kleomenes arrived with a small force. Isagoras gave Kleomenes a list of 700 families to be banished, and Kleomenes drove them out. Then he tried to dissolve the new Athenian Council, intending to put Isagoras and 300 of his friends into power. But the Council resisted, the Athenians spontaneously took up arms, and Kleomenes could do nothing other than seize the Acropolis by force. He had no way to bring in supplies, so after two days the Spartans agreed to

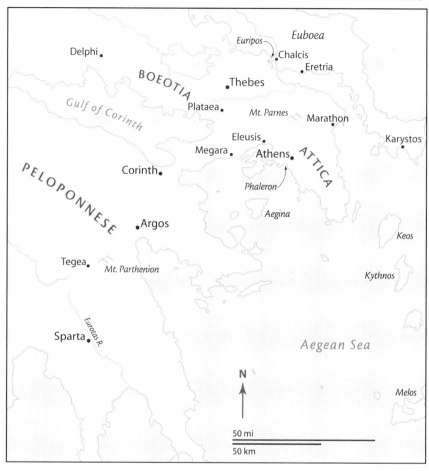

5. Map of southern Greece

a truce giving them permission to withdraw unharmed. The Athenians killed all the non-Spartans they caught. On his way home, Kleomenes took over the sanctuary of Demeter at Eleusis on the western edge of Athenian territory, where he left Isagoras (Figure 5).

The Athenians promptly recalled Kleisthenes and his friends. They must have feared that Kleomenes would return with a larger army. What to do? The Spartan alliance included most of the inhabitants of the Peloponnese or southern Greece, while the Athenians could count as nearby allies only the small town of Plataea. The Peisistratids had received military support from Eretria, Naxos, Thebes, and Thessaly, but after expelling Hippias the Athenians could not rely on help from any of these former friends. Where else could they turn?

The Persian Army

In 507 the Mediterranean world had only one superpower. Modern historians tend to underestimate the Persian army, since much of our evidence for it comes from Greek accounts of two of its rare failures, Xerxes' invasion of Greece in 480 and Alexander the Great's conquest of the Persians in 334. In the late sixth century, these failures were still in the future. How would the Great King's military power have looked to a Greek then?

The Persian and Median infantry, according to the Greek historian Herodotus, had identical equipment: "They wore soft felt caps on their heads, which they call *tiaras*, and multicolored tunics with sleeves, covering their bodies, and they had breastplates of iron fashioned to look like fish scales. On their legs they wore trousers, and instead of shields they carried pieces of wicker [*gerra*], which had quivers hung below them. They were armed with short spears, long bows, and arrows made of reeds. From their belts they fastened daggers, which hung down along the right side." A number of Athenian red-figure vases show scenes of Greeks fighting Persians (two examples appear in Figures 6 and 7). The Persians wear the caps, long-sleeved tunics, and trousers described by Herodotus. They fight with bows, spears, or single-edged curved swords. No iron scales are visible. Some Persians wear corslets that look like padded linen, perhaps the Egyptian corslets that Herodotus says the Persians adopted. The vases also show shields that must be gerra, tall and rectangular. (One is propped upright in Figure 6, and others are held by fighters in Figure 7.) *Gerron* makers cut slits in a rectangular piece of uncured leather and then inserted pliable willow rods into the slits. When the leather dried and hardened, the shield became light and rigid. The different patterns seen on Greek vases resulted from different kinds of slits and perhaps different colors of paint. Made of perishable materials, few gerra have survived, but American excavators at Dura Europos in Syria found two dating from the third century AD.[3]

6. Athenian red-figure cup by the Painter of the Paris Gigantomachy, c. 490–480, showing Greeks fighting Persians (Metropolitan Museum of Art, New York, 1980.11.21; from Eduard Gerhard, *Auserlesene Griechische Vasenbilder, Hauptsächlich Etruskischen Fundorts* [Berlin: G. Reimer, 1840–1858], vol. 3, pl. 166)

The Persians did not originally have cavalry, which Cyrus the Great organized after he defeated the Lydians. On that occasion, he used camels. By the late sixth century, Persian horses were numerous. Estimates put them at not more than 14 hands tall, weighing about 1,000 pounds. The Persians became great horse breeders. No fewer than ten different breeds appear on reliefs at the palace in Persepolis. Tritantaichmes, the satrap of Babylon, was said to have a stud farm with 800 stallions and 16,000 mares. As a result, Persian horses surpassed the best available in Greece. Xerxes demonstrated their superiority in 480 when he held a race

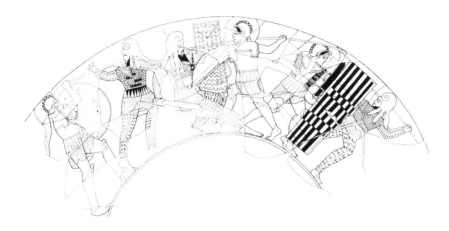

7. Side A of an Athenian red-figure cup by the Painter of the Oxford Brygos, c. 490–480, showing Greeks fighting Persians (Ashmolean Museum, Oxford, 1911.615; drawing by N. Griffiths, © Margaret C. Miller)

among Persian and Thessalian horses. Herodotus reports that "the Greek horses were left far behind."[4]

Herodotus says that Persian and Median horsemen were equipped in the same way as their foot soldiers, except that the horsemen had bronze or iron helmets. In art horsemen have both bows and spears (mounted archers appear in Figure 8). A cavalry officer named Masistios wore a corslet with golden scales under his shirt at the battle of Plataea. After his horse went down, his apparent invincibility puzzled the Greeks until someone realized he had something under his shirt and stabbed him in the eye.

In an inscription on his tomb, King Darius boasted: "As a horseman I am a good horseman. As a bowman I am a good bowman, both on foot and on horseback. As a spearman I am a good spearman, both on foot and on horseback." According to Greek sources, Persians were trained in these skills. The ancient geographer Strabo says that "from five years of age to 24 Persians are trained to use the bow, to throw the javelin, to ride horseback, and to speak the truth." They remained liable for military service up to age 50. Xenophon adds that in practice only the sons of

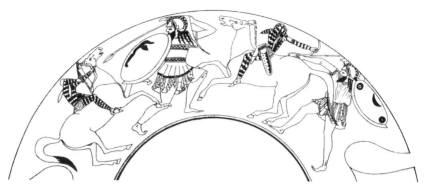

8. Side B of an Athenian red-figure cup by the Triptolemos Painter, c. 490–480, showing hoplites fighting mounted archers (National Museums of Scotland, Edinburgh, 1887.213; from Paul Hartwig, *Die Griechischen Meisterschalen der Blüthezeit des Strengen Rothfigurigen Stiles* [Stuttgart: Spemann, 1893], pl. 55)

great families received this education; Persians who lived on estates in the provinces sent their sons to the satrap's court, where their training was identical to that in Persia. Xenophon has military service proper last from 17 to 27, with liability to conscription lasting for another 25 years.[5]

How did the Persian national infantry fight? It was organized on a decimal system. The largest units of 10,000 comprised units of 1,000 that comprised units of 100 that comprised units of ten. Because one could not shoot a bow while holding a gerron, the front-line man in each file of ten may have held a gerron and fought with a spear or sword to defend the nine shieldless archers behind him. This interpretation fits Herodotus' descriptions of the battles of Plataea and Mycale, where the Greeks apparently have to get past only one line of shields formed into a shield wall.

The Persians would hope to win a battle with a barrage of arrows. They used two kinds of bows. The more common was the Scythian bow, which formed the shape of a Greek capital letter sigma (Σ) when strung. It was about 30 inches long, with a bracing height (the distance from the string to the handle when strung) of about 8 inches. The Persian bow, carried by Persians and perhaps Medes, formed a simple curve with recurved tips. It was longer, about 47 inches, with a bracing height of about 9 inches. Both bows shot arrows made of reed with socketed bronze heads weighing 0.1–0.2 ounces each. The most common was a three-winged head about an inch long. Scythian arrows were about 20 inches long, the Persian about 30.

The Scythian bow imparted a maximum kinetic energy on release of 18–36 joules, the Persian 24–52. (For comparison, later English longbows and Turkish composite bows gave an arrow about 50 joules.) An archer's effective range extended to at least 175–190 yards. The most revealing bit of literary evidence is Herodotus' statement that the Persians shot fire arrows from the Areopagos hill in Athens to the barricades at the gate of the Acropolis, a distance of about 500 feet with a vertical rise of about 100 feet. Those archers could have shot a regular arrow at least 250 yards on a level field. They may have been selected for their strength, but if common archers could reach three-quarters of that distance, they could shoot 190 yards.

The arrows would have lost energy quickly. At 55 yards, the Scythian arrow dropped to perhaps 20 joules. Another 55 yards and it was down to 15 joules. By 220 yards, if it went that far, it had only 9 joules. The larger Persian arrows did better: 30 joules at 55 yards, 26 joules at 110, 20 joules at 220. That compares to about 30 joules for a Greek hand-held spear. A Persian arrow shot from 55 yards away had about as much kinetic energy when it hit as an overhand spear thrust did, a Scythian arrow about two-thirds as much. For causing a wound through armor, a bow has some advantage over a thrusting spear, since a spear needs to create a larger hole than an arrow.

Perforation tests have shown that arrows with an energy below 35 joules would not have penetrated bronze armor 0.04 inches or more thick. Greek shields would have been vulnerable to arrows with an energy of 25–35 joules, so Persian arrows might have pierced shields at close range, but Scythian arrows would have done no harm unless they hit an unprotected area. (See chapter 2 for more information about Greek armor.) If a warrior wore a corslet and carried a shield, his chest was well protected against Persian arrows. This conclusion is consistent with the low casualties reported for the Greeks at the battle of Marathon.[6]

Persians could use their cavalry in several ways. Persian horsemen could attack in squadrons, riding across the enemy front from left to

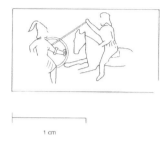

9. Drawing of the seal impression DS 86 from Daskyleion, 479–375 BC (Reproduced from Deniz Kaptan, *The Daskyleion Bullae: Seal Images from the Western Achaemenid Empire* [Leiden: Nederlands Instituut voor het Nabije Oosten, 2002], pl. 257, by permission of Deniz Kaptan)

right, shooting arrows or throwing javelins across their bodies as they went, all the while keeping a safe distance. This is how the Persians first assaulted the Greeks at Plataea. Or they could have charged the infantry head-on and fought at close quarters. They did that (unsuccessfully) at Plataea after their commander Masistios went down, and at the battle of Salamis on Cyprus, where the Persian Artybios' horse had his legs sheared off. They would do better against Greek infantry if they could attack the flanks.

Fighting scenes appear only rarely in Achaemenid art, apart from small seals such as the one illustrated in Figure 9. Deniz Kaptan describes the scene on this seal as follows: "A horseman wearing trousers, corselet, and a bashlyk [headgear made of soft material such as leather and wool] thrusts his spear into the chest of a warrior clad in a knee-length chiton [sleeveless shirt] and a conical helmet with a long tassel. He carries a large round shield in his left hand. Its inside detailing, such as the handgrips, has been carefully indicated." The double-grip shield is typically Greek; the pilos-type helmet with its hanging crest is a rare type most similar to funerary reliefs in Lycia.[7]

A similar scene occurs at the center of a battle painting on the north wall of an early-fifth-century tomb chamber known as Karaburun II in Lycia (Figures 10 and 11). Excavated by Bryn Mawr archaeologists in the 1970s, the tomb awaits final publication. In her preliminary reports, archaeologist Machteld J. Mellink described the scene as "some kind of a

10. Battle scene from the north wall of Karaburun II, early fifth century BC (Photo Department of Classical and Near Eastern Archaeology, Bryn Mawr College, with the permission of Stella Miller-Collett)

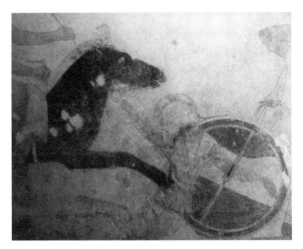

11. Detail of battle scene from Karaburun II after further cleaning (Photo Department of Classical and Near Eastern Archaeology, Bryn Mawr College, with the permission of Stella Miller-Collett)

12. Battle scene on a painted wooden beam from Tatarlı, c. 475–450 (Courtesy Lâtife Summerer)

Persian war in which the Greeks are the losers." The tomb owner, presumably the rider portrayed in the middle, wears a purple long-sleeved tunic over purple trousers tucked into his blue shoes. He rides over a fallen archer as he stabs a warrior armed with a two-handled shield, corslet, helmet, and shin guards. As in the scene on the seal, an eastern horseman uses a spear to kill a warrior armed with a Greek shield. Whether or not these scenes show particular historical events—more likely the horseman died fighting—they provide a nice balance to the vases painted by Greeks. Here Persian horsemen kill Greek hoplites.[8]

Another fascinating battle scene comes from a burial mound near Tatarlı in Phrygia. In the 1960s looters sawed in two the wooden beam on which it was painted (Figure 12). The beam ended up in the Archäologische Staatssammlung in Munich, where it remained largely unnoticed until a German scholar, Lâtife Summerer, rediscovered it. It shows a Persian force, coming from the left, defeating a Scythian force coming from the right. In the center, the Persian commander pulls the Scythian leader forward by his beard as he stabs him in the stomach with a dagger—a stock execution scene in Achaemenid art. The Scythian shot through the neck, the fallen Scythian shot in the back, and the horse shot in the chest show that archers won the battle. The foremost archer shoots from a chariot. Seven mounted and two infantry archers follow, the mounted archers in two lines. The infantry archers shoot the Persian longbow, the others the Scythian or composite bow. The painting is dated on stylistic grounds to the mid-fifth century. Though the Persians are not fighting

Greeks here, the painting illustrates how the Persians might have hoped to win at Marathon, where the Athenians could not match them in archers or horses.

How large was the Persian army? Herodotus' great catalogue of all the ethnic contingents in Xerxes' army, including 1,700,000 infantry, 80,000 cavalry, and 200 camel riders and charioteers, gives the impression of a most heterogeneous force, since all the contingents are described as wearing their native equipment. The Ethiopians, for instance, have leopard skins, lion pelts, and bows more than six feet long. The Sagartian horsemen have no weapons other than lassoes and daggers.[9]

This catalogue records a parade army rather than the fighting army. In his descriptions of fighting, Herodotus mentions only Persians, Medes, Kissians, Sacae, Baktrians, and Indians, all equipped in much the same way as the Persians. Where then did the parade army come from? Perhaps Xerxes brought small numbers of ethnic contingents for his military reviews. Or perhaps some of the Egyptians, Medes, and Sacae were not recruited in Egypt, Media, and central Asia, since the Persians maintained ethnically diverse garrisons and colonies throughout the empire. Some of the native contingents may have included those to whom the Persians granted lands in the satrapy in exchange for military service. We know, for example, of Persians living near Sardis who rallied to the satrap's aid when the Ionian Greeks revolted in 499.

Such a parade, designed to flaunt imperial power, reminds me of the International Festival at the college where I teach, if I may "compare small things with great." Once a year, students who have come from abroad, including sons and daughters of U.S. citizens living abroad, set up displays with photos and flags, dress in their country's traditional style, and serve samples of their native cuisine. On other days I would have a hard time distinguishing most of these students from the majority student population, since they dress in much the same way and eat much the same food.[10]

Just as an International Festival can make a student body seem more diverse than it is, so Xerxes' parade portrayed his army as more diverse than his actual fighting force was. The same applies to Darius. When Herodotus says that Darius set up inscriptions at the Bosporus in 513 listing all the peoples participating in his expedition to Scythia, we should not take him literally. The total of 700,000 men reflects Darius' boast about his empire's total military capacity rather than a statement about how many men actually went on the campaign. A generation later, Xerxes claimed to be able to raise a million men more.

The Persian military had an intimidating record. In addition to the conquests by Cyrus the Great (c. 559–530) and his son Cambyses (530–522), the 15 years of the current king, Darius (522–486), had seen further victories and advances. In the year after he became king, Darius' armies fought 19 battles against rebels. In the trilingual inscription below the monumental relief he had cut into a cliff at Bisitun, more than 300 feet above the road, Darius boasted that he killed 34,425 enemies in the greatest of these battles (Figure 13).

Darius had then defeated the Sacae (Scythians) in central Asia, capturing the Scythian king Skunkha, whose image was added to the Bisitun relief. In the east he went on to conquer India. In the west he took the major islands off the coast of Asia, as well as the Greek cities on the Hellespont, which submitted peacefully. In 513, he invaded Europe. Greek writers heard more about Persian activities when they came closer to Greece. Herodotus devotes most of his fourth book to this first European campaign, which he portrays as a colossal failure. If Darius wanted to annex Scythia, he failed. But the expedition looks rather different if he was really after the timber, gold, and silver resources on the north coast of the Aegean and crossed the Danube River only to deter the Scythians

13. Etching of the cliff at Bisitun by Auguste-Alexandre Guillaumot after a drawing by Pascal Coste (From Eugène Flandin and Pascal Coste, *Voyage en Perse de Mm. Eugène Flandin, Peintre, et Pascal Coste, Architecte, Entrepris par Ordre de M. le Ministre des Affaires Étrangères, d'après les Instructions Dressées par l'Institut* [Paris: Gide and Baudry, 1851], pl. 16; photo, Asian and Middle Eastern Division, New York Public Library, Astor, Lenox, and Tilden Foundations)

from raiding the coast. He returned without bringing the Scythians to battle. As he made his way back to Asia, he left a Persian named Megabazos in command of a large army. Megabazos campaigned in Thrace, bringing "every city and every nation" under Persian control—at least those along the coast, for some peoples were left independent. He pushed toward the Strymon River, where he met resistance from the Paionians. He deported them to Asia. He demanded and accepted earth and water from the king of Macedon. Not much later, Megabazos' son married the king's daughter. So while Herodotus portrays Darius as barely escaping from the Scythians, the Persian king and his general extended the empire to include what is today European Turkey and parts of Bulgaria and northern Greece.[11]

Before returning to the east, probably in 511, Darius appointed his paternal half-brother Artaphrenes satrap of Sardis and named Otanes military commander of the men on the coast, subordinate to Artaphrenes (sometimes spelled Artaphernes). Otanes conquered or reconquered a number of Greek cities in the Hellespont, captured the islands of Lemnos and Imbros, and may have campaigned again in Thrace, for a gap in Herodotus' text resumes, "he enslaved and conquered everyone, accusing some of deserting to the Scythians and others of plundering Darius' army as it returned from Scythia."[12]

By 507, Greeks in Asia and on the northern Aegean coast knew the Persian military well. What's missing is any record of Greeks fighting Persians in the open field. When Cyrus the Great defeated Croesus, king of Lydia, his former Greek subjects fortified their cities. But they did not come out to fight. The Persians built earth mounds against the city walls and captured them one by one, except for Miletus, which had made a treaty with Cyrus earlier, and two others, whose inhabitants abandoned their cities and sailed west. Perhaps only the Greek mercenaries serving under the Egyptian pharaoh Psammenitus when Cambyses invaded Egypt had actually fought Persians. In a great battle, Herodotus says, "the fighting became quite fierce, so that a large number of men fell on both sides, but finally the Egyptians were routed." It would be interesting to know how many Greek mercenaries fought in this battle. Probably thousands, for a generation earlier a large mercenary army of Carians and Ionians

(30,000, according to Herodotus) fought for an Egyptian pharaoh against an army of Egyptian rebels, losing only because they were outnumbered. Eastern monarchs valued Greek mercenaries, but eastern troops could and did defeat them.[13]

Given that no Greeks had withstood the Persians, the Athenians knew that Persian friendship would deter anyone thinking of attacking Athens. How likely were they to get it? What did they know about the Great King and his policies?

Darius, the Great King, King of Kings, King of Persia, King of Lands, the Son of Hystaspes, the Grandson of Arsames, an Achaemenid

Darius had become king at the age of 28, probably by leading a successful conspiracy to assassinate Cambyses' brother and successor. That may not have been common knowledge in Greece. Darius went to great lengths to have his version of events accepted. Herodotus' account agrees in broad outline with Darius' inscription at Biṣitun. In Darius' version, the god Auramazda bestowed the kingship on him after Cambyses murdered his brother, an imposter claiming to be the brother revolted, and Cambyses died a natural death. Darius and a few friends then killed the imposter and restored the kingship to his family. He claimed to be descended from Achaemenes, who was also said (though not before the reign of Darius) to be an ancestor of Cyrus. To strengthen his claim to be related to Cyrus, he married three of Cyrus' daughters (two of whom had been married to Cambyses) and one of Cyrus' granddaughters.

The young ruler showed himself as ruthless in keeping as he was in getting the throne. He faced many rebels, whom he called liars. They came not from the fringes of the empire, but right from its heart: Elam, Babylonia, Media, Parthia, Margiana, even Persia. He punished them publicly and brutally, as he boasted in the Bisitun inscription: "I cut off his [Fravartish's] nose, ears, and tongue, and tore out one eye. He was held in fetters at my palace entrance; all the people saw him. After that, I impaled him at Ecbatana; and the men who were his foremost follow-ers, those I hanged at Ecbatana in the fortress." Darius made sure people

14. Etching of the Bisitun relief by Nicolas-Auguste Leisnier after a drawing by Eugène Flandin (From Flandin and Coste, *Voyage en Perse de Mm. Eugène Flandin, Peintre, et Pascal Coste, Architecte*, pl. 16; photo, Asian and Middle Eastern Division, New York Public Library, Astor, Lenox, and Tilden Foundations)

knew what happened to anyone who opposed him. He circulated the text of the inscription throughout the empire. The relief at Bisitun shows Darius, standing with his foot on the chest of one recumbent rebel, facing a line of smaller rebel leaders, chained together at their necks (Figure 14). Darius continued to portray himself as a warrior throughout his reign. His coinage regularly shows him as an archer.[14]

Several projects illustrated Darius' power in monumental form. He built his own new palaces at Persepolis and Babylon, then rebuilt the palace at Susa and continued Cyrus' construction at Pasargadae. He finished the canal from the Nile River to the Red Sea begun a century earlier, a canal that was almost 150 feet wide, 16 feet deep, and 50 miles long.

To pay for these projects, Darius reorganized the tribute system. Herodotus notes that Darius was nicknamed the *kapelos* (retailer) because he put a price on everything, and contrasts his system of fixed tribute paid in gold and silver to the earlier system of "gifts" used by Cyrus (the "father") and Cambyses (the "master"). Scholars dispute the accuracy of Herodotus' description of the satrapies and their tribute; the details of Achaemenid finance are extraordinarily scattered and complex. But such details are beside the point: Compared with the little Greek city-states, the Great King commanded virtually unlimited resources—that much any Greek would know.

In foreign affairs, Darius proceeded with some caution. Before campaigning, he typically sent scouting missions. They are attested for the Indus River valley, Scythia, and the coasts of Greece and Italy. By 507 Darius' armies had campaigned in all three areas, and he had shown his willingness to use his fleet against Greek cities.

In short, Darius had the resources to help Athens and had shown interest in expanding into mainland Greece. But with submission came obligations. The Athenians must have known that the fate of anyone who turned against the Great King—anyone who became a liar—was not pretty.

The Athenian Embassy in 507/6

Because Athens had no chance against the Spartan coalition, the Alkmeonids faced a fourth exile. Dreading that, they persuaded the Athenians to seek help from the closest Persian satrap, Darius' brother Artaphrenes, at Sardis. "The Athenians"—by which Herodotus ought to mean a vote of the Athenian assembly—"sent envoys to Sardis, wanting to form an alliance with the Persians." Perhaps ten men went, one from each of the new tribes. They would have sailed through the Cyclades to Samos and then to the mainland at Ephesus. From Ephesus they would have walked for three days, about 60 miles all told.[15]

Visualizing the Achaemenid city of Sardis is difficult, despite 50 years of excavation. It apparently lay mostly to the east of what has been uncovered so far. The Persians had looted Croesus' fabulously rich city. On the other hand, Cyrus named a treasurer for Sardis in addition to a satrap, which suggests that the city remained wealthy. Forty years after the conquest, it must have regained much of its prosperity, since it thrived as the capital of the Persian satrapy of Sparda (Ionia). Athenians knew it as "Sardis rich in gold."[16]

Before reaching the city gates, the ambassadors walked past some of Sardis' houses, built of reeds or mud brick with reed roofs. They may have seen two altars on the west side of the city outside the line of the walls: one to Artemis, at the site of the later Hellenistic temple, and one to Kybele, a third of a mile to the north, a small, old altar reconstructed during the Achaemenid period. They probably glanced over at a sanctuary of Kybele near the site of the later synagogue, where a marble model of a temple with a statue of Kybele was found, the earliest Achaemenid sculpture discovered at Sardis (c. 540–530).

They may also have passed a formal garden, a Near Eastern tradition. In the late fifth century, Cyrus and Tissaphernes both planted gardens at Sardis. It seems likely to me that after 40 years of Persian rule there would have been one already in the late sixth century. Archaeologists at Persepolis have explored one such Persian garden, with paths and plants laid out in straight lines leading to colonnaded pavilions. Stone watercourses irrigated exotic flora. Such a formal garden would have put a Persian stamp on the Sardian landscape.

The fortification walls surely impressed the Athenian visitors. At the time of the Persian conquest, Sardis had a massive wall, larger than any contemporary wall in Greece: 65 feet wide at the base, as much as 115 feet tall, built of mud brick on a stone socle that kept the brick from getting wet and turning back into mud. In the excavated section, this wall was demolished in the mid-sixth century and rebuilt on top of the destruction debris. The stone faces of this wall were filled with rubble, most likely with mud brick on top.

The ambassadors made their way up to the satrap's residence in Croesus' palace on the acropolis, past another fortification wall, this one the Lydian wall protecting the acropolis. It too must have been impressive, for Cyrus captured the acropolis only when some of his men scaled the almost vertical face at an undefended point. His first satrap held out here against the Lydian rebels in the 540s, as did Artaphrenes later against the Ionians who revolted in 499. Croesus' palace survived into Roman times, but the only trace of it identified by archaeologists is a possible terrace wall.

Probably a little out of breath after the steep climb, a little awed by the view of the fertile plain below, and more than a little impressed by the strength of the acropolis and its fortifications, the Athenian ambassadors entered the palace. If they hoped for Persian help, I doubt that they came into Artaphrenes' presence before they were told to offer earth and water.

The king did not make alliances with equals; he generously accepted the submissions of inferiors.

Scholars have fussed about the precise significance of the custom of giving earth and water, which we hear about only in Herodotus. Did earth and water, in the Iranian world view, represent humility and inviolability, a humble desire to submit irrevocably? Were earth and water part of a ritual, with an oath taken while standing on one's own ground? Were earth and water connected to the king's role as the good gardener responsible for the fertility of the soil? Did earth and water signify the source of life and, in the Lydian (and now Persian) conception of sovereignty, the king's assertion that he was the custodian of the basis of human life everywhere on earth? Or is the phrase simply Herodotus' shorthand for complete submission, surrendering control of one's earth and water to the king?

Herodotus regularly says that the king asked his opponents to give him earth and water—the Scythians, the Macedonians, the Athenians now, all the Greek cities later. Whatever its precise meaning, the gift of earth and water acknowledged the king's superiority. It was a formal submission that left open what one's future obligations would be. For example, Darius invited the Scythians to give earth and water and then discuss terms with him. These terms could include tribute (perhaps called "gifts" if the subject proposed an amount acceptable to the king), military service, and the provision of appropriate resources to the king or his representatives if they came to the subject territory. Giving earth and water did not automatically mean the imposition of a garrison or a tyrant, or even of tribute.

All this was surely no surprise to the ambassadors. The Athenian colonists in the Chersonese, the strip of land along the European side of the Hellespont, must have submitted to the Persians, since they participated in Darius' European campaign. By now, enough Greeks had either submitted or been conquered that the Athenians must have considered in advance whether they would give earth and water and what terms they would propose. Unfortunately Herodotus does not give details, though he implies that the ambassadors reached agreement with Artaphrenes after giving earth and water. They swore an oath and left for home, no doubt pleased with their success.

CHAPTER 2

Athens' Victories over the Boeotians and Chalcidians

Kleomenes' Big Invasion

Believing that the Athenians "had treated him outrageously in words and actions," Kleomenes did just what the Athenians feared he would do. In the spring of 506, he collected a large army drawn from the entire Peloponnese. An unusually strong Spartan king accustomed to getting what he wanted, Kleomenes had failed the previous summer because he had only a small force, a mistake he did not intend to repeat. With the Peloponnesians invading Attica from the west, he arranged for the Boeotians to attack from the north and the Chalcidians from the east. The nightmare had begun.[1]

Herodotus' catalogue of the Greek hoplites (heavy-armed soldiers) at the battle of Plataea in 479 gives some idea of the numbers potentially involved: 5,000 Spartans, 5,000 other Lacedaemonians, 1,500 Tegeans, 5,000 Corinthians, 600 Orchomenians, 3,000 Sicyonians, 800 Epidaurians, 1,000 Troizenians, 200 Lepreans, 400 Mycenaeans and Tirynians, 1,000 Phleiasians, 300 Hermionians, and 3,000 Megarians, for a total of 26,800 Peloponnesians, not counting light-armed (whom Herodotus reckons at seven for each Spartan and one for each of the others). Herodotus does not give a figure for the Boeotians, nor do we know how many cities the Boeotian League included in 506. In 424 the league had 7,000 hoplites and 10,000 light-armed at the battle of Delion. Herodotus lists only 400 Chalcidians at the battle of Plataea, but in 506, before the Athenians took much of their land, the Chalcidians had thousands of hoplites. In the Archaic period, Chalcis' rival Eretria had 3,000 hoplites and 600 horsemen, so Chalcidian manpower must have been comparable.

The invaders massively outnumbered the Athenians. Despite Kleisthenes' creation of a citizen army based on the new system of ten tribes—the military aspect of Kleisthenes' legislation that probably alarmed the Spartans—the Athenians had fewer than 10,000 fully armed hoplites in 506. They later sent 8,000 hoplites to Plataea at a time when they had at least 500 marines serving in the fleet. Even if they had as many light-armed as they had hoplites, the Athenians faced an overwhelming numerical disadvantage.

The invaders advanced simultaneously on all three fronts. The Athenians decided to ignore the Boeotians and Chalcidians for the time being and deployed against the Peloponnesians. But when the armies were about to fight, the Peloponnesian force disintegrated. First the Corinthians went home, then Demaratos (the other Spartan king who shared the command with Kleomenes) departed, and finally all the other allies dispersed as well.

This is a remarkable chain of events. For starters, it is surprising that the Athenians would be willing to fight against a force so much larger than their own. In general, Greeks refused to fight when outnumbered by a ratio of more than three to two. Facing greater odds, they either fled to the hills or prepared for a siege. In 445, the one other time when the Athenians went out to meet a full Peloponnesian invasion, the Spartan king Pleistoanax led his army back home—and was exiled on the grounds that he must have taken a bribe. (Pericles, the Athenian general, entered a large amount in his accounts for that year for "necessary expenses.")[2]

That confrontation in 445 followed a half century of highly successful warfare for the Athenians. In 506 the Athenians did not have a particularly distinguished record as fighters. Their early wars with Eleusis, Megara, and Aegina were small-scale affairs aptly described by words like "raid" and "skirmish." When Peisistratos invaded from Eretria in his third attempt to establish himself as tyrant, he easily defeated the Athenians who came out to oppose him. The one major victory they could point to was the defeat of the Boeotians in 519, when the Boeotians attacked them on their way home from Plataea. In that battle the Athenians were probably not outnumbered.[3]

No less remarkable is the Corinthian withdrawal. Sparta's allies in the sixth century may not have sworn the oath first attested at the end of the fifth, "to follow the Spartans wherever they lead, on land or on sea," but they had joined the campaign. What made them change their minds? Herodotus says they decided they were acting unjustly, without further explanation. A few pages later he reports that a Corinthian made an impassioned speech against Sparta's new plan to restore the tyrant Hippias because the insolent Athenians had become a threat. So perhaps the Corinthians suspected that Kleomenes intended to make Isagoras tyrant. Alternatively, whatever the Corinthians said about justice, they made a calculated political decision, either that they needed Athenian help against Aegina and Megara or that they did not want Athens controlled by Sparta.[4]

Most remarkable is Demaratos' decision to leave. Surely the two kings had discussed their goals prior to the campaign. Demaratos had not previously disagreed with Kleomenes. Would the withdrawal of Corinth have sufficed to change his mind? True, the Corinthians were powerful allies. Yet they constituted no more than a fifth of the Peloponnesian army, not enough to change the odds to favor Athens. I suspect that Demaratos—and the Corinthians—learned something new, something that changed their minds about attacking Athens. And I think we can be fairly sure what that something was. The Athenian envoys had gone only to Sardis, not all the way to Susa. They should have returned in plenty of time for the Athenians to have informed the Peloponnesians about the new Athenian alliance with the Persians. Perhaps they even had a letter from Artaphrenes threatening the Peloponnesians with what he would do if they harmed his allies, something along the lines of the fourth-century King's Peace. It might have read: "King Darius thinks it just that the other Greeks leave his allies, the Athenians, alone. I will make war, both by land and by sea, with ships and with money, against anyone who attacks them."[5]

For Herodotus does not say that the Athenians repudiated the alliance with Persia. He says only that when the envoys returned, they were greatly blamed for giving earth and water, which they had done on their own authority. But when the Athenians voted to send the ambassadors, they must have known they would have to submit to Persia if they wanted Darius' help. What we're dealing with here is a later Athenian retelling of what happened. After the Persian Wars, no Athenian would want to admit that the city had once given earth and water, much less that the Persian alliance had saved Athens from a Peloponnesian invasion. The fourth-century historian Theopompos mentioned the Athenian treaty with Darius as one of the events falsified by Athenian propaganda, but we can still discern its original importance. It saved Athens in 506.

After the Peloponnesian army disintegrated, the Athenians, out for revenge, moved against Chalcis. They headed for the Euripos, the narrowest place in the strait between the island of Euboea and the mainland, about 130 feet wide. Chalcis sits on the Euboean side, 34 miles from Athens as the crow flies. The march to the Euripos over the shoulder of Mount Parnes would have taken at least two days.

Since the earliest known bridge was not built until 410, crossing to Euboea required boats. The crossing can be tricky, for the channel's current, at times as strong as 8.5 mph, changes direction as often as seven times a day. How did the Athenians plan to cross? In the sixth century Athens did not have much of a navy. According to scattered sources, 48 ship-districts were each responsible for providing one ship. These were probably old-fashioned penteconters rowed by 50 men rather than new triremes crewed by 200, but if you add in some other boats it is not hard to imagine the Athenians ferrying their men across in several trips. They might have had help from Eretria, Chalcis' rival on the island of Euboea.[6]

Before the Athenians left the mainland, word came that the Boeotians were hurrying toward the Euripos to help the Chalcidians. The Athenians decided to fight the Boeotians first and turned to meet them.

Greek Warfare

What was this battle like? The conventional view, championed by Victor Davis Hanson in his influential *The Western Way of War: Infantry Battle in Classical Greece,* holds that each Greek hoplite carried about 70 pounds of equipment, almost half his own body weight. Hoplites deployed in a close-order formation that allowed each man about three feet. The two sides lumbered toward each other, smashing together in a loud collision, and then tried to shove their way forward in what Greeks called "the push" (*othismos*). Modern writers envision the push like a rugby scrum on steroids. The rear ranks shoved the front ranks forward, each man jamming his shield into the back or shoulder of the man in front of him. This kind of fight required little skill with weapons, for hoplites simply jabbed or poked with spears and swords. They looked down on archers, slingers, javelin throwers, and the like, who ran fewer risks than the hoplites. As the Spartan poet Tyrtaios wrote,

> For no man ever proves himself a good man in war
> unless he can endure to face the blood and the slaughter,
>   go close against the enemy and fight with his hands.
> Here is courage, mankind's finest possession, here is
>   the noblest prize that a young man can endeavor to win,
> and it is a good thing his city and all the people share with him
>   when a man plants his feet and stands in the foremost spears
> relentlessly, all thought of foul flight completely forgotten,
>   and has well trained his heart to be steadfast and to endure,
> and with words encourages the man who is stationed beside him.
>   Here is a man who proves himself to be valiant in war.
> With a sudden rush he turns to flight the rugged battalions
>   of the enemy, and sustains the beating waves of assault.

And in another poem,

> Our man should be disciplined in the work of the heavy fighter,
>   and not stand out from the missiles when he carries a shield,
> but go right up and fight at close quarters and, with his long spear
>   or short sword, thrust home and strike his enemy down.
> Let him fight toe to toe and shield against shield hard driven,
>   crest against crest and helmet on helmet, chest against chest;
> let him close hard and fight it out with his opposite foeman,
>   holding tight to the hilt of his sword, or to his long spear.

Conventional wisdom says that the Greeks restricted light-armed men to peripheral roles. Though we have few details for the Archaic period, most historians seem confident that battles remained pushing contests for several hundred years, until the Persian Wars.[7]

Supporters of this view have claimed for it the status of orthodoxy, which puts anyone who disagrees in the category of heretics, with all the negative baggage that term conveys. I remain an unrepentant heretic. Just as the orthodox theology of the Christian Church has a history, so does the orthodox view of Greek warfare. Scholars have not always emphasized a mass shove as the essence of Greek battle, nor have they always interpreted it literally. Recent literalists tend to prefer some categories of evidence to others. They privilege literary sources, even later literary sources, over contemporary vase painting. And only recently has the material evidence, particularly the surviving dedications of armor and weapons at Greek sanctuaries, received the attention it deserves.

Let's begin with the weight of the equipment, or *hopla,* that gave the hoplite his name. Most scholars writing in English today put the total weight of this equipment at 70 pounds or more. This figure originated with W. Rüstow and H. Köchly's *Geschichte des Griechischen Kriegswesens von der Ältesten Zeit bis auf Pyrrhos* (1852), where the authors gave a total of 72 pounds. An influential, combative German military historian, Hans Delbrück, adopted their estimate, and the third edition of his *Geschichte der Kriegskunst* (1920), translated as *History of the Art of War* (1975), has made it popular among English-speaking readers. These 72 pounds are German pounds, each equal to half a kilogram or 1.1 avoirdupois pounds. So the original estimate was actually about 79 avoirdupois pounds, a point that the English translation unfortunately missed, for it gives the erroneous impression that Delbrück thought hoplites carried 72 avoirdupois pounds.[8]

Rüstow and Köchly did not weigh museum pieces or attempt to reconstruct the equipment. One reviewer, Theodor Bergk, dismissed their figures as "purely hypothetical attempts." Another nineteenth-century German scholar, Hans Droysen, justified his decision to ignore them by calling them "arbitrary estimates." After all the archaeological discoveries of the past century and a half, especially in the German excavations at Olympia, we can do better. In 1995 Eero Jarva published a restudy of the armor from Olympia, and in 2002 Johann Peter Franz reported weights for various pieces of equipment in the extensive Axel Guttman collection. To account for the corrosion of bronze and the almost complete disappearance of leather and linen, Franz added 33 percent to each weight to approximate the weight of the piece when it was intact. Scholars can also draw on the experience of enthusiasts who have tried to reconstruct various pieces of hoplite equipment. Peter Connolly, a pioneer in this field, now has many followers in groups such as the Hoplite Association in London, the Sydney Ancients, and the Hoplitikon of Melbourne.[9]

Let's examine the equipment piece by piece, focusing on the late sixth and early fifth centuries. A full set of equipment included a helmet, chest protector, shin guards, shield, spear, and sword.

The most popular helmet through most of the Archaic period, the Corinthian helmet, was hammered from a single sheet of bronze and completely covered the head except for eye holes. Jarva finds the usual range to be 2.6–3.3 pounds, with a few as high as 4.4 pounds. Franz gives the corrected weight as 4.6 pounds. The style of this helmet changed over time. In the last quarter of the sixth century, it became harder and thinner. The average thickness was reduced from 0.05 to 0.03 inches, with an increase in the distance between the skull and the helmet to allow for additional padding. The late Corinthian helmets weighed 2 pounds or less; if we add 33 percent for padding, we get 2.6 pounds. Most helmets worn at the battle of Marathon probably weighed even less than that: Early-fifth-century Athenian vases showing Greeks fighting Persians portray the Greeks wearing "Attic" helmets. These had hinged cheek pieces and did not cover the ears. On the painting of Marathon in the Stoa Poikile, the Plataeans wore only a leather cap called a "dog's skin."[10]

A well-preserved early example of a bronze bell cuirass (breastplate) found in Argos, similar to those portrayed on the Chigi vase (Figure 15), has an average thickness of 0.08 inches and weighs 7.5 pounds in its current state. Later examples are thinner, 0.02–0.04 inches. Franz gives the average corrected weight as 10.6 pounds, with a corrected range of about 7.7–12.1.

Bronze plate cuirasses were never the only option. Homer and Alkaios mention padded linen corslets, probably made of wool stuffed between two layers of quilted linen. To judge by Athenian vase painting, a new type called the shoulder-piece corslet had replaced the bell cuirass by about 525. Debate continues about how it was made. Most likely the maker

15. Battle scene from the Protocorinthian olpe known as the Chigi vase, c. 640 (Museo Nazionale Etrusco di Villa Giulia, Rome, 22679; from E. Pfuhl, *Malerei und Zeichnung der Griechen* [Munich: Bruckmann, 1923], pl. 59)

glued together layers of linen cloth. The Hoplite Association has found that using a leather core speeds up construction. Andy Crapper, one of the group's founders, says that after six years of experience he makes an 8-pound corslet by gluing a dozen or so layers of good midweight cloth onto a leather core. Peter Connolly had earlier achieved the same figure. Vase paintings sometimes show bronze scales added to the corslets, either over the whole or only on the right side. Crapper's reconstruction of this composite corslet, fully covered with bronze scales, weighs 15 pounds.[11]

Shin guards were made of a thin layer of bronze to which linen padding was sewn or glued. Jarva concludes that an average pair weighed about 3.5 pounds; Franz gives a corrected average of 3.7 pounds. Like the helmet, the shin guard became thinner over time. Jarva says the late Archaic examples in Olympia and Copenhagen would have weighed less than 1.1 pounds, so correcting by Franz's 33 percent we may set the average weight of a late Archaic pair at 2.9 pounds.

The concave shield was more or less round, approximately three feet in diameter, with an offset rim that allowed it to rest on the warrior's shoulder. He inserted his left arm up to his elbow into an armband in the center and gripped a leather loop at the edge with his left hand. The shield was made of wood. It could be covered with a thin sheet of bronze on the exterior and leather on the interior. To judge by finds at Olympia, these bronze facings began to be used in the last third of the seventh century, about two-thirds of a century after the double handles appear in vase painting (Figure 16 shows an early example of the double grip). Other shields had bronze rims, but the majority had no bronze and have disappeared without a trace.[12]

Three examples have survived with sufficient wood to be identified. One, dated to the mid-sixth century, probably came from a grave in eastern Sicily and is now in Basel. It was made of willow strips 5.5 inches wide, laminated and pegged together. The famous Chigi vase, painted about 640, seems to show this first type, strips of wood laminated across each other in layers to prevent splitting. This type continued in use for a long time, for a fourth-century example found at Olynthos in northern Greece consisted of crossing pieces of wood 2.4 inches wide (unfortunately the remains of the wood were not analyzed). The second, dated to the early fifth century, probably came from an Etruscan tomb at Bomarzo and is now in the Museo Gregoriano Etrusco di Villa Giulia in Rome. It was made of poplar boards 7.9–11.8 inches wide, glued together with no trace of lamination. The third, from Olympia but so poorly preserved that the method of construction cannot be determined, was willow or poplar. Rather soft woods, both willow and poplar tend to dent rather than split, which qualified them for the list of woods recommended for shields by the Roman naturalist Pliny. They weigh roughly half as much as oak and two-thirds to three-quarters as much as lime and pine.[13]

P. Henry Blyth's reconstruction of the shield in the Vatican weighs 13.7 pounds. The bowl varies from 0.3 to 0.4 inches thick, while the side walls are 0.5–0.7 inches. On the low end of the range in diameter (32.3 inches), this shield had a bronze exterior facing and a leather interior lining. The bronze facing added about 6.6 pounds, so an unfaced poplar shield with the same dimensions would weigh only 7.1 pounds.

Craig Sitch of Manning Imperial in Australia, a modern armorer who produces sophisticated reproductions of ancient Greek equipment, makes several shields: one of poplar, 33 inches in diameter, that weighs 9.5 pounds, and another of radiata pine, 33.5 inches in diameter, that's 14.3–15.4 pounds (samples vary). The Hoplite Association in London

16. Battle scene from a Protocorinthian aryballos, c. 690–680, from Lechaion
(Corinth Museum, CP 2096; from C. W. J. Eliot and Mary Eliot, "The Lechaion
Cemetery near Corinth," *Hesperia* 37 [1968]: pl. 102.2, courtesy of the Trustees of
the American School of Classical Studies at Athens)

produces shields made of lime and pine, 36.6 inches in diameter, that are
14.1 pounds. In popular or willow, these last two models would drop under 11 pounds. Sitch's heaviest version, radiata pine 35.8 inches in diameter, faced with brass and lined with leather, is 19.8 pounds. In poplar, this
shield would be at most 15 pounds. So while some late Archaic hoplites
could have carried shields in the 15-pound range, most probably carried a
lighter one, many a much lighter one, under 11 or even under 10 pounds.
For comparison, a Roman *scutum* weighed 22 pounds.[14]

The hoplite's thrusting spear, to judge by vase paintings, varied between seven and eight feet long, with a cornel or ash shaft about an inch
in diameter, an iron spearhead, and a bronze butt spike. Minor Markle
has calculated that an eight-foot spear would weigh two pounds. Adding
a spearhead and butt spike, Jarva estimates the weight of a typical hoplite
spear as about 3.3 pounds. Franz compares Marcus Junklemann's reconstruction of a Roman *hasta*, which weighed 3.5 pounds.

As a secondary weapon, the hoplite normally carried an iron sword.
In the early fifth century, vases show both a straight cut-and-thrust sword,
usually with a leaf-shaped blade, and a curved, single-edged slashing
sword. Extant examples are not well preserved, so calculating the weight
is difficult. Because the preserved half of a single-edged specimen from
Etruscan Vetulonia weighs 1 pound, Jarva thinks the weight of swords
plus scabbards would fall between 3.3 and 4.4 pounds. Franz notes that a
Roman *gladius* weighed almost 5 pounds.

Other clothing, such as a pair of sandals and a shirt, would add another pound or two.

We can now calculate the total weight carried by an Athenian hoplite in 506:

Helmet	2.6 pounds
Corslet	8–15 pounds
Shin guards (pair)	2.9 pounds
Shield	7.1–15 pounds
Spear	3.3 pounds
Sword	3.3–4.4 pounds
Clothing	1–2 pounds
Total (rounded)	28–45 pounds

Earlier warriors, who sometimes wore additional upper arm guards, lower arm guards, belly guards, and the like, made from very thin bronze, could have added a few pounds more. These estimates remain estimates, but they are not arbitrary or purely hypothetical.

The hoplite therefore carried a maximum of about 50 pounds rather than upward of 70. A fully equipped hoplite might have carried no more than 28 pounds. A warrior who went without chest protection and shin guards could have carried only 17 pounds. The minimum Homer's Odysseus said he needed to fight—helmet, shield, spears—would have protected all vital organs. According to the Spartan king Demaratos, the only essential piece of defensive equipment was the shield, and Aristophanes has the Marathon fighters charge simply "with spear, with shield." Men might even have had a choice of shield, for scattered literary sources refer to wicker shields, presumably made of leather stretched over a frame of woven willow rods. This type would have been a lighter alternative to a solid wooden shield. Homer describes just this sort of mix of equipment in the *Iliad,* where at one point the Greeks exchange gear so that the bravest fighters have the biggest shields, the best helmets, and the longest spears.[15]

The central point is that the Greeks kept to U.S. military historian S. L. A. Marshall's recommendation that a soldier's load should not exceed a third of his body weight. A fully equipped warrior at the Euripos in 506 or at Marathon in 490 might have carried a burden equal to a fifth of his body weight, and many would have had less than a sixth.[16]

How did hoplites deploy? Hellenistic sources describing the Macedonian phalanx give the width of file as three feet, but this figure does not necessarily apply to the Archaic or Classical Greek phalanx, which was equipped differently. The three-foot spacing really rests on a passage from the fifth-century historian Thucydides, in which he says that as hoplites advance, "each man, out of fear, brings his uncovered [right] side as close as possible to the shield of the man stationed to his right." But Thucydides does not say how close that was. There is some truth to Mardonios' statement in Herodotus that the Greeks went to fight on "the finest and most level land," but no plain in Greece looked like a Kansas wheat field. The more I walk on uneven Greek plains—broken up by field walls, watercourses, occasional trees, rocks, ditches, huts, farmhouses, and so on—the more I think that while Archaic hoplites might have lined up at three-foot intervals, they would have scattered or bunched when they charged. Scholars have not always paid sufficient attention to other remarks made by Thucydides, who also says that while the Spartans marched in time to the music of a pipe, other Greeks advanced "violently and furiously," and that the formation of large armies tends to break up or scatter in the approach.[17]

Homer provides an appropriate pair of similes in book 16 of the *Iliad*, when the Myrmidons deploy in a tight formation that Homer likens to a solid wall, and then charge like wasps coming out of a nest:

> And as a man builds solid a wall with stones set close together
> for the rampart of a high house keeping out the force of the winds, so
> close together were the helms and shields massive in the middle.
> For shield leaned on shield, helmet on helmet, man against man,
> and the horse-hair crests along the horns of the shining helmets
> touched as they bent their heads, so dense were they formed on each
>   other.
> . . .
> The Myrmidons came streaming out like wasps at the wayside
> when little boys have got into the habit of making them angry
> by always teasing them as they live in their house by the roadside;
> silly boys, they do something that hurts many people;
> and if some man who travels on the road happens to pass them
> and stirs them unintentionally, they in heart of fury

come swarming out each one from his place to fight for their children.
In heart and in fury like these the Myrmidons streaming
came out from their ships, with a tireless clamor arising.

This imagery would work equally well for Archaic and Classical pha-
lanxes. The two sides did not normally reach each other in neat rectangular formations resembling the red and blue boxes that appear on so many
battle plans.[18]

Relatively few vase paintings from the Archaic period show a tight
phalanx formation. As of September 2008, the Beazley Archive Pottery
Database, an electronic database maintained in Oxford, England, listed
1,761 vases that have images of warriors. Only 17, or about one percent,
show warriors in groups. The best known of these is the Chigi olpe,
painted about 640. Both sides have multiple lines, and a piper accompa-
nies the hoplites advancing to the right, as if to illustrate the famous passage in which Thucydides describes the Spartans marching to pipe music.
Each warrior on the Chigi vase has two spears. At the left, where we see
the two spears of a warrior still arming, the shorter one has a throwing
loop, so it is a javelin. In the two battle lines that appear about to clash,
some warriors have a raised finger on the spear they hold horizontally.
These warriors are about to throw their first spear, after which they will
close to fight hand-to-hand. The painter has omitted space.

Vases with hoplites in groups of three or more show men standing
still, advancing, running (sometimes perhaps in a race in armor). They
do not show fighting. Vases that show hoplites fighting—there are hundreds of them—do not show tight formations. As François Lissarrague
remarks, "the first representation of the phalanx seems also to be the
last," for the other images do not have a pipe player, do not show both
sides, and do not show more than one line of hoplites.[19]

It would be fascinating to have the larger wall paintings of battles,
such as the famous painting of Marathon in the Stoa Poikile. German
archaeologist Wolf-Dietrich Niemeier is currently excavating one at Kalapodi in Phocis. He describes it as a mid-seventh-century battle painting
comparable to the Chigi vase, but on a much larger scale. The only photograph I have seen shows two hoplites advancing close together from the
right; whether there were more, and more lines, remains to be seen.

How did hoplites fight? They began their advance with spears held at the slope on their right shoulders, spearheads upward. They lowered them on command to an underhand thrusting position. During the march they might sing. During the charge they yelled a war cry, something like *eleleu* or *alala*. No conclusive evidence shows that Greek armies collided on the run. The ancient historians regularly speak of armies coming "to hands" or "to spear." The slow Spartan advance, in particular, does not fit the shock tactics that modern historians imagine. In the *Iliad*, the two sides approach each other tentatively, often throwing spears at a distance before some fighters get within an arm's reach.

Opinions differ on whether hoplites delivered their initial blows underhand, with the thumb forward, or overhand, with the thumb rearmost. The Spartan warriors in the movie *300* fight with an underhand grip, which has the advantage of requiring no change in hand position as the soldiers lower their spears, charge, and fight. But in vase paintings soldiers in lines about to engage wield their spears overhand, which would permit a more powerful thrust; only in duels do we see underhand grips. Perhaps the debate is misguided, and we should not look for uniformity. Individuals might have preferred different grips.

For all the prominence of the othismos (push) in modern discussions, the three great Classical historians Herodotus, Thucydides, and Xenophon use the word in battle contexts exactly three times: twice in Herodotus, once in Thucydides, and never in Xenophon. At the battle of Thermopylae in 480, there was an othismos over the body of the Spartan king Leonidas; at Plataea in 479, there was a long fight before the two sides came to othismos; at Delion in 424, there was an obstinate struggle with an othismos of shields. The upshot is revealing: The word for the shove supposed to be the essence of Greek battle occurs once in a description of Greek fighting Greek. There it does not stand alone, but is modified by "of shields." From these few passages, it is hard to be sure that Thucydides' othismos of shields is any more literal than Herodotus' othismos of words, a phrase Herodotus uses twice.[20]

A century ago, readers did not take the word literally. Consider Herodotean scholars. In his translation (1858), George Rawlinson used "a fierce struggle" for Thermopylae and "a hand-to-hand struggle" for

Plataea. In 1904 George C. Macauley translated the same passages "a great struggle" and "justling" (= jostling). In his 1908 commentary on the last three books of Herodotus, Macan wrote that "Hdt. seems to use *othismos* for fighting at the closest quarters (without special reference to its etymological sense)." In the Loeb edition (1921), Alfred Denis Godley offered "a great struggle" and "blows at close quarters." In his 1938 *Lexicon to Herodotus,* still the standard work, John Enoch Powell rendered othismos as "hand-to-hand combat."[21]

Thomas Hobbes (1628) rendered the Thucydides passage, where the text reads literally a "fierce fight and othismos of shields," as "the rest made sharp battle; standing close, and striving to put by each others' bucklers." He gives a more literal alternative, "bearing each other down with their shields," only in a note. Richard Crawley (1874) produced "engaged with the utmost obstinacy, shield against shield." Benjamin Jowett (1881) translated "a fierce struggle and pushing of shield against shield." In the 1920 Loeb edition, Charles F. Smith used "stubborn conflict, with shield pressed against shield."

It is not easy to find the image of a rugby scrum in these translations. Nor were historians yet thinking of Greek battles as shoving contests. Delbrück, for instance, wrote that: "In such a phalanx two ranks at most can participate in the actual combat, with the second rank stepping into the holes of the first at the moment of contact. The following ranks serve as immediate replacements for the dead and wounded, but they exercise principally a physical and moral pressure. The deeper phalanx will defeat the more shallow one, even if on both sides exactly the same number of combatants actually manage to use their weapons." By "physical pressure," Delbrück did not mean shoving by the rear ranks. On the next page he said that Greeks did not put unarmored men in the rear ranks because "the realization that they could not really expect to receive any true support from these rear ranks would have seriously weakened the drive, the forward thrust of the foremost ranks, in which, of course, the value of the rearmost ranks normally lies." If battles were shoving matches, more men in the rear, whether armed or unarmed, would have helped. Delbrück must mean that by their reassuring physical presence the rear ranks supported the front ranks and encouraged their advance.[22]

How then did the rugby model come to be the standard view? The earliest use of the rugby analogy that I have found is in George B. Grundy's *Thucydides and the History of His Age,* originally published in 1911: "Under ordinary circumstances the hoplite force advanced into battle in a compact mass. . . . When it came into contact with the enemy, it relied in the first instance on shock tactics, that is to say, on the weight put into the first onset and developed in the subsequent thrust. The principle was very much the same as that followed by the forwards in a scrummage at the Rugby game of football." Grundy's further explanation of his idea is curious, to say the least: "People who are unacquainted with military history do not understand the importance of mere avoirdupois weight in close fighting. A regiment of big men meeting a regiment of smaller men in a circumscribed space, such as, for example, a village street, will almost certainly drive the latter back. . . . In the fifth century the appreciation of it [the weight factor] would seem to have been at least imperfect. It was not till [the battle of] Leuktra [in 371] that the Greeks really learnt this particular lesson in the military art." Of course Greek battles did not take place on village streets, and the Greeks knew their own military history. If weight was so important in Archaic and Classical battles, how is it possible that the Greeks did not appreciate it until the fourth century?[23]

Grundy found a follower in William J. Woodhouse. In his 1933 book *King Agis III of Sparta and His Campaign in Arkadia in 418 B.C.,* Woodhouse wrote that "a conflict of hoplites was, in the main, a matter of brawn, of shock of the mass developed instantaneously as a steady thrust with the whole weight of the file behind it—a literal shoving of the enemy off the ground on which he stood." Here is the earliest clear statement I have found of the view that *all* hoplites pushed, not merely the first few rows, as Grundy's rugby analogy might have suggested. (Only the eight forwards, not all 15 players on a team, participate in a rugby scrum.) The context for this passage is Woodhouse's odd discussion of Thucydides 5.71, where Thucydides says that soldiers kept close to their right-hand neighbor's shield out of fear. Woodhouse labeled this "notion . . . , to put it bluntly, nothing but a fatuous delusion and stark nonsense." He claimed to understand the real explanation: Hoplites advanced with their shields held straight across their chests, forcing them to slant to the right as they walked.[24]

Not surprisingly, the great commentator on Thucydides, Arnold W. Gomme, objected to this dismissal of the experienced Greek general's word: "A Greek battle was not so simply 'a matter of brawn, a steady thrust with the whole weight of the file behind it—a literal shoving of the enemy off the ground on which he stood' (did the back rows *push* the men in front?), as Professor Woodhouse supposes. It was not a scrummage. The men all used their weapons, and had their right arms free." But no publicity is bad publicity. Despite Gomme's sarcasm, the rugby analogy caught on. By the 1970s it had become the standard view of how Greeks fought. Its defenders now describe it as the "natural" reading of the texts.[25]

It is true that, unlike the noun *othismos,* the verb *otheo* (push) and its compounds occur frequently in the classical historians. One side frequently pushes the other back. The rugby model takes these verbs literally. But before we assume that Greek writers meant this pushing literally, we should consider two points. First, they sometimes use the verb "push" figuratively. When Herodotus says that Miltiades pushed away the Apsinthians by walling off the Chersonese (modern Gallipoli) peninsula, he is not speaking literally. When Herodotus refers to the Athenians pushing the Persian back so that the battle was no longer for their territory but for his, he is not speaking literally. When Herodotus says that the Greeks at Plataea pushed back the Persian cavalry, he is not speaking literally.[26] So it is at least possible that when historians use the word "push" in battle contexts, they do not mean it literally.

Second, the Greeks inherited this word *otheo* from Homer. A word does not always mean the same thing. But if it has a well-established meaning in Homer's battle contexts, the burden of proof rests on those who believe it means something else in the Classical historians' battle narratives. If Homer describes mass shoving, the natural interpretation is that the historians do too. But if he does not, the natural interpretation is that they do not either. W. Kendrick Pritchett, the leading Greek military historian in the 1970s and 1980s, opted for the former. "The *othismos* is as common in Homer as it is in later hoplite warfare," he opined, "although the noun is not used." In his description of Homeric fighting, Pritchett said, "they pushed, leaning their shields against their shoulders . . . while they thrust with swords and spears." But this combination never occurs in the poem. Pritchett cited two passages for the leaning of shields on shoulders. Neither mentions pushing. He cited six passages for the thrusting with swords and spears. Only one mentions pushing.[27]

The one passage that mentions both thrusting with weapons and pushing comes in *Iliad* 13. The Greeks are massed together closely in what sounds like a hoplite phalanx as Hektor attacks:

> But when he met the dense phalanx
> he came close and stopped. The opposing sons of the Achaians,
> pricking him with swords and leaf-headed spears,
> pushed him away from them; he shivered as he retreated.

Here the Greeks are fighting inside their camp wall with their backs to their ships. A small group of nine champions, each one named by the poet, rallies together. Homer does not mention shields; the stabbing and the pushing happen simultaneously. He means that the Greeks used their weapons to force Hektor to retreat, slowly—pushed back, as opposed to routed. A figurative push makes equally good sense in the other passages Pritchett cites as evidence of a mass shove in the *Iliad*.[28]

In his description of the battle of Koroneia in 394—one of the literalists' favorite passages—Xenophon uses the verb "push" while alluding to a passage in Homer that does *not* use it. "Clashing their shields together," Xenophon says in his *Hellenika*, "they pushed, they fought, they killed, they died." This compressed sentence alludes to a scene that occurs twice in the *Iliad*. Xenophon uses the same verb in "clashing their shields" that Homer does:

> Now as these advancing came to one place and encountered,
> they clashed their [leather] shields together and their spears, and the
>   strength
> of armored men in bronze, and the shields massive in the middle
> clashed against each other, and the sound grew huge of the fighting.
> There the wails of despair and the cries of triumph rose up together
> of men killing and men killed, and the ground ran with blood.

The allusion is clearer in the expanded version Xenophon gives in his *Agesilaos*. Here we have, as in Homer, the peculiar noise of battle, men killing and men dying, and blood on the ground: "Clashing their shields together, they pushed, they fought, they killed, they died. There was no screaming, nor was there silence, but the noise that anger and battle together will produce . . . When the fighting ended, one could see, where they met one another, the ground stained with blood." And what happens next in the *Iliad*? Fighting with javelins. Homer continues:

> So long as it was early morning and the sacred daylight increasing
> so long the thrown weapons of both took hold, and people fell.

If Xenophon has this *Iliad* scene in mind, "push" cannot be a mass shove in either the *Agesilaos* or *Hellenika* passages.[29]

Literalists like to cite passages referring to the importance of weight in Greek battles. But this language can also be figurative. Commenting on the battle of Mantinea in 362, for instance, the first-century historian Diodoros of Sicily says that Thessalian slingers and javelin throwers "practiced this type of fighting assiduously from boyhood and consequently were accustomed to exercise great weight in battles because of their experience in handling these missiles."[30]

In short, while individual soldiers sometimes shoved with their shields, when the Classical historians say that one army pushed the other back, they mean that close hand-to-hand combat resulted in a gradual, step-by-step withdrawal as opposed to a rout. When Xenophon says that at the battle of Leuctra in 371 the Spartans finally retreated, pushed back by the mass, he does not mean a mass shove. Since the 12-deep Spartans were winning initially, they cannot have been engaged in a shoving match with the 50-deep Thebans. Xenophon means that the Spartans were overcome by Theban numbers rather than by any superiority in the Theban hoplites or failure in their own courage.

"All infantry actions," the distinguished military historian John Keegan once remarked, "even those fought in the closest of close order, are not, in the last resort, combats of mass against mass, but the sum of many combats of individuals—one against one, one against two, three against five." If we imagine Archaic battles as multiple hand-to-hand fights, we can take two passages in Euripides as reflecting the essence of contemporary battle, though they are set in the legendary past. In *Phoenician Women* 1380–1420, the rival brothers Polyneikes and Eteokles fight a duel that begins with the blowing of the *salpinx,* an early trumpet that sounded the battle charge. They both advance, crouch beneath their shields, and jab their spears whenever they see the other peeking over the shield's rim, but do no real damage until Eteokles stumbles on a stone, revealing his leg. Polyneikes then stabs Eteokles in the thigh, but exposes his own shoulder as he does so, and Eteokles manages to stab him there. Both break their spears and they fight with their swords, clashing their shields together, until Eteokles does the Thessalian feint, stepping back with his left foot and then, as Polyneikes advances, forward with his right, driving his sword through Polyneikes' belly. As Eteokles bends to strip his brother's armor, the dying Polyneikes jabs his sword into Eteokles' liver. Every bit of this could have happened in a hoplite battle, provided we allow a warrior enough space to take a step back.[31]

In *Herakleidai* 830–842, Euripides describes a battle between the Athenians and the Argives. The trumpet sounds, the two sides begin to fight, the shields make a great noise. First the Argives break the Athenian lines, but then the fighting surges in the other direction and intensifies as they stand foot against foot, man against man. Finally, without any mention of pushing, the Athenians rout the Argives completely. This too might describe an actual battle.

The Classical Greek phalanx, familiar from Thucydides and Xenophon, excluded light-armed fighters such as archers, javelin throwers, and slingers. But if we imagine Archaic warriors fighting as described above, we are free to consider the possibility, or even the probability, that the Archaic Greek phalanx included a variety of fighters, so that it was closer to what we read about in Homer than to what Thucydides describes. Passages in the lyric poets, vase paintings, and finds at Greek sanctuaries support the possibility. As late as 640–600, Tyrtaios appended the following lines to one of his exhortations to hoplites:

> You light-armed men, wherever you can aim
> from the shield-cover, pelt them with great rocks

and hurl at them your smooth-shaved javelins,
  helping the armored troops with close support.

Archaic vases often show archers together with hoplites, and archaeologists have found lead figurines of crouching archers among the Archaic and early Classical dedications at the sanctuary of Artemis Orthia in Sparta. These archers look comparable to the stone throwers and javelin throwers in the Tyrtaios passage, crouching behind the protection of hoplites rather than standing. In the *Iliad,* Homer says Teukros

> took his place in the shelter of Telamonian Aias'
> shield, as Aias lifted his shield to take him. The hero
> would watch, whenever in the throng he had struck some man with an
>   arrow,
> and as the man dropped and died where he was stricken, the archer
> would run back again, like a child to the arms of his mother,
> to Aias, who would hide him in the glittering shield's protection.

A good archer would keep his eyes open for an opportunity, as Paris (Alexandros) did when he knocked three heroes out of the fighting: He hit Diomedes in the foot, Machaon in the right shoulder, and Eurypylos in the right thigh. In close hand-to-hand fighting, such archers would be of little use, but in a more fluid battle a light-armed man would have moments to exploit. A contingent of light-armed archers and slingers, such as the Lokrians, could disrupt an enemy:

> The heart was not in them to endure close-standing combat,
> for they did not have the brazen helmets crested with horse-hair,
> they did not have the strong-circled shields and the ash spears,
> but rather these had followed to Ilion with all their confidence
> in their bows and slings strong-twisted of wool; and with these
> they shot their close volleys and broke the Trojan battalions.
> So now these others fought in front in elaborate war gear
> against the Trojans and Hektor the brazen-helmed, and the Lokrians
> unseen volleyed from behind, so the Trojans remembered
> nothing of the joy of battle, since the shafts struck them into confusion.

I think that the exclusive hoplite phalanx did not exist before Marathon. In Archaic battles, men fought with whatever equipment they preferred and could afford.[32]

So far I have said nothing about Greek horsemen. Thanks partly to the rough, mountainous terrain and partly to the high cost of raising horses, cavalry played a much less important role in Greece than it did east of the Aegean. The Thessalians had 1,000 horsemen, but scholars debate whether the Athenians had any cavalry at all in the late sixth century. Perhaps they had only mounted hoplites who rode to the battlefield but fought on foot. I believe that in 506 the Athenians did have a cavalry force, but only a small one, with fewer than a hundred horses. The Boeotians and Chalcidians probably had more. Though Boeotian cavalry is not specifically attested until the Persian Wars, Homer calls the Thebans "horse-racing Cadmeans," and Boeotia is better cavalry country than Attica. The aristocrats at Chalcis were known as the *hippobotai* (horse feeders), which suggests that they had cavalry. Aristotle says that both the Chalcidians and the Eretrians, their rivals at the other end of the Lelantine plain, used horses in war. According to an inscription seen by Strabo, the Eretrians' Archaic cavalry numbered 600 horsemen, one for every five hoplites. The numbers at the battle of the Euripos might not have been so lopsided, for we do not know what proportion of their horsemen the Boeotians and Chalcidians actually sent into the field.[33]

Like the infantry, Greek horsemen provided their own equipment. Vase paintings show some horsemen with the entire set of hoplite equipment, occasionally even including the round double-grip shield; others have helmets and body armor, but no shield; still others have at most light corslets. They fought with one or more light spears or javelins, a heavy thrusting spear, a sword, or some combination of the above, but not with bows and arrows in the Persian manner. Several recent books have argued for the importance of Greek cavalry, but in the Archaic period it really did not count for much south of Thessaly.

Finally, what sort of training did Greek soldiers have? Sparta had a rigorous program designed to produce good soldiers. It began at age 7 and continued until 18. Even thereafter Spartans had no jobs other than to train for war. State-owned serfs made this training possible because they worked the land, freeing Spartans for other activities. Writing in the fourth century, Aristotle credited their early military dominance to the Spartans' training and the discipline it instilled: "Even the Spartans themselves, as we know from experience, were superior to others only so long as they were the only people which assiduously practiced the rigors of discipline: and nowadays they are beaten both in athletic contests and in actual war. . . . The Spartan training has now to face rivals. Formerly it had none." Outside Sparta, no cities had professional armies or even communal training programs for their citizen soldiers. Men turned out for a campaign; when it ended, they returned to what they had been doing before. But I should stress that the ancient Greeks were much more physically active than most people in the United States and Europe are today. The typical Greek man worked on a farm, walked wherever he went, and ate a lean diet that produced a low body-mass index. Wealthy men who did not do their own farm work spent a lot of time exercising in the gymnasium, exercise that Greek writers say prepared them for war. So the fact that Archaic Athenians had no required group training or exercises before going to war should not fool us into thinking that they were unconditioned for combat. Victor Davis Hanson has an illuminating passage about the "uncanny strength" of potbellied California farmers who in middle age could outwork his athletic friends in their late 20s when they came to visit his family farm.[34]

The absence of formal training should make us try hard to overcome any mental picture we might have of Greeks (Spartans excepted) marching in unison or carrying out complex battlefield maneuvers. In the fourth century, Greek hoplites drilled to do a few simple movements, such as leveling their spears and advancing at the sound of the trumpet, or setting down their shields and standing at ease. Because the front man in each Spartan file was an officer, Xenophon says, the Spartans carried out movements that others found difficult, such as changing from a column into a line of battle. That other Greeks would find such a basic marching maneuver difficult tells us a lot.[35]

In sixth-century Athens, an elected polemarchos commanded the Athenians, who were probably organized after Kleisthenes in ten tribal units, as they certainly were in the fifth century. The tribes probably had their own commanding officers. Scholars debate whether there was any further organization whatsoever.

The Battles of the Euripos

Let us resume the story of the Athenians who marched north after the Peloponnesian invasion of Attica fell apart in 506. Herodotus covers two battles in about two sentences: "The Athenians joined battle with the Boeotians, and decisively overwhelmed them, slaughtering vast numbers and capturing 700 of them alive. Then, on the same day, the Athenians crossed over to Euboea and met the Chalcidians in battle as well. Winning another victory there. . . ." Both fights would have looked more like confused melees than giant rugby scrums. The first, in particular, must have ended quickly, or the Athenians would not have had the energy to cross the Euripos and fight again that day. Perhaps the full Boeotian army did not have time to gather. It is also likely that the Athenians had help from Eretria, a traditional enemy of Chalcis.[36]

The Athenians honored their dead by inhuming or (more likely) cremating them near the Euripos and erecting a mound over their remains, all at public expense. This collective burial is the earliest known example of what became standard Athenian practice, a common grave for men who fought in a common cause. An epigram attributed to Simonides is our only evidence for the burial mound at the Euripos:

Under the folds of [Mount] Dirphys, we were killed, and upon us a
  mound
was piled near the Euripos, at public expense;
not unjustly, for we lost our lovely youth
when we welcomed the rugged cloud of war.

This epitaph fits Kleisthenes' democratic army by defending the use of public funds to raise the mound, heroizing the dead with language that has Homeric echoes, and noting that the Athenians fought willingly. The burial itself imitated private aristocratic family burials in Attica that took the form of mounds, modeled on the burials of Homeric heroes such as Patroklos and Hektor. To honor the fallen, the Athenians raised a mound over the remains of the dead and erected a tombstone, inscribed with the epigram and the names of the dead, on top of the mound.[37]

Herodotus draws a lesson in terms of tyranny versus freedom, one of the great themes of his *Histories:* "So Athens flourished. Now, the advantages of everyone having a voice in the political procedure are not restricted just to single instances, but are plain to see wherever one looks. For instance, while the Athenians were ruled by tyrants, they were no better at warfare than any of their neighbors, but once they had got rid of the tyrants they became vastly superior. This goes to show that while they were under an oppressive regime they fought below their best because they were working for a master, whereas as free men each individual wanted to achieve something for himself." The twin victories paid off handsomely for the survivors. Not only did the Athenians annex border territories in the northwest and the northeast, they also settled 4,000 Athenian citizens on land they confiscated from the Chalcidian aristocrats in the fertile Lelantine plain between Chalcis and Eretria. The Athenians eventually released their captives for two minas each, the standard rate for ransom among the Peloponnesians. At that rate 700 Boeotian prisoners brought in more than 1,300 pounds of silver, to say nothing of the captured Chalcidians or the value of equipment stripped from the enemy corpses. The Athenians put the prisoners' chains on the Acropolis, where Herodotus saw them hanging on walls burned by the Persians in 480–479. The Athenians dedicated a tenth of the ransom in the form of a bronze four-horse chariot, with the inscription:

> The Boeotian and Chalcidian peoples were tamed
> By the sons of the Athenians in works of war,
> Who quelled their arrogance in dark bonds of iron,
> And set up these horses as a tithe for Pallas [Athena].[38]

The Athenians' problems did not disappear. The Thebans soon counterattacked, but were defeated; they then urged the Aeginetans to help them by waging an undeclared war on Athens. Aeginetan raids damaged the Attic coast, including the bay of Phaleron, Athens' harbor. As the Athenians were preparing (building ships?) to take revenge, the Spartans called their allies to a meeting at which they proposed reinstating the deposed tyrant Hippias, so that Athens would be weaker and willing to submit to their authority. The allies did not approve this proposal.

Hippias turned to the Persians. After his brother Hipparchos' assassination in 513, Hippias had married his daughter to the son of the tyrant of a Greek city in Asia, "perceiving that they had great influence with King Darius." Now "he missed no opportunity to slander the Athenians to Artaphrenes and did all he could to bring about Athens' submission to himself and Darius." The Athenians sent ambassadors to Sardis to urge the Persians not to listen to exiles, only to be told to take Hippias back if they wanted security. Some Iranologists find this story suspect on the grounds that it sounds like Athenian propaganda. To justify their participation in the Ionian Revolt, the argument goes, the Athenians told a story in which the Persians broke their treaty first. But since we do not know the terms of Athens' submission to Persia, it is not clear that Artaphrenes violated them in this story. Even if the Athenians had received a guarantee of autonomy, Artaphrenes might have considered himself entitled to advise the Athenians to take back Hippias. In any case the Athenians refused. "By this refusal," Herodotus comments, "their posture as enemies of the Persians became public."[39]

This change in policy paved the way for cooperation instead of hostility with Sparta, but it led to armed conflict with Persia.

CHAPTER 3

The Ionian Revolt

The Outbreak of the Revolt

D uring the winter of 499/8, Aristagoras of Miletus arrived in
Athens to ask for help in the Ionian Greeks' revolt from Persia.
Aristagoras had already visited Sparta, where he had appealed to
Kleomenes without success. In front of the Athenian assembly, he talked
up the riches of Asia and how easy it would be to defeat the Persians,
who fought without spears or shields. He piled on rhetoric about how
the Milesians were originally Athenian colonists and how the Athenians,
great power that they were, ought to protect them. After Aristagoras made
unspecified extravagant promises, the Athenians agreed to send 20 ships,
probably penteconters with 50–80 men each. Echoing Homer, Herodotus says that "these ships turned out to be the beginning of evils for both
Greeks and barbarians." He does not exaggerate. As Maria Brosius put
it, from the Persian perspective "Athens' involvement . . . constituted a
violation of the Persian-Athenian treaty of 507/6."[1]

The trouble in Ionia had started when Aristagoras listened to the
"men of substance" (or, in a less flattering translation, "the fat") exiled
from Naxos, the largest and most fertile of the Cycladic islands. The exiles
asked for the forces they needed to return home. Aristagoras reasoned
that if he played his cards right, he could rule Naxos and the rest of the

Cyclades, in addition to Miletus and the Milesian foothold in Thrace—potentially controlling both the Cycladic and the Thracian silver mines. Darius had granted these mines to Histiaios, the tyrant of Miletus, as a reward for faithful service during the Scythian expedition. When Darius later promoted Histiaios to an advisory post in Susa, he left his cousin and son-in-law Aristagoras in control of Miletus. Some scholars have doubted that Aristagoras could really have hoped to control both the Cycladic and the Thracian silver, but with Histiaios an honored adviser at the royal court, why not?[2]

So Aristagoras told the Naxian exiles that he wanted to help them, but he lacked the resources to defeat the "8,000 shields" and "many long ships" that Naxos had. (The unique expression "8,000 shields" may mean not fully equipped hoplites, but all men able to carry any sort of shield.) Aristagoras therefore asked the exiles to approve a request to his friend Artaphrenes, the Persian governor at Sardis. The exiles agreed, promising to pay for gifts to the Persians and for the expenses of the expedition. They thought these expenses would be low, because they expected the local residents to submit quietly. Exiles often persuade themselves that their popularity back home is actually high—and other outsiders looking for an excuse to meddle believe them.[3]

Aristagoras put the idea to Artaphrenes, stressing Naxos' wealth, proximity to Asia, and potential as a springboard to the other Cycladic islands and even the large island of Euboea, off the coast of Attica. He asked for 100 ships. Artaphrenes raised the stakes, promising that 200 ships would be ready in the spring, once he had secured the king's approval. Perhaps he wanted to make sure that it was a Persian operation rather than a Greek campaign with Persian support. To command the expedition he appointed his cousin Megabates, son of the Megabazos who had conquered Thrace.

Darius had contemplated westward expansion for more than a decade. Before the Scythian expedition in 513, his wife had advised him to let the Scythians wait while he attacked Greece. Darius responded by sending a Greek doctor on a scouting mission with 15 Persians. The spies sailed along the coast of Greece and crossed the Adriatic Sea over to Italy. The doctor then deserted. Darius invaded Scythia.

After the Scythian expedition, Darius had opted mostly for campaigning by land on the Aegean coast (Figure 17). By 500 he controlled the eastern and northern coasts, the route through the Hellespont to the Black Sea, and the most important islands directly off the coast. A naval campaign through the Cyclades was a logical next step.

In the spring of 499, the Persian fleet sailed north from Miletus, pretending to head for the Hellespont. Herodotus heard a story about a quarrel between Aristagoras and Megabates, with the improbable result that Megabates tipped off the Naxians he was about to attack. More likely, they heard about their exiles' activities and prepared accordingly.

The exiles misread the Naxians' resolve. After besieging the town for four months, the invaders had run out of supplies, Aristagoras had spent a lot of his own money, and the Naxian exiles did not have the resources to pay for the expedition as they had promised. Megabates decided to abandon the siege. He fortified a place on Naxos for the exiles and returned to Asia.

Fearing for his own position in Miletus, Aristagoras began to plan a revolt from Persia. Just then, "the man with the tattooed head" arrived with a message from Histiaios. Histiaios had shaved a slave's head, tattooed on it instructions for Aristagoras to revolt, waited for the slave's hair to grow back, and sent him to Miletus with orders to tell Aristagoras to shave the slave's head. George Cawkwell recently declared this story unacceptable in detail, quipping that "if the slave was reliable enough to carry the message on his head, he was reliable enough to carry it in his head." But how would a slave have persuaded Aristagoras that what he had to say really came from Histiaios, without some sign? Why not a tattoo?[4]

When the Ionians asked Histiaios later why he sent this message, he told them that Darius planned to transplant the Phoenicians to Ionia and the Ionians to Phoenicia. Though Herodotus asserts that Darius had no such plan for a population exchange, the Great King may have intended to transplant some Greeks. He later moved Milesians and Eretrians who resisted him, so the Naxians would definitely be candidates. Histiaios may have warned Aristagoras after hearing about big new plans for the west.

Critical scholars frequently fault Herodotus for focusing so narrowly on individuals such as Aristagoras and Histiaios that he fails to see the

17. Map of the Aegean

bigger picture of why the Ionians revolted, not to mention why others followed their example. But Herodotus supplies plenty of threads for weaving a larger, more complex tapestry. Explanations that contradict Herodotus are unconvincing. For instance, the hypothesis that Persian expansion ruined the trading economies of Ionian cities not only contradicts Herodotus, who says that Miletus was at its economic peak; it also does not fit the external evidence of increased monumental building, increased private dedications, and increased silver coinage. The Greeks of Asia prospered under the Persians.

The Greeks did have potential economic grievances. For one, the confiscation of land. The king had granted large estates to Persians willing to resettle in Asia Minor in return for help defending the area, such as the man buried in Karaburun II. For another, the annual tribute. Several late stories suggest that Darius was considered lenient in the amount of tribute he required, but require he did. For a third, required military service. Before 513 this standard requirement had not affected Greeks much, but Darius' Scythian campaign involved tens of thousands of them serving in the fleet. After several smaller campaigns, the Naxian fiasco called upon many Greeks again, as many as 40,000 men for the crews. Though this first attempt to conquer the Cyclades failed, the Greeks could expect it to be repeated. Campaigns to Greece and farther west would require more service.

Herodotus supplies all these reasons for the Ionian Revolt, without trying to oversimplify and name a single, truest explanation. But how did Aristagoras persuade Darius' Greek subjects that they had a chance against the powerful Persian navy? No doubt he suggested that Greeks not yet subject to the Persians would help. No doubt he talked about how their revolt would spur others into action, such as the Hellespontines, the Carians, and the Cyprians (all of whom did revolt), as well as the Lydians (who had revolted in 546), the Babylonians (who had already revolted against Darius once), and perhaps even the Egyptians, whose uprising came a few years too late to help the Ionians. But I suspect that he stressed the opportunity offered by the Persian ships returned from Naxos and docked on the coast. To explain the importance of this fleet requires a digression on Archaic navies.

Archaic Navies

The early history of Mediterranean warships is obscure. No warships of the seventh through fourth centuries have been found. Between 2003 and 2006 the Persian Wars Shipwreck Survey Project—a collaborative venture of the Ephorate of Underwater Antiquities, the Canadian Archaeological Institute at Athens, and the Hellenic Centre for Marine Research—mounted four expeditions hoping to find warships at two places where storms destroyed hundreds of them, as well as at the site of the battle of Artemision. The team used visual observation, sidescan sonar, a submersible vehicle, and two remote-operated vehicles, but failed to identify any warships, though they did recover a spear butt spike, apparently cherished in an amphora by the resident octopus. A trireme, the best type of warship available in the late Archaic and Classical periods, may never be found. Unlike a loaded merchant vessel, whose cargo could sink it straight to the bottom and then protect the wood from marine predators and general deterioration, a trireme carried little but its crew, most of whom would abandon a sinking ship. (Experts estimate that the crew weighed almost half as much as the wooden hull.) When penetrated by an enemy ram, a trireme would be swamped rather than sunk, so that it could be salvaged before it went down. Of triremes that did sink, little will remain.

In the absence of direct physical evidence, scholars depend on images of ships, mostly on Athenian pots (and relatively rare and notoriously difficult to interpret), together with literary sources, mostly Greek and especially Herodotus. At the time of the Ionian Revolt, the penteconter (50-oared ship) and the triaconter (30-oared ship) remained in use, but the trireme had become the top-of-the-line warship. In the fifth century, a trireme had up to 170 rowers positioned in three banks. These rowers powered a cigar-shaped ship, less than 20 feet broad, some 121 feet long, with a bronze-covered ram at its prow. A great debate over the structure of the trireme ended, at least in the minds of most naval historians, with the launching of the *Olympias* in June 1987. Aptly described as a "floating hypothesis" for a fourth-century trireme, *Olympias* resulted from a collaboration between Cambridge philosopher John Morrison and naval architect John Coates. The idea of building a life-size working trireme came up in 1981 over dinner in Britain, probably the one country in the world where enough people care enough about both classics and navies to raise the £750,000 necessary to turn this vision into reality. In sea trials conducted between 1987 and 1994, *Olympias'* oar system proved workable, though the ship's all-day cruising speed and momentary peak speed fell about 30 percent short of expectations. These experiments led to several suggestions for tweaking the design, which, the experts think, would enable a modern trireme to work significantly better.

When was the trireme invented? Controversy continues. It is first mentioned in a poem by Hipponax of Ephesus, c. 540–520. A plausible hypothesis holds that the Carthaginians, spurred by a naval defeat c. 540, invented the oar system; that the Egyptians, the coastal power with the largest financial resources, applied the new oar system to much larger ships; and that the Persians, when they set their sights on Egypt in the 520s, had triremes built to match the Egyptian fleet. Triremes were expensive. They required not only more wood than penteconters, but also sailcloth, ropes, flax soaked with pitch for caulking seams, and bronze for sheathing the ram. They were also expensive to man. Herodotus regularly calculates 200 men per trireme, the Athenian standard during his own day, including 10 marines and 4 archers. In 480 Xerxes' ships included 30 marines in addition to native crews.[5]

How many triremes and penteconters did the Great King have? According to Herodotus, Xerxes had 1,207 triremes with 230 men each, plus 3,000 penteconters with 80 men each, or 517,610 men total. Given that the rowers came only from the coastal areas, these numbers are probably as exaggerated as the numbers Herodotus reports for the land army. At Doriskos, Xerxes reviewed his fleet much as he reviewed his army, asking questions about each contingent and having the answers recorded. Perhaps the numbers for ships should be taken as the *potential* forces, analogous to the numbers for infantry. Herodotus' statement that Darius had 600 triremes on his Scythian campaign would mean that the king's potential strength was 600 triremes, not that he actually had that many with him. Alternatively, we could read 600 as simply meaning a large fleet, since Herodotus gives the same figure for the Scythian expedition, the battle of Lade, and the Marathon campaign.[6]

The Greeks lagged behind the wealthier Mediterranean powers in building new fleets. Shortly after 540, the tyrant of Samos used 100 penteconters to raid and plunder his neighbors. He supported the Persian invasion of Egypt with 40 triremes, the hulls perhaps provided by the Persians. The Corinthians, whose city was famously known as "wealthy Corinth," built the first triremes in Greece. At the battle of Salamis in 480, they had 40. The Aeginetans, another Archaic naval power, had 30. No other Greek city managed more than 16, except the Athenians, who built an impressive 200 triremes after a lucky strike of silver in 483. Earlier the Athenians relied on private owners of penteconters for their fleet, such as it was. In the lingering war against Aegina after 506, they could put to sea only 50 penteconters, until the Corinthians sold them 20 more for a nominal price. Individuals owned the first triremes attested at Athens. The trireme on which Miltiades—the future hero of Marathon—sailed to the Chersonese, as well as the five triremes with which he returned home in 493, were probably privately owned.[7]

In 500 the Greeks had no large fleets of triremes. Aristagoras, ruler of the most prosperous Greek city in Asia, had to ask the Persians for triremes to deal with the Naxians, who had long ships, but apparently no triremes. Yet if the Greeks hoped to defy the Persians, they had to control the sea.

The presence in Ionia of a large Persian fleet offered the rebels an opportunity. "Through guile," Herodotus says (without telling us what the trick was), they arrested many of the Greek tyrants who were commanding contingents in the fleet. The promise of equality under the law turned the tyrants' men into freedom fighters, and the rebels acquired at a stroke 200 good triremes. Only after this fleet had joined the cause was Aristagoras "in open revolt."[8]

The Course of the Revolt

In the spring of 498, the Athenians reached Miletus together with five Eretrian triremes carrying another 1,000 men. Another messenger must therefore have approached Eretria, and we can infer still another from Herodotus' later remark that a city on the coast of Caria had refused the offer of an alliance before the Sardis campaign. I suspect that the Ionians sent messengers in all directions. The Cyprians also joined the revolt early.[9]

The Persians stationed in western Asia had begun to gather. Before they had a chance to do anything, however, the Greeks launched a daring raid on Sardis itself. Sardis' gold would fund many ships. But the Greeks may have had broader goals. They may have aimed to overthrow the ideology of Lydian tyranny, taken over by the Persians. In this ideology,

Kybele, the Mother of the Gods, sustained the ruler responsible for her cult. To create a free Ionia, to overthrow the ruling Persian king, the Greeks needed to replace this goddess Kybele with their own great female deity, Artemis of Ephesus.

Led by Ephesian guides, a large force caught Sardis unprepared and captured the entire city without any resistance. Only the acropolis held out. Then a Greek soldier set fire to one of the houses. The fire spread from one highly flammable reed roof to another until the whole city was in flames. In the great fire, Kybele's sanctuary burned. Unable to get out of the city, the Lydians and Persians ran to an open market. Crowded together, compelled to resist, the Lydians and Persians frightened the Greeks, who returned, by night, to their ships at Ephesus. Persian reinforcements arrived too late to save the city. They caught up with the Greeks at Ephesus. The Ionians deployed their troops, but were defeated with heavy losses. The allies then dispersed to their own cities. The Persians later used the burning of Kybele's sanctuary as justification for burning Greek temples. Achaemenid religious tolerance lasted only as long as a people's loyalty to the Persians lasted.

The Eretrians may have remained in the fight, but the Athenians went home and did not come back. Nevertheless, the naval campaign of 497 began well for the Greeks. They sailed first to the north, where they subjected Byzantium and all the other cities, then south to Caria, where most Carians joined the alliance, and finally to Cyprus. There again the Persians won a battle on land. Though the Ionians won a naval battle, they sailed back to Ionia, abandoning the Cyprian cities to be reduced by siege. Archaeologists have unearthed fascinating evidence at Paphos in western Cyprus, where the Persians constructed a siege mound that crossed a defensive ditch and went right up to the wall. Javelin heads and stone balls found in the mound probably came from the defenders, while Persian archers protecting the mound builders shot the arrows whose three-winged heads were found in concentrations rather than scattered. At Soloi in northern Cyprus, the Persians dug a tunnel beneath the wall and captured the city after a siege of more than four months.

The land war in Asia also turned against the Greeks, who managed no further joint campaigns. Instead, they faced a three-pronged assault led by the three Persian commanders who chased them to Ephesus. The Persians won two battles in Caria and began to recapture the cities in revolt.

Meanwhile the Persians were building warships as fast as they could. In 495 or perhaps 494, they concentrated their land forces into one army, manned 600 ships, and headed for Miletus. The Greeks decided to defend Miletus by sea with every one of their ships, leaving the Milesians to defend the walls. This strategy was sound. At the end of the seventh century, the Milesians had survived 11 years of war with the Lydians, who repeatedly destroyed their crops but had no way to challenge them at sea. If the Greeks could maintain control of the water, they could hope to hold Miletus.

The Greek fleet, 353 triremes in all, assembled at the island of Lade, off the coast of Miletus. When the Persian fleet offered battle, the Ionians put to sea. They later disagreed about what happened next, each blaming the other. Apparently some contingents abandoned the fight and fled before the rest, but the Persians won a complete victory in the end.

After losing this battle, the Greeks managed no more joint activity. In 494, the sixth year after Aristagoras began the revolt, Miletus fell. Its sanctuary at Didyma was plundered and burned. Surviving Milesians were deported and resettled on the Persian Gulf. The Persians kept the plain and the land around the city for themselves. At Athens a play called *The Fall of Miletus* reduced its audience to tears. As they wept for Miletus, the Athenians probably thought just as much about their own future.

One by one the Persians took the rebellious cities. Some submitted, others were captured. The Persians left Samos unharmed—proof, perhaps, of the story that they had guaranteed safety if the Samians abandoned the Greek cause at Lade. The other major islands off the coast were captured and "netted." (Netting meant forming a human chain and walking across the island from one side to the other in order to catch every person on the island—not always literally possible, but the idea is clear.) The Persians carried out their threats. They castrated the best-looking boys, took the prettiest virgins for the king, and burned the cities and their sanctuaries. The fleet continued north all the way to the entrance to the Black Sea, where the Byzantians fled before the Persians arrived. By the end of 493, the Ionian Revolt had passed into memory.

Artaphrenes summoned representatives from the Greek cities to a meeting. He compelled them to agree to submit their disputes to arbitration, rather than, in Herodotus' phrase, "pillaging and plundering one another." Scholars have thought Artaphrenes must have had in mind private squabbles rather than disputes between cities, because so few are known. But as Persians got to know Greeks, they must have realized what a remarkably predatory culture Greeks had. When Chian survivors from the battle of Lade managed to reach the territory of Ephesus, for instance, the Ephesians jumped to the conclusion that they were hostile raiders and slaughtered them all. Artaphrenes coerced the Greeks into accepting the principle of arbitration to resolve their differences. Then he reassessed the tribute on the basis of a new survey of their land. The overall amount each city owed did not change much, but the survey clarified the boundaries. Herodotus links this survey closely to the required arbitration and admits that "these policies contributed to peace."[10]

This Persian settlement, a combination of harsh reprisals and a willingness to listen to Greek concerns, proved quite successful. The Ionians participated as loyal subjects in the Persian invasions of mainland Greece in 490 and 480, when the majority of them fought well at the battle of Salamis. The Ionians did not revolt again until the Greek fleet landed in Asia in 479.

Two Enigmatic Figures: Histiaios and Miltiades

Two Greek tyrants, Histiaios of Miletus and Miltiades of Athens, played puzzling roles in this story of revolt and reconquest. What Herodotus says about their actions and especially their motives probably goes back to what they said themselves or what their enemies said about them. Both tried to present themselves as patriotic Greeks, though both had prospered under Persian rule. Looking at them together illuminates the man who led the Athenians at Marathon.

"It is said," Herodotus reports, that when Darius learned about the burning of Sardis (spring 498), he asked who the Athenians were. Then he called for a bow, shot an arrow into the sky, and prayed, "Zeus [Auramazda, in Persian terms], let it be granted to me to punish the Athenians." He also instructed a servant to say to him three times at each dinner, "My lord, remember the Athenians." After giving these orders, he summoned Histiaios and asked him whether he knew about the revolt: How could it have happened without his knowledge? Histiaios denied knowing anything about it and expressed doubt that the Milesians had really revolted. If Darius would send him to Ionia, he promised to restore order, to hand over Aristagoras, and to wear the same clothes until he made the island of Sardinia a tribute-paying subject of the king. Darius sent him west.[11]

When he reached Sardis and met with the satrap Artaphrenes, Histiaios again denied all knowledge of the revolt. Knowing the truth, Artaphrenes quipped, "You stitched up the shoe, and Aristagoras put it on." That night Histiaios escaped to the coast. He managed to cross to Chios, where the Chians arrested him, thinking he intended to overthrow their government. When he explained, they let him go. He told them he prompted the revolt because Darius had plans for a population exchange between Phoenicia and Ionia. He wrote a letter to certain Persians in Sardis, but his chosen courier turned the letter over to Artaphrenes, who executed the intended recipients. Then Histiaios talked the Chians into helping him get back to Miletus, but by the spring of 497 the Milesians, happy to have gotten rid of Aristagoras, did not want Histiaios back. When he tried to get in by force, he was wounded in the thigh. He persuaded the Mytilenians to give him eight triremes, which he used to seize all the ships coming out of the Black Sea, unless they promised to obey his orders.[12]

After the battle of Lade—during which he remained at Byzantium, preying on merchant ships—Histiaios continued to operate in the northern Aegean, attacking islands that refused to cooperate with him. He landed in Asia to find food for his hungry men. When a Persian force attacked as he disembarked, he allowed himself to be captured, expecting that Darius would save him. The satrap Artaphrenes feared the same thing, so he impaled Histiaios and sent his head to Darius. One can only imagine Darius' feelings when he was given his friend's head. Herodotus says that he issued a rebuke for not bringing Histiaios to him alive. Then he had the head washed and buried, because Histiaios had been a great benefactor to the Persians.

This story might all be true. Histiaios might have resented his gilded cage in Susa, might have wanted to assume the leadership of the revolt, and might have been forced to take up the life of a pirate. But since Herodotus presents him as a self-proclaimed trickster, one cannot help wondering. Histiaios went to Ionia without any additional resources: no additional funds, soldiers, or ships. How did he intend to end the revolt? To judge by what he did, he planned to kill the snake by cutting off its head. With Artaphrenes' help, he could escape from Sardis and pretend to be shocked when his courier, carrying incriminating letters, deserted to Artaphrenes. He could then persuade the Chians to help him get back into Miletus. Once there he could persuade the Milesians that it would be in their best interest to abandon the revolt and resubmit to Darius. He could tell them exactly what Darius would do to them—what, in the event, he did do. Without Miletus, the other Greeks would not sustain the revolt.

This plan worked with the Chians, but not the Milesians. Thereafter Histiaios had to improvise. His luck finally ran out. After everything that had happened, the Great King regarded Histiaios as a great benefactor. If he was not acting on Darius' instructions, at least he was acting in what the king believed to be his interest.

Miltiades, the son of Kimon, was less prominent (Figure 18). His uncle, for whom he was named, claimed descent from the Trojan War hero Ajax. This older Miltiades, the son of Kypselos, won the four-horse chariot race at the Olympic games, a clear indication of his wealth. He came to the Chersonese at the request of the local residents, who found themselves in a difficult war with their northern neighbors. Athens had already demonstrated an interest in the north by conquering a town just across the straits. So it made sense for the locals to look to Athens, where they might find an ambitious man who could bring sufficient reinforcements to win the war. Miltiades ended the peninsula's troubles by building a wall more than four miles long across it. He ruled the area for at least 20 years. When he died, his former subjects honored him with equestrian and athletic contests, as well as with the sacrifices traditionally given by Greek cities to their founders.

Having no heirs, Miltiades left the Chersonese to his nephew. When the nephew was assassinated, perhaps in 515/4, the Athenian tyrants sent

18. Herm of Miltiades, a Roman copy of a fourth-century BC original (Museo Nazionale di Ravenna, inv. no. 347; photo inv. no. AFS-RA001880, by permission of the SBAP-Ravenna [MiBAC-Italia]; further reproduction or duplication by any means is prohibited)

out his brother Miltiades. Born in the late 550s, Miltiades had held the archonship in 524/3, and may have married a Peisistratid, perhaps even Hippias' daughter. He was close to 40 years old, with a son named Metiochos, when he left Athens.

Once he arrived in the Chersonese, the younger Miltiades stayed indoors, pretending to mourn his brother, until the leading men came to pay their respects. Miltiades arrested them all. He then hired 500 mercenaries and had no more trouble with the locals.

Miltiades accompanied Darius' Scythian expedition in 513. When the Scythians asked the Greeks to destroy the Danube bridge they were guarding for Darius and go home, Miltiades favored doing as they suggested, but Histiaios won over the other tyrants by pointing out that they all depended on the Persians for their positions. The bridge remained. Later the Scythians, exasperated by Darius, united and advanced as far as the Chersonese, prompting Miltiades to leave. He remained in exile until the local residents brought him back.

At some point Miltiades conquered the island of Lemnos. The Lemnians had once promised to hand over their land "whenever a ship sails with the north wind and completes the journey from your land to ours on the same day." Miltiades sailed from the tip of the Chersonese peninsula to Lemnos in one day and expelled the inhabitants.[13]

He decided to return to Athens in 493 when he heard that the Persian fleet was approaching. Earlier in the year the Persians had sailed up the Hellespont, "capturing everything on the left bank." Evidently they missed some cities, for after burning Byzantium they sailed back to the Chersonese to destroy those remaining. Herodotus says they subdued all the cities in the Chersonese except the one in which Miltiades lived. He loaded all his possessions on five triremes and set out. He encountered the enemy fleet as he cleared the Chersonese, but managed to escape with four ships to Imbros; the Persians captured the fifth ship, the one commanded by his son Metiochos, whom they took to Darius. Instead of punishing him, the Great King gave Metiochos a house, property, and a Persian wife who bore him children regarded as Persians. Miltiades himself reached Athens safely.[14]

Miltiades was a divisive figure. He was put on trial twice, once in 493 after he reached Athens and again in 489 after he led an unsuccessful attack on Paros. What Herodotus heard about him probably goes back to these prosecutions and defenses. What sense can be made of his career in the north?

Scholars have not sufficiently appreciated how remarkable Metiochos' fate was. It is true that Herodotus regularly describes the Persian kings as generous to defeated enemies. It was a Persian custom to honor the sons of kings even if their fathers had revolted. Yet what Darius did for Metiochos surpasses what Persian kings did for others. His treatment of Metiochos suggests a reward, rather than a display of generosity. It looks to me as if Darius regarded Metiochos—and therefore his father too—as a loyal servant.

Miltiades' presence on the Scythian campaign shows that he had accepted Persian authority. His alleged willingness to abandon Darius in Scythia cannot be confirmed or refuted, but even if it is true that Miltiades favored destroying the bridge over the Danube he would only have been following Darius' own instructions.

It seems likely that the Scythians crossed the Danube after Darius went home, but unlikely that they came as far as the Chersonese. It seems likely that Miltiades left the Chersonese, but unlikely that he was fleeing from the Scythians. The story sounds like a prosecutor's version of what happened. Perhaps it was then that Miltiades went to the court of the Thracian king Oloros to marry the king's daughter, and the Chersonesians who brought Miltiades back from exile served as an honorary escort accompanying bride and groom on their return journey. Perhaps Miltiades and some Chersonesians had joined Megabazos on his campaign in Thrace. Megabazos advanced along the coast before turning inland along the Strymon River. He did not compel the Thracians around Mount Pangaion to submit, which probably means they came over voluntarily. If Oloros was related to the Athenian historian Thucydides son of Oloros, who owned gold mines in Thrace, part of his kingdom was probably in this area. It does not require much imagination to envision Miltiades and Oloros meeting while in Persian service and agreeing to a marital alliance. If the prosecution at Miltiades' trial then charged him with fleeing from the Scythians, he would have found himself in a difficult position. If he wanted to refute the charge of cowardice, he would have to explain how he arranged his marriage while helping to expand the Persian Empire.

Miltiades is not mentioned in connection with the Persians' expedition to Naxos, nor did Aristagoras' purge of the Ionian tyrants reach as far as the Chersonese. Herodotus' blanket statement that the Ionians "sailed to the Hellespont and made Byzantium and all the other cities there subject to themselves" probably did not include Miltiades' towns. By that time Athens had abandoned the revolt.[15]

Miltiades probably took advantage of the disruptions in the Aegean to capture the island of Lemnos. The Persians conquered both Lemnos and Imbros in about 512. If Lemnos was in revolt when Miltiades conquered it, then he did not attack a Persian territory. Like Aristagoras and Histiaios, he might have hoped that Darius would allow a loyal Greek tyrant to expand his area of influence. Lying southwest of the Chersonese, Lemnos was a stopping point on the trade route between Athens and the Black Sea. Imbros, another island on that route, was a safe harbor for Miltiades when he fled in 493, which may imply that he had subdued it as well.

Darius might have allowed this expansion. But at the end of the revolt, his field commanders took a harsh line toward the Greeks. Histiaios lost his head before he had a chance to make his case to Darius. Miltiades may have feared the same fate, especially when he heard that a Greek from Paros had denounced him to the Persians, and even more when the Persian fleet started to capture his cities. Perhaps I am too much influenced by my life with a teenage son, but I can hear a family argument, Metiochos disagreeing with his father, arguing that their main city, Kardia, had not been touched, yielding to his father's demand that they get out while they could, and then deserting and going Persian. Miltiades continued on to Athens. This time, he did burn his bridge.

Miltiades knew what Athens faced. Though Herodotus does not describe the fighting in detail, the Ionian Revolt showed that the formidable Persian cavalry could charge and defeat Greek infantry. The Persians won each of the five known battles on land. Most of the time the Greeks of Asia and the islands did not even go out to fight: They tried to withstand a siege, or abandoned their cities, or capitulated. Islanders could survive a Persian siege—Naxos proved that—but most cities fell to Persian siege techniques. Naxos held out only because the besiegers ran out of supplies. Miltiades knew all this, and must have thought long and hard about what to do when the Persians came. They would come. The Athenians had broken their oaths and attacked Sardis. No Great King would forget.

CHAPTER 4

Darius and the Greeks of Europe

Events in Greece

By the end of summer 493, as the Persians finished securing the European side of the Hellespont and the Aegean coast, Darius instructed the tribute-paying cities on the coast to build warships and horse transports. He also sent heralds to the Greek cities asking for earth and water. His request amounted to a blunt "Are you with us or against us?" All the islands approached by his representatives, including Aegina, submitted. Many mainland cities did too. Thebes later claimed to have been the first to give earth and water.

Two cities reacted violently. Herodotus mentions the fate of the heralds to Athens and Sparta only briefly in a digression to explain why Xerxes did not send heralds to them in 481: "When Darius had sent heralds to these cities some years before, the Athenians had cast these heralds, when they made their request, down into a pit, and the Spartans had thrown theirs into a well; and the heralds were told to take their earth and water to the King from there!" Late sources add some interesting names. Miltiades proposed executing the heralds at Athens, while Themistokles—the man who later devised the winning strategy against Xerxes—proposed executing the interpreter as well.[1]

Why did the Athenians and Spartans respond so harshly to Darius' heralds? Greeks normally treated heralds with respect. Herodotus rejects the idea that the Athenians were punished when the Persians ravaged their land and city in 480, but he blames the death of two Spartans on the wrath of Talthybios (Agamemnon's herald, who was worshipped at Sparta). Why didn't they just refuse to submit and send the heralds on their way?

We know little about Athens after the 20 Athenian ships returned home in 498. Some scholars have seen Athens as deeply divided, theorizing that many Athenians regretted their switch to an anti-Persian policy and thought it might be wise to accept Hippias back, while others remained hostile to Persians and tyrants. It appears, for instance, that the Athenians permitted Hippias' relatives to return. They elected Hipparchos the son of Charmos, probably Hippias' grandson, eponymous archon in 496. An altar to Apollo Pythios dedicated by Hippias' son Peisistratos might belong to the 490s, which would strengthen the case that Peisistratids were back in town.

Where would Miltiades stand? As soon as he reached Athens safely in the summer of 493, his opponents put him on trial. Using an Athenian law that disenfranchised anyone who tried to become a tyrant, they charged him with tyranny in the Chersonese. If the stories in Herodotus can serve as a guide to the prosecution and defense in the case, the prosecutors claimed that the law applied to any Athenian, wherever he was. They argued that Miltiades acted as a tyrant by keeping a permanent force of 500 mercenaries. They claimed that Miltiades was a friend of the Peisistratid tyrants, since Peisistratos had supported his uncle's original trip and Hippias had given Miltiades a trireme. They branded him a coward who had fled from the Scythians, and they faulted him for submitting to Darius. We can also see how Miltiades responded. He reminded the Athenians that his father chose exile rather than life under the Peisistratids, who eventually had him murdered. He said that he hired troops to protect the Chersonese, not himself. He maintained that he was no tyrant and that he ruled no Greek cities. Even if he did, the law did not apply to an Athenian in the Chersonese. And finally, he had acted as independently of Darius as he dared. His flight from the Persians demonstrated his anti-Persian credentials.

He was acquitted. But as a man under some lingering suspicion, Miltiades had good reason to take a tough line against the Persians. He and Themistokles succeeded in persuading the Council to take a strong stand, one that would be difficult to reverse. The execution of the heralds committed the Athenians to fighting Persia.

Spartan history in the 490s is equally opaque. Most of what we hear concerns Kleomenes. The two kings, Kleomenes and Demaratos, had disagreed during the aborted invasion of Attica in 506. Kleomenes listened to Aristagoras in 499/8, but eventually decided against helping the Ionians. He won a great victory against Argos about 494, after which he burned a sacred grove where many Argives had taken refuge. Accused of accepting a bribe not to take the city, he was acquitted, though Herodotus could not tell whether the charge was true or false. Mutual hostility to Aegina, friend of Argos, may have nudged Sparta and Athens together in opposition to Persia. I suspect that Kleomenes, like Miltiades, meant to make an irrevocable decision by killing Darius' heralds. Demaratos would have been irked, judging by what happened next.

When the Athenians heard that the Aeginetans had given earth and water, they thought that the Aeginetans intended to join the Persians in attacking Athens. They went to Sparta and accused the Aeginetans of betraying Greece. Kleomenes promptly crossed over to Aegina and tried to arrest the men most responsible for Aeginetan policy. But Demaratos wrote a letter to Krios, a prominent Aeginetan whose name meant "ram," informing him that Kleomenes did not have the Spartan assembly's support for his actions. Demaratos alleged that the Athenians had bribed Kleomenes. Krios stood up to Kleomenes and refused to let him arrest anyone. Kleomenes asked him his name. When the Aeginetan told him, Kleomenes snarled, "Well then, Krios, cover your horns in bronze, since you are about to encounter great trouble."[2]

Kleomenes returned to Sparta and found that Demaratos had denigrated him while he was away. Furious, Kleomenes found a way to depose his fellow king. Demaratos' father, childless with his first two wives, had tricked a friend into giving him his wife, believed to be the most beautiful woman in Sparta. She gave birth to Demaratos fewer than nine months later. When the king heard the news, he counted the months on his fingers and blurted out, with an oath, "He could not be my own son!" He later came to believe that Demaratos really was his son, born prematurely. When he died in 515, Demaratos inherited the kingship. Now, more than 20 years later, Kleomenes learned that a relative of Demaratos named Leotychidas was willing to accept Kleomenes' policy against Aegina if he replaced Demaratos as king. At Kleomenes' urging, Leotychidas accused Demaratos of being illegitimate. The Spartans decided to resolve the dispute by consulting the Delphic oracle. Kleomenes bribed the priestess to give the answer he wanted. After being publicly mocked by Leotychidas at a midsummer festival in 492, Demaratos left Sparta. After some adventures, he ended up at the court of the Persian king, where Darius welcomed him and gave him property in Asia.[3]

Kleomenes took Leotychidas with him to Aegina, where they selected ten wealthy Aeginetan aristocrats, including Krios, and gave them to the Athenians as hostages. The rest of the Kleomenes story reflects what his friends and enemies said about him. When his plot against Demaratos was discovered, Kleomenes went to Thessaly and then to Arcadia, where he tried to rally the Arcadians against Sparta. The Spartans brought him back in alarm, but he had gone mad. His family locked him into wooden stocks because he kept shaking his staff in people's faces. Somehow he got a knife and "started to mutilate himself, beginning from his shins. Cutting his flesh lengthwise, he proceeded to his thighs, and from his thighs, his hips, and then his sides, until he reached his abdomen, which he thoroughly shredded and then died." Herodotus reports no fewer than four Greek explanations. Many Greeks blamed his death on the fact that he had bribed the Delphic priestess; the Athenians said he had ravaged sacred ground in Eleusis; the Argives said he had executed men who had taken sanctuary in the sacred grove and then burned the grove; the Spartans said he had become an alcoholic after learning to drink undiluted wine from Scythian ambassadors. The alleged madness of Kleomenes has prompted more than a few people, in the modern age of conspiracy theories, to read between the lines: Was Kleomenes assassinated and the plot covered up?[4]

Mardonios

The Ionian Revolt postponed Persian expansion to the west, but it soon resumed. The forces that finished suppressing the revolt in 493 were disbanded. To lead a new expedition across the Hellespont, the king picked Mardonios, who was simultaneously Darius' nephew, brother-in-law, and son-in-law: His mother was Darius' sister, his sister was one of Darius' wives, and he had recently married one of Darius' daughters.

At the beginning of the spring of 492, Mardonios left Susa for the coast, traveling more than 1,000 miles in perhaps two months. After assembling an army and a fleet in Cilicia, he went by ship to the Hellespont while subordinate commanders marched by land. He needed two or three weeks to sail approximately 600 miles to Miletus. As he proceeded up the Ionian coast, Mardonios stopped at the Greek cities, deposed the tyrants, and established democracies. Exactly how long this took we do not know, but the army needed at least six to eight weeks to walk from Cilicia to the Hellespont. It might have been mid-July or even early August before the joint forces crossed to Europe.

Herodotus describes the results as "disgraceful failures" and says Darius replaced Mardonios "since he had failed on his expedition." Does Mardonios deserve such a pejorative legacy? Eretria and Athens were the pretext for the expedition, but Herodotus says the Persians intended "to subdue as many Greek cities as they could." There is no good reason to doubt that Darius intended to conquer mainland Greece. Even if we reject the tale that his wife Atossa had advised him to conquer Greece more than 20 years earlier, plenty of evidence demonstrates an interest in the west: Democedes' reconnaissance mission along the Aegean coast, up the Adriatic, and over to Italy; the request for earth and water from the Athenian ambassadors in 506; Megabazos' campaign in 500, intended to take the Cycladic islands and even Euboea; and Histiaios' promise to capture Sardinia.[5]

Perhaps Darius underestimated the length of time Mardonios would need. If so, Xerxes benefited from his experience. Setting out from Sardis rather than Susa in the spring of 480, Xerxes reached Athens by late summer. Alternatively, Mardonios was sent simply to push as far as he could. The king may already have had in mind the island-hopping expedition that ended at Marathon in 490. A logical strategy would be first to consolidate gains in the northern Aegean, second to conquer the rest of the Aegean islands, and third to punish Eretria and Athens before conquering the rest of mainland Greece.

Mardonios' navy and army operated separately. The navy subjugated Thasos without any resistance before it ran into a powerful north wind as it attempted to sail around Mount Athos. It was said that savage creatures (sharks?), rocks, drowning, and the cold destroyed 300 ships and 20,000 men. This story is credible, though I wouldn't insist on the numbers. The rough coast, sudden strong winds from the north, sharks, cold water brought by a storm, all fit the Athos peninsula, even in summer. Xerxes took extreme measures to avoid a similar disaster: He dug a canal across the peninsula so he would not have to sail around it. The project took three years.

The navy likely had other successes to its credit. After ferrying the army across the Hellespont, it probably visited the other islands in the northern Aegean before reaching Thasos. After the storm, it may have continued west to a rendezvous with Mardonios at the mouth of the Haliakmon-Axios river valley in Macedon.

The infantry proceeded west by land all the way to the heart of Macedon. In Herodotus' phrase, the Persians "added the Macedonians to their already existing host of slaves." The Macedonian king Alexander most likely submitted peacefully, since there is no evidence of fighting with the Macedonians. Macedon became a formal part of the satrapy of Thrace. During the night, a Thracian tribe called the Brygoi attacked the Persian camp. The Brygoi lived east of the Axios River in what is now southern FYROM (Former Yugoslav Republic of Macedonia). Though Mardonios himself was wounded, he counterattacked and did not leave the area until he had subjugated the Brygoi. Herodotus says he later told Xerxes that he advanced as far as Macedon, a short distance from Athens, and "no one came out to face us in battle." From Darius' perspective, the campaign succeeded: "All the peoples as far as Thessaly," Herodotus later admits, "had been enslaved and forced to pay tribute as subjects of the king after the conquests of Megabazos and, later, Mardonios."[6]

Mardonios had set the stage for the invasion of Greece.

Datis and Artaphrenes

During preparations for the next campaign, Darius ordered the Thasians to demolish their city wall and send their long ships to Abdera. Their neighbors (the Abderitans?) had accused them of planning a revolt. Thanks to their gold mines, both on the mainland and on the island, the Thasians enjoyed a regular annual income of 200 talents, or 300 in a good year. For comparison, the first Persian provincial district on Herodotus' list, comprising the Ionians, Magnesians, Aeolians, Carians, Lycians, Milyans, and Pamphylians, paid the Great King a combined total of 400 talents a year. So it is not surprising that Darius took advantage of the opportunity to put wealthy Thasos more firmly under his thumb. The Thasians complied without protest and brought their ships to Abdera, a relatively young city founded by Ionians who did not want to submit to Cyrus. In Darius' day, Abdera accepted Persian sovereignty, and it remained loyal to Xerxes, who was hosted at Abdera on his way to Greece and again on his way back. One citizen quipped that they should thank the gods that the king ate only once a day, for Abdera would have been bankrupted had it been asked to provide lunch as well as dinner. Thasos too remained loyal as well as prosperous, able to spend a rumored 400 talents on the king's dinner in 480.[7]

Darius named two new commanders for the anticipated expedition in 490: his nephew Artaphrenes, son of his brother Artaphrenes, and Datis, a Mede whose ancestry is unknown. Why two? Darius had used single generals before, such as Megabazos in Thrace in 513 and Mardonios in Thrace and Macedonia in 492. Herodotus treats Datis as the real commander, so Artaphrenes might have been sent to keep an eye on him. Alternatively, Artaphrenes might have been put in command of a subsidiary unit, such as the fleet or the cavalry (locals at Marathon later showed travelers what they said were the stone mangers of Artaphrenes' horses). Or Darius might have intended the two to divide their forces at some point, as the three commanders who first chased the Ionian rebels to Ephesus had done.

Datis was a Mede, not a Persian. Cyrus the Great had defeated the Medes, to whom the Persians were related so closely that the Greeks often did not distinguish them. A Greek who took the side of the Persians was said to "medize." Some Medes held powerful posts under Persian kings. Cyrus, for example, left a Mede to finish the conquest of the Greeks after Sardis fell, and when he died of an illness, Cyrus appointed another Mede to replace him. So Datis the Mede's appointment was not unprecedented.

Neither Datis nor Artaphrenes was a particularly young man, since both had sons who commanded contingents of Xerxes' forces in 480. Both men had prior experience with Greeks. A quotation from the lost historian Ktesias, a Greek doctor who worked at the Persian court in the late fifth century, says that Datis returned from the Black Sea in command of the fleet. He had also gone to Sardis in 494 on a mission from the king, for one of the tablets found in an archive at Persepolis reads: "Datiya received 70 quarts beer as rations. He carried a sealed document of the king. He went forth from Sardis [via] express [service], [he] went to the king at Persepolis. 11th month, year 27." Among all the persons receiving rations attested in this archive, only Parnaka (the king's uncle and the chief economic official of Persia) and Gobryas (father of Mardonios) got more than Datiya (= Datis), with 90 and 100 quarts respectively. Because Datis had travel orders from the king, he was on the return leg of a round trip to Ionia that began and ended in Persepolis. The date falls between January 17 and February 15, 494, just before the final campaign. Given this previous service, he would have been well-informed about Greeks before assuming the command in 490. As for Artaphrenes, he had probably lived with his father, the satrap in Sardis during the Ionian Revolt.[8]

The Expedition Departs

Datis and Artaphrenes left the king in Susa in the spring, say mid-March, and brought a large, well-equipped army to Cilicia, the Persians' regular gathering point. The fleet, including ships (re)built as horse transports (the earliest known example of boats carrying horses), met them there. They put the horses on the transport vessels, the army embarked, and the entire force sailed with 600 triremes for Ionia.

So says Herodotus, without any more precise numbers. Simonides, a poet of the early fifth century, mentions 90,000 men; Lysias and Plato, a century later, say 500,000. The writers of the Roman era give 200,000 (Cornelius Nepos) and 600,000 (Justin). Pausanias says that 300,000 died at Marathon. The one source to lower Herodotus' ship numbers is Plato, who speaks of 300 triremes.[9]

No one puts much stock in the later writers. Within a few years the Athenians were boasting that "we alone of the Greeks fought the Persian all by ourselves and not only survived such a remarkable endeavor, but won a victory over 46 nations."[10] Over time, the opponent's numbers multiplied in the telling.

Trying to deduce the size of the Persian land forces from Herodotus is tricky. At the standard Classical figure of 200 men per trireme, Herodotus has in mind at least 120,000 men on the triremes, plus men and horses on the transport ships. But as we saw in chapter 3, 600 may be a stock figure meaning nothing more precise than a large number. Or Herodotus might be using "triremes" loosely. Since triremes had little storage room, supply vessels must have accompanied them. Perhaps Datis had 300 triremes, as Plato says, and 300 other ships. Between 478 and 331, the most common size of Persian fleets is 300 triremes.

In either case, we do not really know how many men these early triremes carried, nor can they have been fully loaded given their mission to bring back Eretrian and Athenian captives. The highest number of soldiers ever attested on triremes is 40. If each trireme had 60 rowers and 40 soldiers, 300 triremes would have had 18,000 rowers and 12,000 soldiers; 600 triremes could have carried 36,000 rowers and 24,000 soldiers.

These figures can serve as outside limits. Some scholars argue for a number on the higher end, believing that the Persians must have planned on fighting the combined forces of Athens and Sparta at a minimum. But the Persians might have expected few Greeks to fight at all, and they could always sail away as long as they controlled the sea. Various scholars have maintained that the 6,400 who eventually died at Marathon represented most of the middle third of the Persian line, implying a total fighting force of perhaps 20,000. But was the Persian center a literal third? Major General Frederick Maurice estimated that the water supply at Marathon could have sustained a force of 16,000 for a week, but not a significantly larger force. To my mind, this is as good a figure as any.

The number of horses is unknown: Estimates have ranged from zero to 10,000, the figure given twice by Cornelius Nepos. Later Athenians converted old triremes into transports that carried 30 horses each. But even if we knew how many Persian ships carried horses (which we don't), they were not triremes, for Herodotus counts them among Xerxes' 3,000 smaller vessels. Most likely the Persian transports carried a handful of horses each.

The transports also carried food and water for the animals. Estimates for the horses' daily rations vary from 12 to 21 pounds of hard fodder, such as barley, and 14 to 55 pounds of green or dry fodder, such as hay. They drank four to eight gallons of water each day, perhaps more at the peak of the sweltering Aegean summer. Persian planners must have anticipated feeding and watering the horses for several months. Springs, rivers, and wells could supply much of the water, but the Aegean islands lacked good pastures, and, in any case, horses shifted suddenly to pasturage can develop debilitating or even fatal colic. The Persians must have brought plenty of grain and hay. As it happens, the Roman naturalist Pliny says that alfalfa hay was introduced to Greece "from Media at the time of the Persian wars that Darius waged."[11] Presumably Persian horse droppings left fertile seeds.

Given the challenges of feeding horses and keeping them healthy, the Persians would have taken enough to counter whatever cavalry they might have to face, but not many more. How many horsemen would they have imagined opposing them? On most islands, there were none to speak of. Homer has Telemachos decline an inappropriate gift from his host Menelaos of Sparta in the following diplomatic words:

> I will not take the horses to Ithaka, but will leave them
> here, for your own delight, since you are lord of a spreading
> plain, there is plenty of clover here, there is galingale,
> and there is wheat and millet here and white barley wide grown.
> There are no wide courses in Ithaka, there is no meadow;

a place to feed goats; but lovelier than a place to feed horses;
For there is no one of the islands that has meadows for driving horses;
They are all sea slopes; and Ithaka more than all the others.

The Lelantine plain between Chalcis and Eretria on Euboea was an exception; the Eretrians had 600 horsemen. I doubt that the Persians had
as many as 1,000. If I had to guess, I'd say 800. They had to take more
than one horse per rider to make up for animals that died or became
disabled.[12]

Darius instructed his commanders to enslave Athens and Eretria and
to bring the captives to him. The philosopher Plato put the orders color-
fully: "Come back with the Eretrians and Athenians, if you want to keep
your head." The plan called for avoiding the long land route around the
Aegean by sailing from island to island through the Cyclades, beginning
with Naxos, perhaps the primary target of the campaign (Figure 19). The

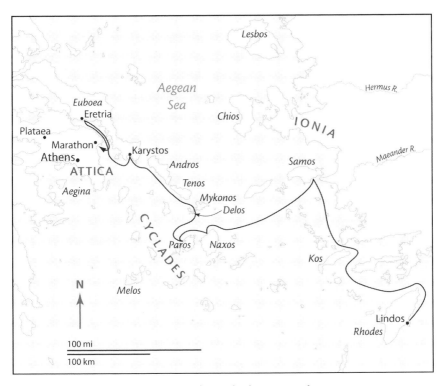

19. Map showing Datis' route in 490 from Rhodes to Marathon

Naxians had opposed the king before either the Athenians or the Eretrians had acted against him; and, as Aristagoras and the Naxian exiles had realized a decade earlier, whoever controlled Naxos would dominate the rest of the Cyclades. But the Persian horses show that the campaign goals went beyond the Cyclades to include at least Euboea. In short, Datis was to carry out the plan Aristagoras had proposed to the satrap Artaphrenes before the Ionian Revolt. Darius tempered aggression with caution, consolidating his current or prior holdings before expanding. After the revolt he reconquered the Aegean coast, adding some of the nearby islands that had supported the rebellion, and then consolidated his grip on coastal Thrace. Now he wanted to secure the remainder of the Aegean islands before tackling the Greek mainland.[13]

Rhodes

The Persian forces saw their first hostile action at Lindos, a city on the east side of the island of Rhodes. The evidence comes not from Herodotus, whose account of the campaign is highly compressed (only a couple of pages until the Persians reach Marathon), but from a monumental inscription cut in 99 BC and excavated by Danish archaeologists at the beginning of the twentieth century. The text records a list of offerings made at the sanctuary of Athena, most of which had been destroyed, and of the goddess's epiphanies. The first epiphany describes how Athena saved the people from the Persian expedition sent by Darius to enslave Greece. The Persians landed first on Rhodes and besieged the Rhodians at Lindos. When the Rhodians had only five days of water left, one of their leaders had a dream in which Athena encouraged him not to surrender, saying she was going to ask her father Zeus for help. So the Rhodians asked for a truce for five days, saying they would surrender peacefully if nothing happened before then. Datis laughed. But when it rained heavily on the acropolis the next day, he made a treaty of friendship with the Rhodians. Saying that the gods protected them, he dedicated to Athena the clothing he was wearing, including his jewelry, as well as a sword and his covered carriage.

The date is not certain. Some scholars have argued for either 497, when the Persians first attempted to suppress the Ionian Revolt, or 495, when the Persians were on their way to the battle of Lade. But the phrase "for the enslavement of Greece" fits 490 best, when the Persians passed Rhodes on their way to Greece.

Others have dismissed the entire episode as fictitious. Of the nine authorities the inscription names, four are otherwise entirely unknown and two are only tentatively identified with known writers. But surviving writers refer to the other three. These three were real authors, and though none is earlier than the fourth century, the basic story is completely credible: A sudden rainstorm relieved the besieged Lindians' thirst. If Herodotus' silence is a hurdle to believing what the inscription says, it's a very low one.

The inscription tells the story from the Lindians' perspective. While the rain saved them from complete surrender, it is evident that they negotiated a deal with Datis. His version would have told how he spared the city when the residents submitted, giving earth and water. Datis then encouraged other Greeks to submit by recognizing the Lindians' god with appropriate gifts. Easterners often dedicated items of personal clothing and adornments. Datis would continue this policy at Delos.

The Cyclades

From Rhodes, the Persian fleet continued up the coast to Samos, not the quickest route to Naxos. Perhaps the Persians needed to rendezvous with additional ships or pick up additional supplies. Or the route may have been a feint: If the Naxians thought that the Persian fleet was once again proceeding north, they might not be ready for an attack.

A rapid advance from Samos caught the Naxians off guard. Remembering what had happened to the Milesians and other Ionian rebels who tried to withstand a siege, the Naxians ran for the hills. Naxos has high mountains (the tallest is almost 3,300 feet) ideal for hiding from invaders, but the Persians caught and "enslaved" some of the inhabitants. That might mean that the Naxians were literally deported and taken away into slavery, or only that they were forced to recognize the sovereignty of the Persian king, since the Greeks conceptualized even high-ranking Persian

nobles as "slaves" of the king. After burning the city and the Naxian sanctuaries, the Persians sailed off. Naxian chroniclers, according to Plutarch,
later maintained that "the general Datis was repulsed after burning [. . .]
to do harm." Despite the gap in the text, it is clear that patriotic Naxians
reframed the story.[14]

The Persians then sailed for the other Cycladic islands. First was Delos. Although it was tiny—three miles long and less than a mile wide—
Delos played a major role in the region as the birthplace of the divine
twins Apollo and Artemis. A sanctuary was established soon after 700.
In the Archaic period the Greeks held a great festival, the Delia, every
four years, with athletic, musical, and dancing contests. The Ionians
and the islanders came with their wives and children. Thucydides says
that "later, naturally enough, most of the contests were stopped because
of misfortune," though the islanders and the Athenians continued to
send choruses and offerings. Whether he means the conquest of Ionia
in the mid-sixth century or the reconquest in the 490s, the holy place
of Delos loomed large in the minds of the islanders and the Athenians
in 490.[15]

Datis sailed to Delos ahead of the rest of his ships. He had them anchor at Rhenaia, an island less than half a mile from Delos. He found the
sacred island deserted. With no mountains to hide in—the tallest hill on
Delos is only 367 feet high—the Delians had fled to a nearby island. When
Datis learned where the Delian refugees were, he sent a herald with this
message: "Holy men, why have you gone in flight and condemned me
without good reason? For I myself have enough good sense to know, and
besides the King has instructed me, not to harm the site on which the two
gods were born, nor the rest of the island or its inhabitants. Therefore
return to your homes and inhabit your own island again."[16]

As he had at the sanctuary of Athena on Rhodes, the Persian commander donated some of his personal ornaments as votive offerings. Inscriptions record a gold necklace Datis dedicated. One even specifies that
it lay "against the wall."[17]

Then he burned 300 talents of frankincense on the altar. The scale of
this offering supports his claim that the king had instructed him to treat
Delos with special care. The offering was so generous—7.5 tons, or 38

camel loads—that scholars usually dismiss it as hopelessly exaggerated. It would be easier to imagine the scene if we knew the dimensions of the altar, but French archaeologists have found no trace of it. There were actually two altars in the sanctuary, one for wheat, barley, and cheese cakes, and the other, composed of the horns of previously sacrificed victims, for burnt offerings. Altars built up of the remains of sacrificial victims could be quite large. The famous altar of Zeus at Olympia, composed solely of ashes, grew to 23 feet tall.

Grandiose as the offering would have been, the Persians had the resources to make it if they wished. The Arabians gave the Persian king an annual gift of 141 camel loads of the stuff. Of course this report might be exaggerated too, but the figure pales in comparison to what the Roman Empire imported: In the first century AD, 7,000 to 10,000 camel loads of frankincense entered the Roman Empire every year. So I am prepared to believe that Datis brought 300 talents of frankincense, which would have fit on a single merchant ship. If it would have taken too long to burn it all, perhaps he simply gave it to the priests for future use. But Datis need not have been in a rush. The twin towers of smoke, one from Naxos and the other from Delos, sent a powerful message to other Greeks. A week spent demonstrating Persian generosity and religious toleration might save many more days later.

Datis may also have needed to wait for ships to arrive from Asia, for when he left Delos he took Ionians and Aeolians with him. These Greeks from Asia did not necessarily row triremes; they might have brought supplies.

Instead of sailing directly to Euboea, Datis divided his forces and sent them in different directions, taking the time to conscript men and take boys as hostages. The residents of the Cyclades islands all complied with Persian requests. Which islands were visited? Certainly Paros, which contributed a trireme to the campaign, and probably the other Cyclades too. Since these islands had already given earth and water to the king, the Persians were confirming, rather than imposing, their authority. They left no occupying troops behind.

When the Persians reached Karystos on the southern end of Euboea, they found a different attitude. The Karystians refused to give hostages or join the campaign against their neighbors, the Eretrians and the Athenians. Evidently they hoped the Persians would move on, for they did not flee into the steep hills from which came the greenish marble later so popular among the Romans. Accepting nothing short of total compliance, the Persians besieged the city and ravaged the land until the Karystians submitted. Perhaps because other Greeks believed that Karystos had voluntarily gone over to the Persians, the residents of Karystos still take pride in this early resistance, even though it did not succeed. The Athenians later used their behavior as an excuse first for extorting money from them, then for ravaging their land, and finally for fighting and conquering them. The fact that Karystos suffered no punishment from the Persians suggests that it capitulated fairly quickly. The longer the siege lasted, the harder it is to understand the later belief that the Karystians had medized.

Waiting for the Barbarian

From the moment news arrived of Datis' attack on Naxos, the Eretrians and the Athenians knew they were in immediate danger. In Persian eyes, both had become followers of the Lie. The Eretrians had surely heard about Aristagoras' proposed expedition to take Naxos, the rest of the Cyclades, and Euboea, an actual expedition foiled only by stubborn Naxian resistance. They had helped the Ionian rebels and may have contributed larger forces and for a longer time than the Athenians did. The Athenians had accepted Persian protection only to reject Artaphrenes' request that they take back Hippias. Then they sent ships to help the Ionians, participated in the attack on Sardis, and killed a Persian herald who offered them a second chance. Whether Darius' servant really reminded him every day to remember the Athenians, as they believed, scarcely matters.

The Eretrians asked the Athenians for help. Eretria was in the more difficult position, since it was on an island. What mainland city would send troops to an island when the Persian fleet controlled the sea? The Athenians could not very well commit their men to Eretria, since Karystos was closer to Attica than to Eretria. If Athenian troops had crossed to Euboea, the Persians could easily have reached Athens before the citizens could return. The Athenians did send the 4,000 colonists who settled on Chalcidian land after their victory in 506.

An inscribed column found just a few years ago in Thebes may explain the availability of these men. In late Archaic letters, this broken text seems to commemorate an otherwise unknown event, the "loosening" of Chalcis. From the Theban and Chalcidian point of view, the 4,000 Athenian settlers had oppressed Chalcis. Perhaps Thebes had loosened or liberated Chalcis, driving the Athenians out.[18]

When the Athenian settlers arrived, they found the Eretrians divided about what to do. Some wanted to flee to the hills, while others pondered betraying the city to win personal rewards. Given this uncertainty, a prominent Eretrian advised the Athenians to go to their own country so they would not die along with the Eretrians. They took this advice, returning not to their farms in the Lelantine plain between Eretria and Chalcis—a confirmation that the Thebans had intervened in Chalcis?—but to Attica, crossing the channel safely before the Persians arrived.

The Eretrians determined not to abandon their city, but to withstand a siege.

The Persian Assault on Eretria

Datis sailed up the strait and landed his ships in Eretrian territory, not right at the city itself, but at three places whose precise location is unknown. The Persians unloaded their horses and prepared to attack. What preparations did they make?

The city was fortified by a strong wall made of stone below and mud brick above. The Persians had to go over, under, or through this barrier. Building a mound against the wall or digging a tunnel under it would have proceeded slowly. The assault must have been more direct, with archers trying to clear defenders from the top of the wall so men could climb ladders or bash the gates with battering rams. So their preparations must have included making rams and ladders. The ladders had to be built on the spot after the attackers could see the height of the wall: too tall, and the ladders would have been easy to throw off; too short, and the climbers would not have reached the top. (Think of the besieged Plataeans preparing to escape from a siege in the Peloponnesian War, counting bricks in the Spartans' circumvallation wall again and again to get the height of the ladders right.)[19]

Even with skilled archers doing their best to clear the wall, men climbing ladders were exposed and vulnerable. If they were knocked off, the fall might be their last. In his *Phoenician Women,* Euripides describes the fate of one such attacker vividly:

> He crept up having drawn up his body under his shield,
> Passing up the smooth rungs of the ladder.
> Just as he reached the cornice of the wall
> Zeus struck him with his bolt; the earth rang
> So that all were terrified. From the ladder
> He was hurled, his limbs spreading apart,
> Hair toward heaven and blood toward earth.
> His arms and legs like the wheel of Ixion
> Spun; the fiery corpse fell to earth.

Herodotus describes the assault as "fierce." In six days, many fell on both sides. On the seventh day, Euphorbos son of Alkimachos and Philagros son of Kyneas, both prominent citizens according to Herodotus but otherwise unknown to us, "betrayed their city and surrendered it to the Persians." Were it not for the sequel, one might think this sentence a pejorative description of a negotiated settlement. But the Persians looted and burned the sanctuaries and enslaved the people, so Euphorbos and Philagros must have opened a gate or arranged to leave part of the wall undefended or performed some other such traitorous action. The king later rewarded them with land, perhaps—if the Gongylos whom Xenophon described as "the only Eretrian to medize" was one of their relatives—near Pergamon, where Xenophon met Gongylos' descendants.[20]

The Persians deported 780 Eretrians, including old men, women, and children. Logistics ruled out taking the entire population by ship to Asia. For the moment, the Persians deposited the prisoners under guard on the little island of Aigilia in the strait between Euboea and Attica.[21]

The campaign so far had gone as planned.

CHAPTER 5

The Armies Arrive at Marathon

Decisions at Athens

One target remained. Athens was part of Datis' assignment all along, as the presence of an Athenian adviser, the deposed tyrant Hippias, shows. Whether or not Datis intended to restore him to power—Hippias was by now an old man, nearly 80—he would be an invaluable resource for the campaign in Attica.

Datis rested his men for several days. He gave the Athenians one more chance to surrender. His messenger told the Athenians that not a single Eretrian had escaped, for as Plato puts it, his soldiers "had joined hands and swept Eretria clean as with a net."[1]

The Athenians faced a difficult choice. Though they had sent messengers "in all directions" to ask for help, only Sparta and Plataea had responded positively. The Spartans had at least 5,000 hoplites, the best warriors in Greece, and seven times that many light-armed, but they lived 150 miles from Athens. Plataea was closer, just across the border in Boeotia, but also much smaller. Only 600 Plataean hoplites and 600 Plataean light-armed fought in 479 at the battle of Plataea, for which they should have produced every available man since it was fought in their own territory. Despite being allied to Athens for a generation, they could not be expected to send more than 1,000 men.[2]

What then to do? Capitulation would mean death or deportation for many and loss of freedom for all. Could they withstand a siege? Naxos had managed to hold off the Persians for four months in 499. In less than half that time, the Persians would need to sail east before the stormy season began, for it was already August or even September. But would the Athenians remain loyal as they watched the Persians trample their vines, chop down their trees, grab their movable property, and burn their houses outside the city? Eretria had just been betrayed.

For Athens, unlike Eretria, fighting was a real option. The largest of all Greek city-states, Athens had 9,000 or 10,000 troops according to late sources. Herodotus gives no numbers for the Athenians at Marathon. His Athenians have 8,000 hoplites plus about 8,000 light-armed at Plataea, at a time when the Athenians were also manning 200 or so triremes. If we calculate ten hoplite marines per trireme, the Athenians had 10,000 hoplites and 8,000 light-armed. There ought to have been as many available for Marathon. Unfortunately, we do not know whether the 4,000 men who returned to Athens in 490 from Chalcis remained in Athens in the 480s, in which case the survivors among them would have been included among the men available in 479, or returned to Chalcis, in which case they would not have counted among the Athenians available for Plataea. If they were not counted at Plataea but were present at Marathon, the Athenian total would rise to 22,000.[3]

The Athenians had been talking about what to do for weeks if not months. The Persian envoys appeared before the Council of 500, where a proposal might be formulated and debated before it went to the Athenian assembly for a decision by majority vote. Miltiades made the motion.

He had been elected general in the spring of 490, perhaps because of his experience with the Persians. Just what experience he had is not certain, beyond the time he spent waiting at the Danube for Darius to return from Scythia. He was no tyrant in Athens. He served as one of ten generals the Athenians elected annually, one from each of the ten Athenian tribes, starting in 501. The titular commander of the army remained the traditional polemarchos. In 490 the polemarchos was Kallimachos of Aphidna, whose voice was to prove critical, even if he was no longer the field commander of the army.

Miltiades proposed that as soon as they learned where the Persians had landed, the Athenians take provisions, leave the city to the god, and go out to meet the barbarians. To maximize Athenian numbers, he offered freedom to any slaves willing to fight.[4]

The motion carried.

The Persians Land at Marathon

When they learned that the Athenians refused to submit, the Persians started to sail across to Marathon (Figure 20). No ancient evidence supports the suggestion that they timed the attack to coincide with a religious festival at Sparta when the Spartans could not send out an army. Nor is there any reason why the Persians should fear the Spartans so. All the Spartans had done in the past was warn Cyrus to keep his hands off the Greeks of Asia. When he ignored their threat, the Spartans had done nothing.

Herodotus gives two reasons why Hippias led the Persians to Marathon: It was the most suitable place in Attica for horses and it was closest to Eretria. Picky readers have objected that it was neither. The plain of Phaleron was better for horses; Oropos was closer to Eretria. But no place in Athenian territory was better for horses *and* closer to Eretria.

Hippias had in fact invaded Attica here before. Almost 60 years earlier, he accompanied his father, Peisistratos, on his return from exile. Peisistratos and sons collected money and men in Eretria, crossed to Marathon, and then marched on Athens via the same route followed by the Lambrakis Peace Marathon today. The first third of the trek follows a fairly flat path south along the coast, then there's a turn to the west and an uphill climb for a long middle third, and the last stretch goes downhill to the city. Peisistratos surprised the Athenian forces resting after their midday meal at Pallene, about two-thirds of the way to Athens, and routed them completely.

Hippias hoped for a repeat performance.

After rounding the promontory of Kynosoura, the Persian ships backed into the shore and tethered to stones or stakes on land. When he reached the beach, Hippias began to sneeze and cough. One particularly

20. Map of Attica and Euboea

violent cough sent a loose tooth right out of his mouth. He searched in
the sand, but it had disappeared among the many brown and white pieces
of rock that cover the beach. He could not find it. He then rethought his
dream from the previous night, when he dreamed he was sleeping with
his mother. At first he had interpreted the dream to mean that he would

recover his rule and die in his native land, but now he groaned and said, "This land is not ours, and we shall not make it subject to us, either, for my tooth now has my share."[5]

Moving the entire force from Eretria to Marathon, unloading men, horses, and supplies, and setting up camp took several days. Plutarch says that the booty captured after the battle included "silver and gold piled up, all kinds of clothing and innumerable other goods in the tents and captured ships." Since Herodotus says nothing about the booty at Marathon, Plutarch might have extrapolated this description, not unreasonably, from what Herodotus does say the Greeks captured in Xerxes' camp after the battle of Plataea: "They found tents adorned with gold and silver, couches gilded with gold and silver, golden mixing bowls, libation bowls, and other drinking vessels. On the wagons they discovered sacks in which they saw cauldrons of gold and silver. And they stripped the bodies lying there of their bracelets, necklaces, and golden daggers, but they paid no attention at all to the embroidered clothing. . . . Later, well after these events, the Plataeans found chests made of gold and silver as well as other goods [that presumably had been buried in the camp]." As the Great King, Xerxes would have traveled more opulently than Datis and Artaphrenes, but Persian nobles did not travel lightly.[6]

The Persian nobles and horses probably camped in the plain of Trikorynthos by the Makaria spring, the best source of water in the plain (see the next chapter). Others probably slept on the beach or under the ancient predecessors of the umbrella pines there now.

The Oath That the Athenians Swore When They Were About to Fight against the Barbarians

If the Athenians had lookouts and fire signals, the news reached the city a few minutes after the Persian ships landed. The generals had the trumpeter blow his trumpet to summon the men to the usual marshaling place, the gymnasium of Apollo Lykeios east of the city. We do not know how many of the 18,000 to 22,000 available men answered the call. If the Athenians sent 16,000 men to Plataea in 480, they ought to have had at least as many at Marathon. The late sources that mention 9,000 or 10,000 Athenians probably counted only citizen hoplites required to serve on the basis of their wealth (ability to afford armor). Sometimes, however, the Athenians declared a campaign that welcomed all volunteers, whether they were fully equipped or not. Marathon was surely one such campaign. To magnify the glory of the victory, Greek writers understate Greek numbers even as they exaggerate Persian numbers. As William Mitford observed in the eighteenth century, "later writers have not less contradicted probability in diminishing the Grecian than in exaggerating the Persian force."[7] The numbers were probably about even.

When the men had gathered and sorted themselves into their ten tribes, they sacrificed to the gods and prayed for victory. They then performed a unique ceremony. They placed their shields over the sacrificed animals, bringing each shield into direct or indirect contact with a victim, so that soldiers would see on their shields a bloody warning of what would happen to them if they broke their vows. The piles of shields also demonstrated their solidarity in this crisis. At the sound of the trumpet, they swore to fight to the death, not to desert their officers, to follow the generals' commands, and to bury their dead on the battlefield. They guaranteed special treatment for their allies Sparta and Plataea, even if they became enemies, and kept the door open for other cities to join the fight. They invoked blessings if they kept their word, but curses if they broke it: "If I keep true to what has been written in the oath may my city be free from sickness, if not, may it be sick; and may my city be unravaged, but if not, may it be ravaged; and may my [land] bear, but if not, may it be barren; and may the women bear children like their parents, but if not, monsters; and may the animals bear young like the animals, but if not, monsters." This oath became the template for a more famous oath, the Oath of Plataea that all the Greeks swore before the last great battle of the Persian Wars.[8]

The March to Marathon

From Athens, two main routes lead to Marathon. The shorter way goes north to Kephisia, skirts Mount Pentelikon to the west, climbs to the village of Stamata, and then descends to the plain of Marathon either through the Avlona valley, passing Vrana, or between Mount Kotroni and Mount Stavrokoraki, passing modern Marathona. European travelers in the early nineteenth century followed this route on horseback. (The Turks governing Athens regarded anyone on foot as a lowly peasant.)

As a student at the British School in Athens in 1930, Nicholas G. L. Hammond walked to Marathon and back to Athens on the same day, taking the even more difficult variation of this route, over the top of Mount Pentelikon. He reached Marathon in six hours and returned in seven. He believed he would have made even better time by going through Stamata. When he became a distinguished Oxford historian, he maintained that the Athenians went via Stamata. He recognized that the route was difficult, but he thought that each Athenian would have found his own way over the hills rather than marched in column along a path.

The other main route is the one taken by Peisistratos in reverse, passing between Mount Pentelikon and Mount Hymettos, turning east over the hills to the coast, proceeding north along the coast, and entering the plain of Marathon in the southwest. This route is longer, about 25 miles versus 22, but easier. It is the better choice for a large force. If Datis had tried to march quickly on Athens, he would have taken the coastal route and the Athenians would have intercepted him. I feel certain that the Athenians took the longer, easier coastal route. As historian Peter Green writes, no commander in his right mind would "have first stripped Athens of defenders, and then obligingly left the front door open, as it were, while he led his troops up the back lane."[9]

Since they were not leaving their own territory, the Athenians probably took less with them than they would have if they were going farther afield. At a minimum, they transported armor, weapons, and some provisions. An ancient Greek, smaller than his modern counterpart, needed about 3,000 calories a day. The standard daily ration of one Attic *choinix* of barley or (less often) wheat, weighing about 1.9 pounds, provided some 2,800 calories. Men got the remainder from onions (soldiers' packs reeked of onions), cheese, salted meat or fish, and perhaps figs. The total daily ration weighed two to three pounds. They probably brought wine, too, since they normally drank wine mixed with water.

They probably also brought camping supplies (not necessarily tents, since the weather would be hot and dry), tools, and medical supplies. For cooking, men needed either stone hand-mills, which might weigh over 60 pounds, or lighter wooden mortars and pestles, and pots or griddles or grills. Tools might include rasps for smoothing spear shafts, files for sharpening weapons, carpenter's tools, shovels, mattocks, axes, and sickles, plus plenty of extra straps, for as Xenophon notes, "when straps break everything stops, unless you have extras."[10]

The typical hoplite did not carry all this himself. He had a porter, usually a slave. And the Athenians had "coworkers in war," otherwise called "under-the-yokers," oxen and mules and donkeys. These animals might pull two-wheeled carts or larger four-wheeled wagons, but they would move more quickly if they simply carried packs on their backs.[11]

When the Athenians reached the plain of Marathon, they camped at the sanctuary of Herakles. Greeks often camped at sanctuaries because they offered a critical resource during hot Greek summers: water. This particular sanctuary had another appealing feature. It blocked the coast road to Athens (see next chapter).

No sooner had the Athenians set up camp than the Plataeans joined them with every available man. If they numbered as many as the 1,000 mentioned by the later sources, the figure includes light-armed.

Philippides

Before they left Athens, the generals sent Philippides, a professional distance runner, to Sparta. Probably running barefoot, Philippides reached Sparta the day after he left Athens—that is, he covered roughly 150 miles (on the most likely route) in not more than about 36 hours. If the story once seemed incredible, it does no longer. In 1982, two RAF officers ran from Athens to Sparta in 34 and 35.5 hours, demonstrating that Philippides could have done what Herodotus says he did. Starting in 1983, runners have competed in an annual Spartathlon. A Greek, Yannis Kouros, set the course record of 20:29 in 1990, but hundreds of people have completed the race in less than 36 hours.

Philippides' route was not easy. He began on the Sacred Road through the Kerameikos cemetery to Eleusis, the sanctuary of Demeter on the western edge of Attica. Then he followed the coast through the Megarid to the isthmus, including the track along the Skironian Cliffs, where the legendary Athenian hero Theseus was said to have avoided the giant Skiron's kick and then pushed him off the cliff. After Corinth he would have turned south, tackling much hillier country in the Peloponnese. He probably crossed the Argolid plain and continued over Mount Parthenion (3,986 feet) to Tegea.

On the far side of Mount Parthenion, Philippides experienced an epiphany of the god Pan. Pan was an Arcadian deity, represented as part human, part goat. As Philippides later reported, Pan fell in with him, called him by name, and told him to ask the Athenians a question. "Why do they pay no attention to me, though I like them and have already helped them many times and will do so again in the future?"[12]

When he reached Sparta, Philippides asked for help. "Spartans," Herodotus reports that he said, "the Athenians beg you to rush to their defense and not look on passively as the most ancient city in Greece falls into slavery imposed by barbarians. For in fact Eretria has already been enslaved, and thus Greece has become weaker by one important city." In reply, the Spartans expressed their willingness to help, but said that they could not act yet. It was the ninth of the month, and a law prevented them from marching until the moon was full. The law in question probably applied only to the month of Karneia, during which the Spartans celebrated the festival of Apollo that gave its name to the month. Scholars of an earlier generation tended to dismiss Spartan religious qualms as specious excuses for inaction, but today it is generally recognized that the Spartans paid particular attention to the gods in their military life.[13]

Herodotus may not have understood all the Spartans' concerns. Indeed, Philippides may not have heard them. The philosopher Plato says that the Spartans were hindered by a war against the Messenians, that is, against their helots, most of whom came from Messenia, the region across Mount Taygetos west of Sparta. For all his brilliance Plato was not a very good historian. Some scholars have been reluctant to believe him here because no other literary evidence directly mentions a helot revolt in 490. But various stray bits of evidence add up to a case for a revolt at this time. The best is an inscription found on a statue base for a Spartan dedication at Olympia. Pausanias saw and quoted this very inscription, which he says was set up at the time of the second Messenian revolt. The usual candidate is the famous revolt after the earthquake in the 460s. The letter forms on the inscription, however, look decidedly earlier than 460 and would fit a revolt in 490. Of course, Pausanias could be wrong; the inscription does not actually mention the Messenians. But worries about homeland security would help explain why only 2,000 Spartans set out from Sparta after the full moon. They reached Attica remarkably quickly, on the third day after they started. So their religious scruples were entirely sincere.[14]

Philippides had a mixed report to take back to Athens. Human help was coming, but not yet. Would the god Pan make good on his promise?

CHAPTER 6

The Plain of Marathon

Geography

The plain of Marathon has changed a great deal in the 200 years since Lord Byron mused there and Ottoman Turks still ruled Greece. In the days of early European travelers, Marathon retained an unspoiled, wild look. Richard Chandler, who visited Greece in the mid-eighteenth century on behalf of the Society of Dilettanti, noted that "this region abounds in wolves." He sounded no less frightened of the "large and fierce" dogs that guarded his party as they roasted a kid goat for supper and slept under a bare rock on Mount Agrieliki. Marathon positively inspired Rev. Edward D. Clarke in 1801:

> And if there be a spot upon earth pre-eminently calculated to awaken the solemn sentiments which such a view of Nature is fitted to make upon all men, it may surely be found in the *Plain of Marathon;* where, amidst the wreck of generations, and the graves of antient heroes, we elevate our thoughts towards HIM "in whose sight a thousand years are but as yesterday;" where the stillness of Nature, harmonizing with the calm solitude of that illustrious region which was once a scene of the most agitated passions, enables us, by the past, to determine the future. In those moments, indeed, we may be said to live for ages;—a single instant, by the multiplied impressions it conveys, seems to anticipate for us a sense of that Eternity, "when time shall be no more"; when the fitful dream of

human existence, with all its turbulent illusions, shall be dispelled; and the last sun having set in the last night of the world, a brighter dawn than ever gladdened the universe shall renovate the dominions of darkness and of death.[1]

A visit to Marathon became part of the standard tour in Greece. On Monday, April 11, 1870—the same year Heinrich Schliemann first visited Marathon—Lord Muncaster's party left Athens at 5:45 a.m. in two carriages, accompanied by four mounted soldiers supplied by the Greek government. The group included four Englishmen, two women, a six-year-old girl, an Italian with his servant, and a Greek guide. They took the coast road, the only route suitable for carriages. Muncaster's journal records that they reached the Soros about 11:00 a.m. and had a picnic. The gentlemen walked to the shore and looked for Persian remains. About 2:30 p.m. they started back to Athens. At about 4:30, as they entered a wooded part of the road, they heard gunshots and soon found themselves prisoners of the Arvanitakis gang, one of the most notorious bands of klephts (thieves).

Events quickly spun out of control. The brigands released the females and sent Lord Muncaster to get ransom for the men. They also demanded amnesty, which the Greek government declared unconstitutional. Greek soldiers attacked the klephts, who moved north toward Dilesi, hoping to reach the Turkish border. They shot prisoners who could not keep up. Early on Friday morning, April 22, Muncaster learned that the four Englishmen and their Italian friend were dead. The following Sunday, Muncaster made his way through a crowd in Athens to see something exposed on a gallows. He soon identified seven of his captors' mutilated heads.

In the crowd of boisterous vacationers who populate the coast of Marathon on summer days now, it is as hard to imagine the solitude Clarke experienced as it is to imagine being kidnapped by brigands or fighting in a battle, unless you climb up one of the mountains that surround the plain. From above it remains evocative. The bay has a pleasing, crescent-shaped curve, unbroken except for a slight bump near the middle, an irregularity that only emphasizes the harmony of the whole. It is easy to imagine the Persian fleet rounding the thin Kynosoura (Dog's Tail) peninsula that shelters the bay from northeast winds and unloading on the long, sandy beach known as Schoinia.

But appearances can deceive. It would be unwise to assume that the ancient Greek coast looked pretty much as it does today, or as it did in 1800. The modern visitor to Thermopylae, to take an example familiar from recent books and movies, may feel disappointment, for the site of the Spartans' last stand now sits three miles inland instead of blocking a narrow path along the cliffs. Sediment brought down by the Spercheios River has pushed back the Malian Gulf. Recent work by geologists suggests some important changes at Marathon, too.

Schist and marble mountains surround the plain. From the southwest, proceeding counterclockwise, they are Agrieliki (altitude 1,827 feet), Aphorismos (1,555 feet), Kotroni (771 feet), Stavrokoraki (1,043 feet), Lingovouni (1,089 feet), Terokorifi (1,227 feet), Mavrokorifi (738 feet), Megali Korifi (866 feet), Drakonera (794 feet), and the Kynosoura peninsula (164 feet).

Water bringing down sediment from these hills created the alluvial plain below. The most prominent of the watercourses is, or was, the Charadra. The Charadra arose on the northern side of Mount Parnes. When rain fell, the Charadra grew as it proceeded to the southeast. Before the Marathon Dam cut off the water supply in the late 1920s, the Charadra could rush with deadly force. Colonel William Leake reported that "in the autumn of 1805, the torrent carried away some of the houses of the village of Seferi [on the right bank below Marathona], and destroyed cattle and corn-fields in the great plain below." Edward Dodwell said that in 1806, if I understand him correctly, the Charadra overflowed, "sweeping away a mill that was upon its banks, and depriving several individuals of their lives."[2]

Even if it flows irregularly, a powerful torrent can move an impressive quantity of material. The Marathon Charadra created an alluvial fan or fluvial delta system. At the Soros, the ground level has risen ten feet. The alluviation increases as one moves northeast from the southwest corner of the plain. W. Kendrick Pritchett, who was as much an expert on Greek topography as he was on military history, reported that wells southwest of the Soros are dug only 23 feet deep, while near the Charadra they go down 66 feet. Most recently the Charadra continued more or less directly to the sea, entering it roughly in the middle of the bay. C. G. Higgins, an expert in groundwater geomorphology who accompanied Pritchett on one of his visits to Marathon, observed that the Charadra had at times flooded along the slopes of both Mount Kotroni and Mount Stavrokoraki. He found the heaviest scarring along the base of Mount Stavrokoraki, suggesting that the Charadra once drained to the northeast. Two drawings made more than 200 years ago support this claim. Louis-François-Sébastien Fauvel's sketch made in 1792 shows the Charadra hugging Mount Stavrokoraki and reaching the sea northeast of where it does today (Figure 21); in Giovanni Battista Lusieri's drawing from 1801, the Charadra zig-zags downhill between Kotroni and Stavrokoraki and then turns east, disappearing behind Stavrokoraki rather than continuing to the sea (Figure 3 in the Introduction). But since three different core sample studies have found that the Great Marsh does not contain much fluvial deposit, most of the time the Charadra passed through the middle of the plain. The northern end has its own story.

Because it was a dynamic system, we cannot tell where the Charadra ran in 490, nor can we tell how much of an obstacle it posed to men or horses. During the dry summer it should not have posed any great difficulty to either. Crossing it before the battle, in other words, should have been possible for either Persians or Greeks. Crossing it while fighting or retreating might have been more of a problem. Since no ancient source mentions the Charadra, it probably did not play a significant role in what happened.

Water also reached the plain through springs. The most important of these are the springs at the base of Mount Agrieliki (which fed a small marsh until the Rockefeller Foundation paid for a canal to drain it in 1933), several small springs at the other side of the bay below Mount Drakonera, and above all Megalo Mati, which still gushes powerfully where a spur of Mount Stavrokoraki juts out toward the Megalo Helos (Great Marsh). The remains of an old pumping station remind the visitor that this spring once supplied water to Athens. A concrete pillbox shows that the Germans considered it worth protecting as recently as World War II. Megalo Mati is the Makaria spring mentioned by Pausanias.

The coastline has shifted over time. Greek geologists interested in the effect of the Marathon Dam deduced from aerial photographs that the coast at the former Charadra outlet receded 328 feet between 1938 and

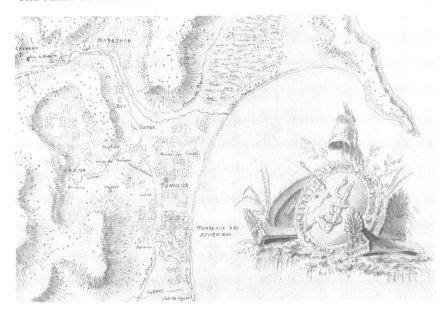

21. Sketch of Marathon drawn by Louis-François-Sébastien Fauvel in 1792 (Collection Barbié du Bocage no. 1341, Bibliothèque Nationale de France)

1988, since the river no longer brought down sediment to counteract the rising sea level.

How has the coast changed since 490? In broad terms, the history of the plain seems to be as follows. So much water froze during the last great ice age that at its height, 20,000 years ago, the global sea level dropped almost 400 feet. When that ice melted, 10,000 to 8,000 years ago, the sea level rose. The water probably reached all the way to the hills. Since then rushing water coming down from the mountains in the Charadra and other, smaller torrents has pushed the shore back out by depositing sediment. How fast this happened and whether the trend ever reversed before the construction of the dam depends on many things. Increased rainfall would lead to more alluviation, for instance, decreased rainfall to less. Deforestation leading to erosion would increase the size of the plain. The region is tectonically active; an uplift would expand the land, while the opposite would bring in the sea. Currents can move sand along the coast. Rising sea level would counteract alluviation.

At the southern end of the plain, Pritchett found reason to think that the shore moved inland between the Archaic period and the Roman period, and has since moved back out. He found Archaic and Classical sherds in clay or sandy soil in one place near the coast. Since the surrounding alluvium had none, he guessed that he had found a burial mound. The Roman buildings now 160 feet inland sit on a layer of clay above beachrock, so they may have been on the coast. Pritchett supposed that the land once extended farther out; he notes "heavy formations of beachrock" extending out into the bay. On British Admiralty Chart 1554, the contour lines in the bay suggest that the delta once extended farther out opposite the Soros. Indeed, the sketch of the plain published by George Finlay in 1839 shows just such a bulge in the coast, though it is small. Hauptmann von Eschenburg, who surveyed the plain for the German map project *Karten von Attica* in the winter of 1884, also shows a projection of the coast in the middle of the bay. All this suggests that the coastline has moved, but does not tell us where it was in 490. "Our greatest need at Marathon," Pritchett rightly said, "is for a geophysical map prepared by scientists who have permission to drill."[3]

For the northern end of the plain, we have just that. In fact we have more than one. In the 1980s and 1990s, several teams drilled holes to study the history of the Great Marsh. These studies aroused more interest than most because of the controversy over the construction of a rowing center for the 2004 Olympics. The studies reached similar broad conclusions. The northern end of the plain had its own alluvial fans created by torrents from the hills, but the hills in the east are lower and the torrents weaker than the powerful Charadra river in the west. Largely bypassed by the Charadra system, the eastern plain developed more slowly. Ten thousand years ago, the sea extended much farther inland than it does today. But after about 4000 BC, eastward littoral transport brought sand and gravel from the Charadra delta and began to form a barrier beach. This barrier gradually shifted southward. By 490, it was still some 1,600 feet farther inland than it is today.

When did the beach close off a lake that turned into a lagoon that turned into the Great Marsh? On the basis of carbon-14 dated cores drilled at the western edge of the Great Marsh, Cecile Baeteman concluded in 1985 that the area did not become entirely dominated by a fluvial system until 530 BC or AD 590 (two peat layers, though close to each other, had distinct dates). More recently, a team led by Kosmas Pavlopoulos drilled boreholes and dug trenches in the western part of the marsh, slightly east of Baeteman's. They found that communication with the sea was perennial until about 1550 BC. For the next thousand years, freshwater and saltwater conditions oscillated. At times freshwater from springs dominated, but at other times salt water penetrated most of the lake. Since about 550—uncomfortably close to the date of the battle, given the margin of error for carbon-14 dating—the area has no longer been inundated by salt water. The best study, though still unpublished, may turn out to be Richard Dunn's, since Dunn drilled holes across the Great Marsh rather than only on its western side. He concludes that in 490 the area was a shallow lake or lagoon open to the sea. His results match the ancient testimony of Pausanias, who describes a marshy lake connected to the sea. After Pausanias' visit, the area became less lake and more marsh; before his visit, it would have been less marsh and more lake.

It remains uncertain whether in 490 the connection to the sea was wide enough and deep enough to permit Persian ships to enter the lake. A trireme had a rather shallow draft. Unmanned, the modern trireme *Olympias* has a draft of 3.3 feet; fully manned, it is 3.9 feet. So if Dunn and Pausanias are right, some of the Persian ships might have sheltered in the lake (see Figure 30 for a battle plan based on Dunn's reconstruction of the topography).[4]

Ancient Descriptions of Marathon

Herodotus does not describe the plain. He says only that the Greeks camped at the sanctuary of Herakles and pursued the Persians until they reached the sea. Fortunately, that energetic ancient traveler Pausanias visited Marathon in the second century AD. He gives the following description:

> There is a deme called Marathon, equidistant from the city of Athens and Karystos in Euboea. It was at this place in Attica that the barbarians landed, were defeated in battle, and lost some of their ships as they put out to sea. On the plain is the grave of the Athenians, and on it are tombstones inscribed with the names of the dead, arranged by tribes.

There is another grave for the Plataeans of Boeotia and for the slaves, for slaves fought then for the first time. There is a separate monument for one man, Miltiades the son of Kimon. . . . A trophy of white marble has also been made. Although the Athenians say that they buried the Medes, because the gods require a human corpse to be buried in the earth, I could not find any grave, for there was neither a mound nor any other trace to be seen, as they carried the corpses to a trench and threw them in any which way. At Marathon is a spring called Makaria. . . . At Marathon is a lake, for the most part marshy. Into this ignorance of the roads made the foreigners fall in their flight, and it is said that this accident was the cause of their great losses. Above the lake are the stone mangers of Arta-phrenes' horses, and marks of his tent on the rocks. Out of the lake flows a river, affording near the lake itself water suitable for cattle, but near its mouth it becomes salty and full of sea fish. A little beyond the plain is the Hill of Pan and a remarkable Cave of Pan. The entrance to it is narrow, but farther in are chambers and baths and the so-called "Pan's herd of goats," rocks shaped in most respects like goats.

Can these places and monuments be located? Any reconstruction of the battle depends on the answer. Let me take them up in turn.[5]

The Herakleion (Herakles' Sanctuary)

Ancient Marathonians claimed that they were the first to recognize Herakles, son of Zeus, as a god. The only fifth-century source that may give a hint about the location of his sanctuary, Pindar, says in his victory ode for Aristomenes of Aegina that Aristomenes also won "in the *muchos* [nook, corner, recess] of Marathon." If by this phrase he means not that Marathon was a corner of Attica but that the sanctuary was in the corner of the Marathon plain, Pindar provides a clue.[6]

For anything else we have to look hundreds of years later. Accord-ing to Lucian of Samosata, writing in the second century AD, Herakles' temple was "near" the tomb of Eurystheus. Where was the tomb of Eu-rystheus? Strabo narrates Eurystheus' death as follows: "Now Eurystheus made an expedition to Marathon against Iolaus and the sons of Herakles, with the aid of the Athenians, as the story goes, and fell in the battle, and his body was buried at Gargettos, except his head, which was cut off by Iolaus, and was buried separately at Trikorynthos near the spring

Makaria below the wagon road. And the place is called 'Eurystheus' Head.'" If Lucian knew this story, was he thinking of Eurystheus' head or his body when he spoke of Eurystheus' tomb? Since there is no known Herakleion at Gargettos, on the other side of Mount Pentelikon, the better bet is the resting place of Eurystheus' head near Makaria. But the Athenians cannot have camped in the northeastern part of the plain, as they came from Athens after the Persians landed at Marathon. So Lucian must have used "near" loosely. He is not much help for locating Herakles' sanctuary.[7]

Scholars have suggested no fewer than a half dozen possible sites for the Herakleion, where the Greeks camped:

1. In 1876 an early topographer, H. G. Lolling, identified the stone enclosure in the valley of Avlona, known today as *Mandra tes Graias* (Old Woman's Sheepfold), as the sanctuary's boundary.
2. In their *Commentary on Herodotus* (1908), W. W. How and J. Wells favored the convent of St. George on the spur of Mount Aphorismos above Vrana.
3. Greek archaeologist Giorgios Soteriades advocated a large irregular enclosure just north of the chapel of St. Demetrios.
4. N. G. L. Hammond suggested the south end of Mount Kotroni as a possible site.
5. W. Kendrick Pritchett championed the mouth of the Vrana valley.
6. American archaeologist Eugene Vanderpool put the Herakleion in the region of Valaria, just north of the smaller marsh.

Of these six, the first four are no longer serious candidates. The stone enclosure turned out to be part of the estate of Herodes Atticus, a wealthy Athenian of the second century AD. Sites two and four lack any evidence of an ancient sanctuary. The wall of site three might very well be modern. Of the two remaining sites, one has foundations of a small temple and of a larger building, perhaps also a temple, but no inscriptions to connect the buildings to Herakles. The other has inscriptions relating to Herakles, but no foundations. Neither can be positively ruled out. Either could be described as in a recess or corner of the valley.

At the mouth of the Vrana valley, Soteriades excavated the foundations of a small temple, 36 by 20 feet, north of the chapel of St. Demetrios. In 1969 Pritchett published a photograph of a larger foundation about

1,000 feet north of the chapel of St. Demetrios and about 330 feet west of Soteriades' temple. He argued that this corner of the plain was devoted to sanctuaries and graves. The temple foundations could belong to Athena Hellotis, Dionysos, or Apollo Pythios; ancient sources attest sanctuaries at Marathon for each of these gods. Or one of the foundations might belong to Herakles. A Herakleion here would make sense for an army coming by the shorter route from Athens via Stamata. A natural route would bring the Plataeans here too. The camp would protect the shorter route to Athens and flank the coastal route.

Soteriades saw an inscribed stone in the courtyard of a house in Marathona. The homeowner told Soteriades that he discovered it in 1930 in his vineyard just north of the smaller marsh. The stele had two Archaic inscriptions. When he published them in 1942, Vanderpool dated the inscription on the back to the early fifth century on the basis of its letter forms. It contained regulations for the Herakleia, the contests held in honor of Herakles. Though damaged, the first 12 lines of the inscription can be read. They say: "For the Herakleia at Marathon a board of commissioners are to hold the contest. Thirty men are to be chosen for the contest from among those present, three from each tribe, who are to promise in the sanctuary to help in arranging the contest to the best of their ability and who are to be not less than thirty years of age. These men are to take the oath in the sanctuary over victims. To serve as steward [illegible]." In 1966 Vanderpool revealed what he had thought a quarter century earlier but refrained from saying out of respect for Soteriades, who had given him permission to publish the inscription. Vanderpool suggested that the stone's findspot indicated the Herakleion's approximate position. The inscription turned up only a few yards south of where the nineteenth-century German survey of Attica, the *Karten von Attika,* noted a foundation and building fragments.[8]

Not all scholars were persuaded, since the stone might have been moved from its original position. Then, in 1972, a second inscription was discovered built into a late Roman building in the same area. This inscription is a simple dedication to Herakles. As one colleague remarked to Vanderpool when he heard the news, "Two Herakles inscriptions are more than twice as good as one Herakles inscription."[9]

There remains one more relevant inscription, the one containing the Marathon epigrams. Greek epigrapher Angelos P. Matthaiou recently clarified this important text. In his interpretation, based on the discovery of a new fragment, the epigrams formed part of a cenotaph erected in Athens, a replica of the monument erected on the mound at Marathon. One of the epigrams refers to the Athenians standing in front of "the gates." Matthaiou connects this phrase to the dedicatory inscription mentioned in the previous paragraph, where he interprets a difficult phrase as referring to the Herakleia Empulia (the games in honor of Herakles at the gates, deriving the adjective "Empulia" from *pule* or gate). A Herakleion at the relatively narrow southern exit from the plain would be "at the gates." Compare Thermopylae, the hot gates, an even narrower road on the coast.

In my judgment, the best choice based on current evidence is Vanderpool's site. An Athenian camp there would have blocked the main road to Athens.

The Deme of Marathon

The deme or village of Marathon is even more elusive than the Herakleion. In population Marathon was the ninth largest of the 139 Athenian demes. So where was it? Archaeologists and topographers have found nothing definitive, which is perhaps not surprising in a plain with so much alluviation. In less than a decade, Pritchett advocated no fewer than three different sites. In 1965, he commented that "whoever suggests a site for the deme of Marathon today does so on a purely speculative basis."[10]

The candidates are:

1. Marathona, between Mount Kotroni and Mount Stavrokoraki.
2. The left bank of the Charadra between Marathona and the plain.
3. The flat ground at the foot of Mount Agrieliki, about 1.6 miles from the coast and east of the cemetery below the chapel of St. Demetrios.
4. At the southeast foot of Mount Kotroni, at the north end of the Vrana valley.
5. Vrana, at the back of the Vrana valley.
6. Vrexisa, the smaller marsh at the southwest entrance to the plain.

7. The area known as Plasi, on the right bank of the Charadra at the coast.

Only the last two remain serious contenders today. The first four, however plausible they have seemed to some topographers, have yet to produce sufficient remains for a deme site. Vrana was a cemetery, not a deme. The finds at Vrexisa so far have mostly been Roman. The most likely candidate, therefore, is Plasi, where the Charadra entered the sea in 1884, when Hauptmann von Eschenburg surveyed the plain for the *Karten von Attica*. On the bottom left corner of sheet 18 (Drakonera), von Eschenburg indicated potsherds, building remains, and foundations. He saw more ancient remains here, in fact, than anywhere else in the plain. In a lecture on December 4, 1886, he declared that the site had to be the deme of Marathon. In the early 1970s, Spyridon Marinatos made some preliminary excavations in the area "on a line parallel to the shore towards the North and East, for half a mile." He found "ruins and crossing walls almost everywhere," about one and a half to three feet beneath the surface. Though the datable finds were all several hundred years later than the battle, he concluded that "it is now fairly certain that the deme of Marathon existed on this site."[11]

Vasileios Petrakos has suggested one other possibility: There was no village of Marathon. The residences might have been dispersed, rather than clustered together in a single village. I see no way to rule out this possibility. But on balance, Plasi seems to me the best candidate—with one twist, admittedly speculative. Perhaps much of the deme is now under water. If the delta once extended farther into the bay, as argued above, then the remains of earlier houses might have washed out to sea as the eastward littoral movement ate away the land on which they sat.

The Grave of the Athenians

The prominent mound known as the Soros is the only candidate for the Athenians' grave. The early travelers all focused on it. It has been excavated (I use the term loosely) four times.

In October 1788, the French antiquarian Fauvel opened the mound as he hunted for antiquities. For eight days he had ten men dig in the middle, where they reached the level of the plain. They dug two other holes as well, to the right and left of the large one, both five or six feet deep. Fauvel cut quite a swath—E. D. Clarke reported that it was visible from the mountain behind Marathona, "like a dark line traced from the top towards the base"—but he did not find what he was looking for. Lord Byron heard that Fauvel found "few or no relics, as vases, & c." In his 1897 biography of Fauvel, Philippe-Ernest Legrand says that "nothing is found for his trouble, and Fauvel, mortified by his failure and harassed by the owner of the land, discontinues his research."[12]

On June 24, 1802, Lord and Lady Elgin, on board the frigate *Narcissus,* "came in sight of Marathon and saw the barrow on the shore, under which it is supposed the Athenians who fell in battle against the Persians were buried." Lady Elgin described their visit in a letter to her mother. On the 25th the sailors pitched a tent for them, surrounding it with pillars they found scattered. After dinner, she wrote, "we visited the mound of earth which Fauvel had partly opened; our ship's crew dug in another direction and discovered a few fragments of pottery and some silver rudely melted into a small mass." The next day three other Englishmen joined the party, including one Captain Leake, the future colonel. They explored the entire plain before sailing off together on the 29th without digging deeper in the mound.[13]

Nameless followers of Fauvel and Elgin, termed "speculators in antiquities" by historian George Finlay, left the mound "half dug open" by the 1830s. On May 12, 1836, the Greek minister of education, Iakovos Rizos Neroulos, sent the following memorandum to the Provincial Directorate of Attica: "Being informed that foreign travelers passing via Marathon are frequently excavating, with the help of the locals, in the very tumulus [mound] of those Athenians who fell in the battle (the so-called Soros), in order to find arrow heads, and wishing this most ancient monument of Greek glory to remain untouched and untroubled, we ask you to issue as quickly as possible the necessary orders to the municipal authority of Marathon, so that it is not allowed for anyone on any pretext to excavate the afore-mentioned tumulus or the other monuments on the field of battle." An engraving published by Christopher Wordsworth in 1838 gives a vivid impression of the mound's sorry state (Figure 22).[14]

22. Engraving of the Soros in the 1830s, designed by Captain Irton and engraved by G. W. Bonner (From Christopher Wordsworth, *Greece, Pictorial, Descriptive, and Historical* [London: Orr, 1839], 113)

In 1883, Heinrich Schliemann, the excavator of Troy and Mycenae, sank a 13-foot square trench into the top of the Soros, and a second one, half as large, into the eastern side. He dug the central shaft through the mound to a depth of 6.5 feet below the level of the plain, where he believed he hit virgin soil. The eastern shaft filled with water and had to be abandoned when only half that far below modern ground level. Concluding that the Soros had nothing to do with the battle in 490, Schliemann suggested that it was a prehistoric mound from the nineteenth century BC.

Then in two seasons of excavations in 1890 and 1891, Greek archaeologist Valerios Staes demonstrated beyond reasonable doubt that the tomb held the cremated remains of Athenian soldiers. It might seem incredible that anything was left to find, but no one had dug deep enough. Thirteen feet below the plain Staes found a funeral pyre on a brick-lined tray, with ashes and charred bones and black-figure pottery not later than the early fifth century (Figure 23). Apparently foreseeing that skeptics might challenge his veracity, Staes published an affidavit signed by himself and four

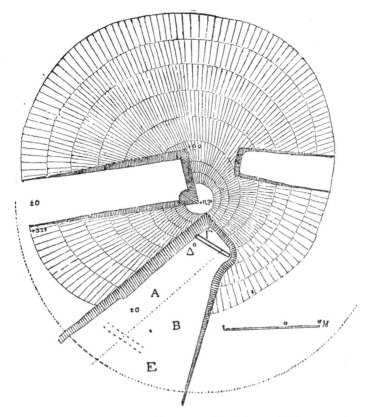

23. Drawing of Staes' excavation of the Soros. The delta marks the cremation tray.
(After V. Staes, "Ho en Marathoni Tumbos," *Athenische Mitteilungen* 18 [1893]: 49)

distinguished scholars who vouched for his findings: P. Kavvadias, H. G.
Lolling, K. Metsopoulos, and G. Kaveraou.

For the past century, scholars have almost unanimously accepted the
Soros as the burial mound of the Athenians. It has played a major role
in some battle reconstructions for two reasons. First, Pausanias says that
the Athenians were buried "on the spot." Second, Hammond maintained
that Persian arrowheads found in the fill of the mound show that the
earth in the mound came from within bowshot of the Persian battle line.
Both claims deserve scrutiny.[15]

It might seem that Greeks would bury their battle dead in the closest convenient spot—closest, that is, to where they fell, or where most of
them fell. But that is not what usually happened. The best comparison is
probably the burial of the Sacred Band who fell on the Greek right wing
at Chaironeia (338). They were buried all the way across the plain, under
the ugly stone lion. The point was to make a memorial that would be noticed. At Marathon, the Athenians might have erected the Soros where it
would have the greatest visual impact, perhaps at a fork in the path from
Athens leading left to Oinoï (up the pass between Mount Kotroni and
Mount Stavrokoraki) and right to Marathon, Trikorynthos, and Rhamnous. Pausanias' phrase "on the spot" need not be taken literally, for he
is comparing those buried at Marathon with all the other Athenians who
died in battle and were buried just outside Athens' Dipylon Gate along
the road to the Academy. By "on the spot" he might mean at Marathon
instead of outside the Dipylon Gate.

As for the arrowheads, the more one looks into them the more puzzling they become. Early travelers made quite a sport of finding arrowheads in the Soros. In 1801, E. D. Clarke wrote, his party "had no sooner
reached this *Tumulus,* which stands about six furlongs from the shore,
than we entered a passage which had been recently excavated towards its
interior [a footnote says this excavation was said to be Fauvel's]; and in
the examination of the earth, as it was originally heaped from the Plain to
cover the dead, we found a great number of arrow-heads, made of common flint. . . . We collected many of these."[16]

Edward Dodwell says that he "found in the large tumulus some fragments of coarse pottery, and a great many small arrow heads of black flint,
which probably belonged to the Persian army." He then cites Herodotus
for Ethiopians in Xerxes' army having stone arrowheads and concludes
from Pausanias' description of the statue of Nemesis at Rhamnous that
Datis had Ethiopians in 490 as well. (Pausanias says that Pheidias carved
the statue from a block of Parian marble that the Persians brought to
Marathon to make a trophy; with her right hand the goddess held a cup
on which were carved Ethiopians.) On the next page Dodwell says that
Marathon "is the only part of Greece where I found arrow-heads of flint;

those of bronze are common on the spots where battles have been fought." Common, but he evidently found none of bronze in the Soros.[17]

Sir William Gell wrote that "The tumulus, supposed that of the Persians [*sic*], toward the centre of the plain . . . consists of a large heap of earth, in which are found arrow heads of brass, and others of flint, apparently such as were used by the Ethiopians, who joined the Persian invaders, according to Herodotus." Thanks to his use of the passive voice, it is uncertain whether Gell found bronze as well as flint arrowheads himself, or was reporting what he had heard.[18]

Colonel Leake's reports are curious. Hammond quotes him selectively, giving the false impression that Leake gathered bronzes while his servant collected flints: "In the 1820s Leake's servant gathered 'a great number of small pieces of black flint at the foot of the mound,' which Finlay realized were from modern threshing instruments. Leake himself found 'many brazen arrowheads, about an inch in length, of a trilateral form' in the soil of the mound's surface." Here Hammond combines passages from two different books describing two different visits.

Leake visited Marathon first on June 26–29, 1802, when he met Lord and Lady Elgin, and again on January 29, 1806. In *The Demi of Attica*, he describes what must be his first visit: "[I found the mound] composed of a light mould mixed with sand, amidst which I found many brazen heads of arrows, about an inch in length, of a trilateral form, and pierced at the top with a round hole for the reception of the shaft. There were also, in still greater number, fragments of black flint, rudely shaped by art, and which in general are longer than the arrow-heads of brass. All these were probably discharged by the Persian bowmen, and, having been collected after the action, were thrown into the grave of the Athenians, as an offering to the victorious dead, who thus received the first marks of those heroic honours which were ever afterwards paid to them by the Marathonii."

In his *Travels in Northern Greece*, Leake describes his brief second visit quite differently. He writes that while he was on top of the mound, "my servant amused himself in gathering, at the foot of the barrow, a great number of small pieces of black flint which happened to strike his observation. These flints are so numerous, and have been so evidently chipped by art into their present form, like gun-flints, that there is good reason for believing them to have been the heads of arrows discharged by the Persians who fought at Marathon, and to have been interred with the Athenians, after having been gathered from every part of the plain, after the battle: Herodotus shows, that some of the Barbarians were armed in this manner, though his remark is applied not to the army of Darius, but to that of Xerxes. . . . I have heard that arrow heads of bronze have also been found here, but we searched for them without success." These words sound as if Leake found no bronze arrowheads, either in 1806 or previously. I cannot explain these conflicting statements. This puzzle about bronze arrowheads matters because, as Hammond noted, the flint pieces turned out to be parts of wooden threshing sleds, not arrowheads at all.[19]

If it seems unclear whether the early travelers found bronze arrowheads, it is as certain as these things can be that Schliemann and Staes did not. Neither mentions them. Though their reports sound amateurish by current standards, I cannot imagine that they found arrowheads and kept quiet about them. Bronze arrowheads would have supported Staes' identification of the cremated bones as those of the Athenian heroes.

What then of the "Marathon" arrowheads now in London (38 bronze and 10 iron) and Karlsruhe (35 bronze)? Elisabeth Erdmann's careful study of the Karlsruhe specimens divided them into four types and collected comparanda for each. She concluded that three of the types fit the era of the Persian Wars (the fourth type is later), but she stressed that her comparisons do not confirm that the arrowheads in Karlsruhe came from Marathon. Indeed E. J. Forsdyke, in his much earlier paper on the Marathon arrowheads in the British Museum, thought they were "much more likely to have been accumulated in a modern shop. Arrowheads no doubt find a readier sale as relics of a famous victory than on their own merits, and it would probably be found that Marathon has always been an attractive source of curiosities for the traveler. It ought not to be accepted as a provenance for ancient weapons without good evidence of their discovery." We have little evidence at all for the provenance of these arrowheads. When Saumarez Brock donated 10 of them to the British

Museum in 1906, she said that "her father, Admiral Brock, had dug them out of a grave in the plain of Marathon in 1830." Hammond thought the grave was "no doubt the mound," but there were lots of graves at Marathon, some of which have entirely disappeared. And even if Admiral Brock did find arrowheads in the Soros, they do not confirm the early reports of bronze arrowheads. All 10 are iron.[20]

In short, the Soros contains the ashes of Athenians who died in the battle, but it does not tell us where they fought. It is all too likely that the early reports of arrowheads were based mainly on the pieces of flint, and that some or even all of the bronze arrowheads said to be from Marathon did not come from the Soros. The absence of arrowheads among the finds of Schliemann and Staes makes it unlikely that the ingredients of the Soros included the ground on which thousands of Persian arrows fell.

The Tomb of the Plataeans?

In the 1970s, Spyridon Marinatos excavated five burial mounds at Vrana. While four were prehistoric, the fifth proved to be Late Archaic. The half of the mound that Marinatos excavated contained 11 males, ten adults and one boy about ten years old. Only two of the burials were cremations. Gravestones marked several of the inhumations, one of them crudely inscribed in Ionic letters (the dialect favored at Athens). Marinatos judged the pottery indistinguishable from the finds in the Soros. Based on the ceramic evidence and the absence of female bodies, he identified this mound as the tomb of the Plataeans who died in the battle. Archias, he thought, was an officer whose friends preferred the Ionic alphabet to the Boeotian; he took the ten-year-old to be a military messenger. Believing it unlikely that the Plataeans and freed slaves would have been buried together, Marinatos proposed to emend a single word in Pausanias by a single letter (*heteros* to *heteroi*), which would give "other graves for the Plataeans of Boeotia and for the slaves" instead of "another grave for the Plataeans of Boeotia and for the slaves."

Scholarly response has been mixed. Marinatos found nothing conclusive. Skeptics have argued that the mound is too far away from the Soros (about 1.6 miles) for the length of the Greek line, and too far out of Pausanias' path as he passed through the plain on his way to Rhamnous. A better candidate, they suggest, would be the mound seen by the early travelers near the Soros. (Since it has completely disappeared, this hypothesis cannot be tested.) Why are most individuals here inhumed, when the Athenians cremated all their corpses? Perhaps this is simply a family tomb in an area known to be a cemetery.

Whether or not the mound contains the Plataeans, it does not help us reconstruct the battle. The burial site does not have to be anywhere near where they camped or fought and died. It might have been chosen as the most appropriate place to honor Plataean heroes, along the route Plataeans would have taken to Marathon.

The Monument of Miltiades

About 650 yards north of the Soros, the early travelers saw the ruins of what the locals called Pyrgo (*pyrgos* = tower). Leake described it as "the foundations of a square monument, constructed of large blocks of white marble," and suggested it was all that was left of the monument of Miltiades. The marble blocks had all disappeared by 1890, leaving only a foundation of bricks and mortar. Vanderpool thought that the Pyrgo was most likely a medieval tower made of ancient blocks. They could have come from Miltiades' monument or from one of the sanctuaries. No other candidates have emerged for this monument.[21]

The Trophy

In 1966, Vanderpool explored the remains of a medieval tower beside the chapel of Panagia Mesosporitissa in the northeastern part of the plain. The chapel stands midway between the modern shore and the base of Mount Stavrokoraki, a few hundred yards from the western edge of the lake or marsh. Early travelers had noticed ancient marble blocks built into this tower. Vanderpool found one monumental Ionic capital, fragments of at least five column drums (two others, reported by travelers as lying on the ground some distance away, have disappeared), a battered bit of sculpture, and a number of step and orthostate blocks. Vanderpool

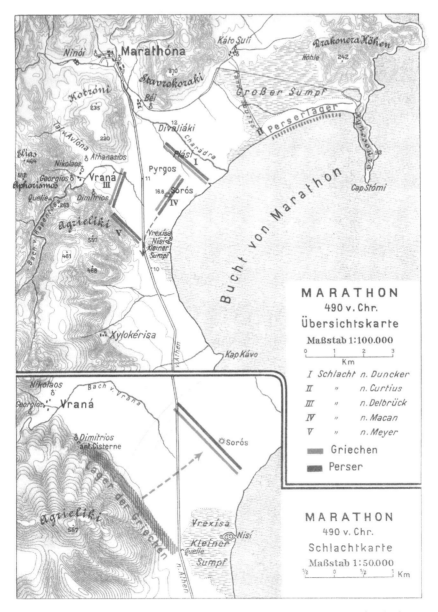

24. Johannes Kromayer's map of Marathon, showing early hypotheses for the location of the battle. Kromayer's own hypothesis appears at the bottom. (From Kromayer, "Drei Schlachten aus dem Griechisch-Römischen Altertum," *Abhandlungen der Philologische-Historischen Klasse der Sächsischen Akademie der Wissenschaften* 34 [1921]: pl. 1)

believed these to be the remains of a single Ionic column, 33 feet tall, datable by the style of the capital to the second quarter of the fifth century (475–450). He therefore endorsed Leake's suggestion that we have pieces of the Marathon trophy mentioned by Pausanias. He thought it commemorated the place where the greatest number of Persians died.

The tower sits on rubble and mortar foundations, not, so far as Vanderpool could determine, on top of ancient foundations (he dug small trenches on each side of the tower down three to six feet without reaching the foundations' lowest level). Odds are, though, that so many blocks were not moved far. The ground rises slightly, but not enough to make it worth moving large blocks any great distance to get to this spot. I believe the Marathon trophy stood here.

The word "trophy" comes from the Greek *tropaion*, which derives from *trope* (turn). On the day of a battle, victorious Greeks erected trophies—captured armor and weapons hung on a tree or post—at the place where the enemy turned and ran. The Athenians evidently replaced the temporary trophy with a marble Ionic column that became one of their proudest monuments. Aristophanes and Plato, among others, refer to it. For the reconstruction of the battle, the trophy is the single most critical topographical marker. It should mark the battle's turning point, not necessarily the place where the greatest number of Persians died. It makes irrelevant the earlier debate about how the battle lines were oriented (Figure 24), for the fighting took place well to the east of the Soros.

Before the 2004 Olympics, the Greeks built a replica column in marble next to the remains of the tower. Standing on top of a three-stepped platform, it commemorates the place where the Greeks and Persians met and where the Persians turned to flee.

The Trench with the Persian Dead

Six hundred years after the battle, Athenians assured Pausanias that their ancestors had buried the Persian dead. He deduced, or was told, that they were thrown into a trench. He could find no trace of them. Von Eschenburg may have done better during the seven months he spent surveying Marathon. He reported that "in the vineyard belonging to Skouzes a large quantity of remains of bones was found, haphazardly placed, which seem to belong to many hundreds of dead. I thank for the information Mr. Skouzes' steward, an intelligent young Greek under whose direction the vineyard was planted. I myself dug at the edges of the vineyard and found that this area full of remains of bones extends as far as the marsh." Though it would be nice to have confirmation from a proper archaeological excavation, in all probability von Eschenburg discovered the remains of the Persians, dumped unceremoniously into the ground. The Greeks had no reason to bury the Persians anywhere other than where they fell.[22]

The Spring of Makaria

I have already mentioned the identification of Makaria with the powerful spring at the northwest corner of the marsh. The geographer Strabo locates it below the wagon road to Trikorynthos (modern Kato Souli). Leake reported "traces of ancient wheels" on the rocks in the pass between the base of Stavrokoraki and the marsh, a passage Clarke described as "hardly wide enough to admit of two persons abreast of each other." At the end of the nineteenth century, J. G. Frazer found it only slightly broader: "hardly wide enough for two horses to pass each other."[23]

The Mangers of Artaphrenes' Horses

Leake noted a "small cavern . . . which has in some places the appearance of having been wrought by art" in the side of Mount Drakonera, east of the lake; he suggested that it might be the stone mangers mentioned by Pausanias. More plausibly, in his 1898 commentary on Pausanias, J. G. Frazer noted "some shallow, niche-like excavations in the rock, not unlike mangers," halfway up the hill above Kato Souli, and thought that locals had named them the mangers of Artaphrenes' horses. This local tradition may have no more historical significance than the names tour guides give to stalagmites in caves, but it is likely that the Persians kept their horses near the Makaria spring, so that the Persian headquarters was in the plain of Trikorynthos, as Leake suggested.[24]

The Cave of Pan

Visited by some early travelers, this cave was rediscovered in 1958 about two miles west of modern Marathona. Greek archaeologist Ioannis Papadimitriou explored the cave, which is identified by an inscription recording a dedication to Pan and the Nymphs, and found that human activity there began in Neolithic times. Papadimitriou believed that people abandoned the cave after the Mycenaean period and only began to use it again after the battle. It has no importance for the reconstruction of the battle. It does show that Pausanias did not proceed directly through the plain on the road to Rhamnous farther up the coast, which means that his account is not inconsistent with Marinatos' proposed identification of the Tomb of the Plataeans.

A Short Description of the Plain in 490

After visiting Marathon, Edward Lear wrote to his sister from Athens on July 19, 1848: "The place like all such in Greece is quite unchanged by time, & the exact points of the battle are as exactly to be followed as those of Waterloo." This letter is a cautionary tale against such confidence, for Lear continued, "A vast tumulus still marks the site of the buried Persians [*sic*]." But any reconstruction of the battle must rest on the best possible understanding of the topography, even if it remains less certain than Lear supposed. Here's my best understanding (Figure 25).[25]

Surrounded by mountains, the alluvial plain of Marathon extended farther out to sea in the southwest than it does today, while the coastline in the northeast ran farther to the north. The Kynosoura promontory protected the eastern end of the bay. The barrier beach may or may not have closed off the shallow lake that later turned into the Great Marsh. Athenians could get to Marathon either by the coast road or by the shorter route around the other side of Mount Pentelikon, past Stamata, and down to the plain via (modern) Vrana or (modern) Marathona.

In August or September, the torrents would have been dry. Rain seldom falls in Attica during the summer. Both Greeks and Persians depended on springs and wells. There were good springs both in the southwest,

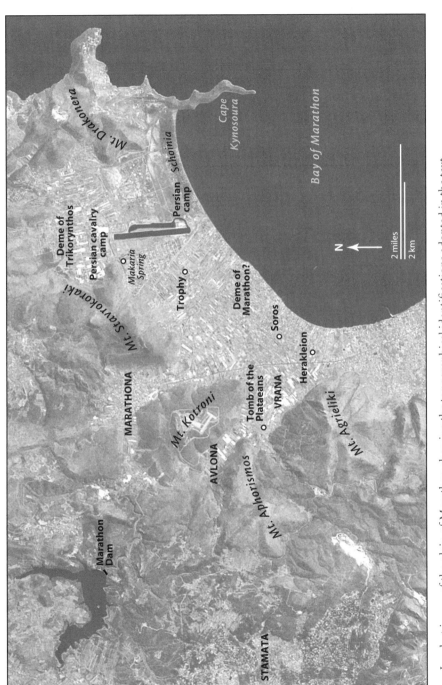

25. Landsat image of the plain of Marathon showing the topographical identifications adopted in the text

which later supplied the small marsh, and in the north and east, around the lake. The village of Marathon most likely lay on the coast in the middle of the bay, where the delta used to extend farther out. The path or paths of the torrents in 490 cannot be known because these dynamic systems have changed course many times. Since no source mentions them, they are best left aside when reconstructing the battle.

Ancient writers described the plain as *liparos* (shiny, oily, wealthy), *ennotios* (wet, moist), and *elaiokomos* (olive-rearing). In the eighteenth century, Richard Chandler rode through "some very thick corn [grain] of most luxuriant growth." By the time of the battle, the grain harvest had ended. The olive trees grew primarily on the hillsides, but Cornelius Nepos mentions "scattered trees" on the battlefield. With grapevines, olive trees, fruit trees, houses or outbuildings, watercourses, and boundary walls here or there, the plain would not have looked like a manicured parade ground.[26]

The sanctuary of Herakles sat at the "gates," just north of the narrow exit from the plain in the southwest. Neither the Soros nor the mound Marinatos identified as the tomb of the Plataeans helps to locate the fighting, though the former is certainly the resting place of the Athenian dead and the latter might hold their Plataean allies. The two sides met where the marble trophy stood, well out in the plain near the chapel of Panagia Mesosporitissa.

It remains to discover how and why the battle came to be fought there.

CHAPTER 7

When Marathon Became a Magic Word

The Athenian Generals Debate

Though the Athenians and Plataeans had hurried to Marathon and secured the southern end of the plain, the Spartans had not yet arrived. The ten Athenian generals differed in their views about what to do next. Half thought their numbers were too few to fight, while the other half wanted a battle. Herodotus says that Miltiades persuaded the polemarchos Kallimachos to cast the deciding vote.

It is now up to you, Kallimachos, whether you will reduce Athens to slavery or ensure its freedom and thus leave to all posterity a memorial for yourself which will exceed even that of Harmodios and Aristogeiton. For from the time Athenians first came into existence up until the present, this is the greatest danger they have ever confronted. If they bow down before the Medes, it is clear from our past experience what they will suffer when handed over to Hippias; but if this city prevails, it can become the first among all Greek cities. I shall explain to you how matters really stand and how the authority to decide this matter has come to rest with you. We 10 generals are evenly divided in our opinions, some urging that we join battle, others that we do not. If we fail to fight now, I expect that intense factional strife will fall upon the Athenians and shake their resolve so violently that they will medize. But if we join battle before any rot can infect some of the Athenians, then, as long as the gods are impartial, we can prevail in this engagement. All this is now in your hands and depends on you. If you add your vote for my proposal, your ancestral land can be free and your city the first of Greek cities. But if you choose the side of those eager to prevent a battle, you will have the opposite of all the good things I have described.

Kallimachos' vote broke the tie. The Athenians would fight. Nevertheless, the battle did not happen immediately, because the ten generals took turns commanding for each day, and the generals in favor of fighting yielded their days to Miltiades. He did not take the field until his own day of command came around. We do not know how long the delay was, but if we take Herodotus' plural "generals" seriously, Miltiades waited for at least two and as many as nine days. Why? What really broke the stalemate?[1]

Miltiades' speech—composed by Herodotus, of course, not a transcription of what was actually said—echoes the pre-battle speech Herodotus has Dionysios of Phocaea make before the battle of Lade, the battle that, for all practical purposes, ended the Ionian Revolt. Both speeches stress the decisiveness of the moment. Both draw a sharp distinction between slavery and freedom. Both contain, word for word, the phrase "as long as the gods are impartial." At Lade, many of the Greeks abandoned the fight. Would Athenians lose their courage and submit now? That fear was real, but Herodotus does not support J. B. Bury and Russell Meiggs' idea that "bad news on the political front from Athens" persuaded the generals to risk a battle. Miltiades urges fighting *before* such bad news could arrive.[2]

The speech may contain a clue about how Herodotus thought Miltiades planned to win. What does Herodotus mean by the expression "as long as the gods are impartial," or more literally, "if the gods distribute equal things"? Is it more than a pious *inshallah* or "God willing"? He might be thinking psychologically: If the gods keep us from panicking, we can win. This interpretation would make sense of the fact that Philippides' vision prompted, after the battle, a formal cult of Pan in Athens. Pan caused panics. But the Persians did not panic at Marathon; on the contrary, they fought for a long time. So perhaps the idea is rather that Pan prevented panic among the Athenians, since Herodotus says that be-

fore Marathon "even to hear the name 'Medes' spoken would strike ter-
ror into the Greeks."[3]

Or we might accept Jon D. Mikalson's suggestion that the phrase
means "if the gods make it a fair fight." Then the question becomes: How
did Miltiades plan to secure a fair fight? If the Athenians advanced into the
open plain, they became vulnerable to Persian cavalry. Would that be a
fair fight, if the Athenians could not match the Persian cavalry? Wouldn't
the fight be on more equal terms after the Spartans arrived?[4]

According to one of J. A. R. Munro's ingenious ideas, the Persians
forced Miltiades' hand. In the first edition of the *Cambridge Ancient History*, Munro maintained that the Persians had divided their forces. Datis
landed at Marathon while Artaphrenes landed at Eretria. "It was the sailing of the Persian ships from Eretria," Munro wrote, "that determined
the day of the battle. . . . News had arrived that Artaphernes was moving,
and no doubt that his cavalry was embarked, for either Marathon or Phalerum. At Marathon the cavalry would heavily weight the scale against
the Athenians, at Phalerum it could make a dash for Athens, or rout the
Spartans, if it met them on the plain. . . . The critical moment had come;
the Athenians must strike instantly, now or never." This vivid account,
unfortunately, grew out of Munro's own imagination. No source suggests
that the Persians divided their forces to attack Athens and Eretria simultaneously. In fact Plutarch says specifically that Datis landed at Marathon
"with his entire force."[5]

There must be another answer. Miltiades must have seen an opportunity to exploit—an opportunity that would not wait for the Spartans.

"The Cavalry Are Apart"

After emphasizing the Persian cavalry when he describes preparations
for the campaign and the landing at Marathon, Herodotus does not mention horsemen in his battle narrative. According to another old hypothesis (which Munro favored in an earlier article), Herodotus does not mention them because they were no longer there. On this view, Datis decided
to leave a covering force on land, embark his cavalry and half his infantry,
and sail to Athens, where he hoped either to catch the city undefended

or to find pro-Persian Athenians who would betray it. Tipped off by Io-nians that the horses and half the infantry were on the ships, Miltiades attacked and won. Though this idea rests on what Charles Hignett called "no evidence worthy of the name," it has proved remarkably resilient. Two videos about the battle broadcast on the History Channel in 2004, for instance, present the embarkation of the horses as fact.[6]

Scholars favoring this hypothesis cite three passages, one in Herodotus, one in Cornelius Nepos' biography of Miltiades, written more than 400 years after the battle, and the third in the Suda, a Byzantine Greek histori-cal encyclopedia compiled in the ninth or tenth century.

Andrew R. Burn pointed to Herodotus' statement that after the battle the Athenians hurried back to Athens "as fast as their feet would carry them." To Burn, this haste meant that the Persians had already begun to embark on their ships before the battle. But neither the Persians nor the Athenians could have reached Athens until the following day. Herodotus' comment on the Athenians' speed tells us nothing about when the Per-sians began to embark.[7]

Nepos has Datis invading with 200,000 infantry, but fighting with only 100,000. Nepos apparently thought that only half of Datis' infantry engaged. But he does not say that the other half had returned to the ships, and he describes Datis' horsemen as fighting, not reembarking.

So the notion that the Persian cavalry did not participate in the battle really rests on an entry in the Suda under the heading *choris hippeis* (the cavalry are apart). R. W. Macan said of this passage, "It is certainly re-markable that with the authority which is chronologically the end of the *catena*, one new grain of gold is added to the circle of tradition." In his translation of the paragraph, James A. S. Evans indicates different pos-sibilities where the meaning is not certain:

> When Datis invaded Attica, men say that the Ionians, when he had with-drawn (*or* gone away), came up inland to a wooded area (*or* climbed trees) and told (*or* signaled) the Athenians that their horses were apart (*or* away *or* brigaded by themselves, *or possibly* off on a separate mission). And Miltiades who took note of their departure (*or* understood what they were up to), attacked and won a victory. Thus the aphorism is said

26. Roman sarcophagus, third century AD, showing the fight at the ships (Photo courtesy of the Civici Musei di Brescia)

of those who break up (*or* destroy) battle order (*or* an army detachment, *or possibly even* an army).[8]

Does the Suda truly offer a grain of gold? In addition to its unknown authorship, late date, and unknown source, the passage presents several other difficulties. It does not say clearly where the horses were or what they were doing. It does not mention ships. It does not explain why the Athenians would need to hear anything from the Ionians. With hills all around, the Marathon plain offers ready visibility. The Athenians ought to have seen for themselves where the horses were. The story reeks of Ionian propaganda. Who benefited from it? The Ionians who accompanied the Persian expedition, but here at the moment of crisis show their loyalty to the Greek cause. I suspect the story was first told somewhere in Ionia.

Some evidence—late, but not as late as the Suda—suggests that horses *were* present at the battle. More than 600 years after the battle, Pausanias reports that locals heard horses neighing and men fighting every night. His contemporary, the orator Aelius Aristeides, says that the Athenians captured the horses. More tentatively, there is artistic evidence too: The Brescia sarcophagus, which may derive from the painting of the battle in the Stoa Poikile, includes a horseman (Figure 26), and the south frieze of the temple of Athena Nike, which may also derive from the great painting of Marathon, shows hoplites fighting mounted Persians.[9]

All in all, the Suda passage is best put aside. Its staying power derives more from the perceived inadequacies of Herodotus than from its own clarity or pedigree. Other evidence cannot be said to support it. If an explanation of how the Athenians won the battle is consistent with the Suda, or explains the aphorism's origin, well and good, but the Suda is no firm foundation on which to rest a reconstruction. It may be true, as Burn claimed, that "it would have received more respect in our age of *Quellenkritik* [source criticism] if the writer had only quoted, as the book often does elsewhere, the name of his source." Or it may not, if the writer had only a poor authority or none at all.[10]

Miltiades' Plan

If the proposed division of Persian forces is rejected as a modern invention without sufficient support in the sources, then what did break the stalemate? One suggestion is that the Persians threatened to take the coast road to Athens, but the location of the Greek camp at Valaria rules out that possibility. The Persians would have had to go right through the camp. But it did not block the more difficult route via Stamata. To cover that route as well, the Greeks had to advance not only in front of the Vrana valley, which would cut off one entry to the Stamata route, but also to Mount Stavrokoraki, in order to cut off the other entry up the pass between Mount Kotroni and Mount Stavrokoraki. To cover both land routes to Athens, in other words, the Athenians had to cross the broadest part of the plain.

To protect their flanks as much as possible, the Athenians would have wanted to reach the shortest line between Mount Stavrokoraki and the sea. That line would have passed right by the trophy. The formation there would have extended almost 1.5 miles, a length of line that some previous writers have considered feasible. Herodotus says that the Greek center was stretched thin, but the wings were strong. A force of 18,000, eight deep on the wings and four deep in the center third, would have covered 1.5 miles with a file width of three feet. Fewer would have sufficed in a looser formation, as I think possible.

The Greeks' challenge would be to cross the widest part of the plain before the Persian cavalry slowed or halted their advance, leaving them sitting ducks to be shot down by Persian archers. (If Richard Dunn turns out to be right in his hypothesis that the delta extended farther out in 490, the plain was much broader in the middle than it is now, and the risk even greater. But this is hypothesis; he did not bore holes in the southern half of the plain.) No Athenian commander would have marched out into the plain without some plan for dealing with the Persian cavalry. What was Miltiades' plan?

Miltiades had had several days to observe the Persians deploying on the plain, as they surely did, ravaging Athenian land and offering to fight. He had a sense of how early in the morning they started and how long the deployment took. The Persians tethered and usually hobbled their horses at night. To get them ready for action, the grooms had to untie them, give them feed and water, and put on their saddlecloths and bridles. The fourth-century historian Xenophon, who had served with Persians, comments that this preparation is difficult at night. So we should imagine them starting no earlier than first light.[11]

If the Persian high command and the horses camped in the valley of Trikorynthos north of the lake, as Leake and Hammond have suggested, the cavalry had to make its way single file along the narrow road between Mount Stavrokoraki and the Makaria spring. The effect would be something like what happens on a modern highway that suddenly shrinks from four lanes to one. If it took only five seconds for each horse to pass the spring, a cavalry force of 600 would need 50 minutes to ride through the bottleneck. Ten seconds each would mean an hour and 40 minutes.

I believe that Miltiades planned to get inside his enemy's decision cycle. If the Greeks could reach the Persian infantry before the Persian cavalry deployed in the plain, it would be too late for Datis to do anything about it. The Greeks could fight on equal terms.

The Run for Eight Stadia

The tactical plan outlined above makes sense of Herodotus' narrative, particularly of the famous run. The Greeks ran to cross the plain before the Persian cavalry could reach them.

Herodotus says that the Athenians advanced *dromoi* (at a run) for eight *stadia*. He uses the word *dromoi* four times in a single paragraph. Other fifth-century evidence confirms the importance of this run. The lost painting of the battle in the Stoa Poikile showed the Athenians and Plataeans closing with the enemy for hand-to-hand combat, with the Plataeans, distinguished from the Athenians by their caps, each coming to help "as fast as he could." In other words, the painting showed both the Athenians and the Plataeans charging at a run, with the Plataeans identifiable not by their running but by what they had on their heads. Another confirmation comes from the comic poet Aristophanes, who says that the Athenians "ran out with spear and shield" to fight the barbarians. After the battle, archaeologist Sarah Morris writes, "the image of a running warrior in armor became a symbol of the Athenian victory over Persia" (Figure 27).[12]

A Greek *stadion* was always 600 Greek feet, but the length of a foot differed from place to place. It varied from about 10.9 inches at Halieis, where the stadium was 548 feet long, to as much as 12.6 inches at Olympia, where the stadium was 630 feet. Most likely Herodotus heard this story from Athenians; on the Attic standard (one Attic foot = 11.7 inches), eight stadia would be about 0.9 miles.

Since Hans Delbrück published *Die Perserkriege und die Burgunderkriege* in 1887, most scholars have refused to believe the Athenians ran this distance on the grounds that, as Delbrück later put it, "Such a run is a physical impossibility: a heavily equipped unit can cover at the most 400 or 500 feet (120 to 150 meters) at a run without completely exhausting its strength and falling into disorder."[13]

The skeptics have differed over whether Herodotus exaggerated the speed or the distance. One solution is to translate dromoi as "at the quick step," that is, 120 steps per minute, each step 2.5 feet, or a pace of 3.4 miles per hour (mph). But in an article published in 1919, W. W. How collected the occurrences of dromoi in Greek historians and argued persuasively that "at the quick step" is too slow. How favored "double-time," in modern terms 180 steps per minute, each step three feet, or a pace of 6.1 mph.

Delbrück himself argued against the distance, citing current Prussian military practice, which restricted men carrying a load of 64 pounds to

27. Painted clay plaque, c. 490, showing a running hoplite carrying a shield with a satyr (Pan?) as the shield device. The plaque originally read "Megakles *kalos*" (Megakles is good-looking), but "Megakles" was erased and "Glauketes" substituted. (Acropolis Museum, Athens, no. 67; Ministry of Culture, A' Ephorate of Prehistoric and Classical Studies)

running two minutes, walking five minutes, and running two minutes. They ran at a speed of 6.1–6.5 mph. Delbrück reported that the director of the Military Central Physical Training School confirmed to him personally that two minutes would be the most that a column with field equipment could run and still reach the enemy in condition to fight. Since Delbrück believed that a Greek hoplite carried 15 pounds more than a Prussian soldier, he concluded that the amateur Athenians ran at most 400 or 500 feet.

In the 1970s, two professors at Pennsylvania State University tried to test the Marathon run's feasibility, both in the field and in a human performance laboratory. In 1973, Walter Donlan and James Thompson asked ten male college students, each carrying 15 pounds (including a nine-pound shield), to run a mile at a 7 mph pace. Two students failed to finish the distance, and only one, a member of the varsity track team, was judged able to fight after the run. Donlan and Thompson did not report their data on energy expenditure and heart rate, but they said: "It was calculated that for a subject to run the measured distance carrying a total weight of 13.6 kg (30 lbs.), including the nine-pound shield, would require 90–95 percent of his maximum capability. While this is not an unusually high figure for well-trained men to run a mile, relatively untrained men would have experienced considerable difficulty." In 1977, they had 13 students, similarly equipped, run 565 yards in 2:45, again at a 7 mph pace. This time they reported that the students reached 93 percent of their maximum work capacity. Again they did not report their data, but by using "established formulae" they concluded: "Given a total panoply weight of 50–70 lbs. (including a 15-lb. shield, carried isometrically), a grade of approximately 2 1/2% (which simulates uneven terrain), and a reduced rate of 5 mph for 1.5 minutes, well-conditioned men can traverse a distance of 220 yards with sufficient energy reserves to engage in combat."[14]

Mistaken assumptions vitiate these experiments. Instead of 7 mph, the test ought to be done at the slowest pace that would still qualify as a run. Physiologists distinguish walking and running gaits on the basis of the duty factor (the fraction of the stride duration for which each foot is on the ground). When the duty factor is greater than 0.5, a person is walking, whereas if the duty factor is less than 0.5, the person is running. Put another way: To walk, a person must have at least one foot in contact with the ground at all times. If there is a moment when neither foot is on the ground, the person is running. To go faster, people walk with longer and quicker steps until they reach 4.5 mph, when they spontaneously change gaits from walking to running. This pace falls between quick-step and double-time. It is well below that used by Donlan and Thompson.

The other mistaken assumption in the Penn State tests relates to the weight hoplites carried. As I showed in chapter 2, by the end of the sixth century a fully equipped hoplite carried 30–50 pounds instead of 50–70, as Donlan and Thompson assumed. So the tests and calculations ought to be done at a pace just over 4.5 mph instead of 7 and a load of 30–50 pounds instead of 50–70.

But even if we redid the experiments, they would never settle the argument to everyone's satisfaction. It is debatable how similar U.S. college students are to ancient Greek farmers, as I learned a few years ago when I had a student who wanted to rerun the tests as a summer research project. I agreed to work with him and helped him apply for a summer research grant at Davidson College. The faculty selection committee turned him down with the comment that the tests would not prove anything. How can college students who drink soda loaded with sugar, eat a high sodium diet, and work out for 30–60 minutes a day be compared with farmers who drank wine mixed with water, ate a lean diet with little meat, and walked almost everywhere they went?

We ought to look at soldiers in the field rather than students in a lab. Delbrück should have asked his Prussian army sources about a slower pace with less weight. He did know about a French captain named de Raoul who claimed to have trained a platoon from the French 16th Infantry Regiment with great success in the winter of 1889–1890. With each man carrying a rifle, a saber, 100 rounds of ammunition, and rations, the platoon covered 12.7 miles in 106 minutes, a pace of 7.2 mph. In another performance they carried field equipment for 6.8 miles in 80 minutes, a pace of 5.1 mph, and proceeded to target practice, in which they bested all their rivals. Delbrück scorned these claims, suggesting that even if they were true, de Raoul had worked with only a small number of carefully selected men. Athenian farmers, fishermen, charcoal burners, potters, and sculptors, he said, would have had neither the time nor the energy to train for running.

De Raoul's claims are not unparalleled. I give two twenty-first-century examples from two different countries:

- Lieutenant Colonel J. C. C. Schute recently reported on a British battalion challenged to move 15 miles with 66 pounds in less than 3.5 hours (that is, faster than 4.3 mph) and again 15 miles with 44 pounds in less than three hours (that is, faster than 5.0 mph) and then to attack with full battle procedure. Schute reported that the "vast majority" of the battalion passed this test.[15]
- To qualify for the Expert Infantryman Badge in the modern U.S. army, soldiers carrying a 35-lb backpack and a rifle have to cover 12 miles in three hours or less. That's an average of 4 mph.

A modern Delbrück might object that only particularly fit soldiers meet these standards. To get a better sense of what might be more typical, I e-mailed all of the Davidson College ROTC graduates for the past 30 years and asked them about running with weight. I received replies from more than 50. With one exception, they were confident that troops carrying 35 pounds could run a mile and then fight. Some of their comments:

- Captain Bob Beard '77: "It was quite common to train by jogging with full equipment, and sometimes wearing chemical gear. I was on active duty from 1977–1980. Given the 'jog' pace of running in a tight formation, I don't think you would be overly fatigued after a mile to continue into battle."
- Captain Bob Blair '98, who served with an infantry unit in 1999: "We discouraged troops from running with weighted rucks, but many did on their own, often with 30 or more pounds, at a jogging pace (around 5 mph). It's fairly common, and for multiple miles. . . . I ran with that weight for 7 miles on one occasion in training."
- Lieutenant Colonel David Dale '76 described training at the 82nd Airborne Division's Recondo school. He remembered running 3 to 5 miles each morning, carrying approximately 30 pounds and running 8- to 9-minute miles. He said that afterward he was drained, but "like anything else we quickly improved our stamina and by graduation (10 days or so) it became just another daily task."

- Based on his polling of old colonels, Colonel Will David '84 thinks that "it would be entirely possible for a formation to run a mile in battle gear. . . . When you look at a well-conditioned unit, most of the soldiers can complete a 12-mile Expert Infantry Badge road march in less than 2:30 with gear weighing about 30 pounds. Many soldiers would be in the 2 to 2:15 range. When you drop down to a 6-mile road march, it is common to see times of about an hour."
- Lieutenant Colonel Rocky Kmiecik '85 wrote from Iraq to describe his combat load (51 pounds plus water) and a run of about 6,800 feet he did once through palm groves chasing a group of insurgents. Though winded at the end, he walked out of the groves and continued on patrol. "For training," he said, "most units have a standard ruck march (usually a jog) where the soldiers carry a 35- to 40-pound load over a 20 kilometer [12 mile] course and must complete it in under 3 hours."
- 2nd Lieutenant Myles MacDonald '79 reported on his experience as an armor officer in a tank battalion stationed in northern Bavaria from 1980 to 1983. "We routinely ran 5 miles/day in boots in an 80-man formation after a half hour of calisthenics. Once a week we did it as a battalion with 600 people in formation. . . . Every couple of months we did 2 miles in gas masks wearing MOPP suits." They ran at 4 to 4.5 mph wearing gas masks, 5 mph for the battalion run, and 4 to 6 mph for the company runs. MacDonald said it was hard to stay organized above 5 mph or so. "Within that limit, running 10 minutes with 20 to 30 pounds 3 feet apart is no sweat. Add peer pressure and adrenalin and I suspect you'd be warmed up to fight on arrival."
- Captain Grier Martin '91 described experiences in college, Air Assault School, the army reserves, and Afghanistan. His sense: "Thirty-five pounds is not so bad to keep up a slow steady run. Fifty-five starts to get heavy."
- Major David Rozelle '95 wrote: "Modern body armor and combat equipment, without even adding a ruck-sack load, is a minimum of 50 pounds. Our field soldiers train for this kind of weight as part of their physical training and adapt to the extra burden before deploying to a combat zone. With that weight it is common for men to run in excess of one mile, climb walls, and even maneuver through various obstacles. If a soldier is properly conditioned, it is not a problem."
- Colonel Jack Summe '78 said: "The U.S. Army is big on running and a great deal of our special forces focus . . . conditioning training on running with weighted rigs. I have been assigned to Ft. Bragg, NC and commanded both an Airborne Battalion and an Airborne

Brigade there. . . . I have seen soldiers running on weekends carrying full backpack loads (approx 35 to 55 pounds) or while wearing a flak jacket or body armor with plates (20 to 30 pounds). . . . We routinely run 3 to 5 miles daily with no extra weight, but could easily run with 20 to 30 pounds of equipment for 1 to 2 miles with no deleterious effect. We also accomplish routine (monthly) "ruck" marches (fully loaded backpack—55 pounds, weapon and load bearing belt or harness) of up to 12 miles. During many of these marches, you might see a soldier run for 2 to 3 miles to make up time. . . . After 28 years of service in the military, I can confidently state that I could throw a 35-pound ruck on my back today and go out and run a mile with very little negative effect."

• Major David Taylor '91 emailed from Iraq: "Present-day U.S. Infantry troops train to move 12 miles with a 35- to 50-pound load, in less than 3 three hours (4 mph), and fight upon arrival."

If our soldiers today can manage 12 miles at 4 mph, ancient Greeks carrying a comparable load could have done one mile at 4.5 mph. It is true that men today are bigger. But we should not underestimate the work capacity of farmers accustomed to doing hard physical labor all their lives. Ancient Greeks could have charged 0.9 miles at a pace that could be described as dromoi, though "jog" would probably better describe their speed than "run." The competitors in the race in armor (*hoplitodromos*) at Olympia would have run faster, since the race was only two stadia. (The length of this Olympic event does not prove, as some have suggested, that hoplites cannot have run farther, any more than the 100-meter dash shows that no one can run a marathon.)

Delbrück clinched his argument against the long run, or so he thought, with the battle of Pharsalos. When Julius Caesar's Romans charged at Pharsalos, Pompey had his troops remain stationary, confident that his enemies would lose their formation and exhaust themselves as they ran. Caesar's veterans realized the danger, checked their charge about halfway, and caught their breath before charging again. Caesar does not actually say how far apart the two battle lines were. (Delbrück assumed 600 to 700 feet by analogy with an earlier confrontation in Spain.) And Caesar's legionnaires were more heavily equipped than the Greeks at Marathon. If Pharsalos shows anything, it shows that warriors might spontaneously stop to catch their breath. Anyone who doubts that the Greeks at Marathon could have jogged eight stadia is free to believe that they stopped (just out of missile range?), caught their breath, and made their final charge.[16]

The charge did not have to maintain a tight formation. Herodotus uses the word *athrooi*. Though the standard Greek-English dictionary translates athrooi here as "in close order," it is better understood as "all together." In a nearly contemporary parallel, the poet Pindar has the leaders of the Cadmeans run quickly athrooi in their bronze armor, but here they are running into the infant Herakles' bedroom and so running "all together" or "all at once" rather than "in close order." Or take Thucydides' account of the Plataeans escaping from their besieged city on a dark and stormy night: They proceeded athrooi along the road toward Thebes.[17]

Herodotus says that the Persians were surprised to see the Athenians charging without the support of archers or cavalry. The important point is not that the Persians had archers and cavalry or that the Athenians did not yet have archers or cavalry. The point is that the Athenian archers did not fight as archers or their horsemen as horsemen. Because the Persians had Hippias as an adviser, they knew what sort of forces the Athenians had, and the Athenians knew that they knew. So either Herodotus had a source (an Ionian?) who knew that the Persians were surprised to see the Athenians charging without their archers and cavalry, or his source conjectured that the Persians were surprised to see the Athenians charging without their archers and cavalry. Either way, the passage implies that Athens had archers and cavalry but did not use them as such. The Athenians charged "all together," hoplites and light-armed and dismounted horsemen, all with spears or swords. In his *Knights,* Aristophanes says that Demos—a personification of the Athenian common people—"competed with the Medes in the sword-dance for the land at Marathon." I would like to think that a red-figure cup by Douris shows this charge, with a hoplite and an archer, both armed with spears, running together (Figure 28).[18]

A great irony of Marathon historiography is that so many modern writers have explained the running charge by the presence of Persian

28. Interior of an Athenian red-figure cup attributed to Douris, c. 490, showing
two running warriors, one armed as a hoplite, the other dressed as an archer but
carrying a spear. (Johns Hopkins University Museum, Baltimore, B8; from Paul
Hartwig, *Die Griechischen Meisterschalen der Blüthezeit des Strengen Rothfigurigen
Stiles* [Stuttgart: Spemann, 1893], pl. 22.2)

archers while explaining the Athenian decision to fight by the absence of
Persian cavalry. Herodotus mentions neither archers nor horses in his
battle narrative. He stresses the run for eight stadia. Archers would explain a charge for one stadion, approximately the range of Persian bows,
not eight. Only the presence—or rather the near presence—of the cavalry
explains the long charge. The Greeks had to cross the plain and engage
the Persian infantry before the Persian cavalry could attack them.

A Reconstruction of the Battle

On the evening before his day of command, Miltiades explained his plan to the other generals and circulated the orders to prepare for battle in the morning. Like the English king in Shakespeare's *Henry V*, he made the rounds himself, offering encouragement. He told them they were going to seize the initiative. They would surprise the Persians by a bold advance, crossing the plain and closing to close quarters before the Persian cavalry could stop their advance. He suggested that his men leave unnecessary weight behind. He asked them, Do you need your shin guards? Could a slave or poor friend wear your corslet, while you rely on your shield?

The men woke early. They had a fortifying cup of wine and water. An owl, some said, flew over—a good omen since the owl was the bird of Athena. The polemarchos Kallimachos sacrificed, looking for good omens. Campground sacrifices were a normal part of Greek warfare; the seer studied the flames as well as the internal organs, especially the liver, of the sacrificial victims.[19]

When the seer declared the sacrifices favorable, the generals gave the orders to arm and begin deployment. The usual way to give such orders was by blowing the trumpet. Aristotle compares its sound to that of a trumpeting elephant. Others likened it to the braying of a donkey. The Persians would have heard it and realized the Greeks were going to act. So perhaps the Athenian generals planned a quieter way of starting their deployment at Marathon.

As Kallimachos took his traditional position of honor on the right wing, the Athenian tribes "followed after as they were counted." Last came the Plataeans, who took the left wing.[20]

The Athenians made their line equal to the Persian formation in length, Herodotus says, keeping both wings strong but thinning the middle of the line, where the men were only a few ranks deep. Some recent writers have deduced that the Persians moved first, so that Miltiades could see the length of the Persian line as it advanced and adjust his own. But the Greeks could have observed the size of the Persian force on earlier days. If the Persians deployed first, they would not have been in the act of preparing (Herodotus uses the imperfect *pareskeuazonto*) when the Greeks charged.[21]

The Greeks deployed in front of their camp, perhaps originally eight men deep throughout. As the line wheeled out into the plain, the Plataeans headed for the base of the hills on the far, northern side, while Kallimachos kept close to the shore or headed for the inland edge of the village of Marathon. As a result—did Miltiades foresee it?—the center stretched thinner than the wings.

When a report reached Datis that the Greeks were moving, he was delighted and gave orders for the Persians to prepare for battle. Their preparations began later and so lagged behind the Greeks, as Miltiades had anticipated. The Persians had not gone to sleep expecting to fight the next morning. They had something to eat and drink, dressed, checked their equipment, and began to take positions west of the lake. They were in no hurry. No Greek force had ever charged a Persian army. Datis expected to have plenty of time.

The Greeks continued advancing for some 2.5 miles from the Herakleion, until they were less than a mile from the Persian line they saw forming before them (Figures 29 and 30). Here they paused and dressed their lines. Perhaps some men took off their shin guards or their sandals or even their corslets, to save weight. They would have preferred to continue walking, but Miltiades realized that they did not have 20 minutes to reach the Persian lines. Perhaps the first Persian cavalry appeared on the plain. If the Greeks didn't close with the Persians soon, if they didn't jog, the Persian cavalry would reach the plain and be on them. So the seer made the final battle-line sacrifice, the *sphagia*.

The noun *sphagia* and the verb *sphagiazesthai* (to perform *sphagia*) have the same linguistic root as the verb *sphazein* (to pierce the throat). Greeks made this sacrifice at the last moment before they charged. The act required no altar and no fire. It was quick. The seer stabbed the animal's neck and watched the blood flow. He used the same sword he would soon wield against the enemy. Sphagia could turn out badly; in that case another victim would be sacrificed. But there was less concern with divination at this last, emotional moment than there had been with the sacrifice in camp. The act of sphagia meant, as Michael Jameson put it, "O gods!

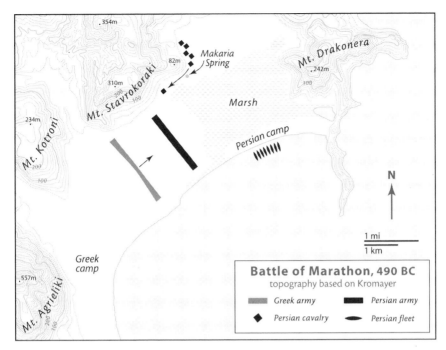

29. Reconstruction of the battle, based on the modern shoreline in Johannes Kromayer's map

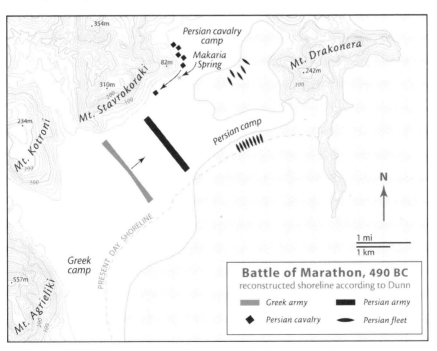

30. Reconstruction of the battle, based on Richard Dunn's reconstructed shoreline.

We destroy this life. We wish to kill and not be killed. Support us." Or even more succinctly: "We kill. May we kill."[22]

At this critical moment, Kallimachos vowed, on behalf on the Athenian people, to sacrifice one female goat to Artemis Agrotera (of the wild) for every enemy killed. The Spartans regularly sacrificed a goat to Artemis Agrotera immediately before charging. The goddess had a temple at Agrai just outside the city of Athens, but the Athenians are not otherwise known to have sacrificed to her before battle. They may have decided to imitate the Spartan custom this time because they were about to face skilled Persian archers. Artemis the hunter was an archer; her cult statue showed her with a bow.[23]

As soon as the sacrifice was good, Miltiades raised his arm, pointed at the Persians, and shouted *Hormate kat' auton* (Rush at them). The trumpet blew for the charge. The men yelled and began to jog. Herodotus says they were the first Greeks to run all together into a battle. The challenge was not to follow a "rabbit" and run faster than planned—a danger familiar to many a marathon runner today (including me) who, full of adrenalin, has started too fast and regretted it later. Perhaps the officers put mature men in the front line and ordered the others not to pass them. At a jog, they would have covered eight stadia in no more than 12 minutes.

The Persians thought the Greeks were insane to be charging without cavalry or archers, but they prepared to receive the charge. They set up a barricade of wicker shields, as they did at the battle of Plataea, and readied their bows and arrows from behind the shield wall. When the Greeks came within range of the Persian archers, "it was impossible to see the sky because of the arrows," as Aristophanes puts it. The arrows provided an incentive to keep up the pace but did not break the charge.[24]

When the Athenians reached the Persian line, the hand-to-hand fighting lasted "a long time." How long is anybody's guess. The only other direct evidence is Aristophanes' *Wasps,* which says that the Athenians pushed the enemy back "towards evening." Athenian tradition remembered a tough fight "with spear, with sword . . . standing man by man," not a quick resolution. Modern guesses have ranged from a few minutes to an hour or so, at most three, but if we include the advance, the hand-to-hand fight, the pursuit, the fight at the shore, and the return to camp, the battle must have lasted at least six hours.[25]

Herodotus describes the fighting in one down-to-earth paragraph: no singing dust clouds, no apparitions of women shouting so loudly that the entire force could hear them, not even a vision of Pan or Herakles. The single remarkable occurrence noted by Herodotus was the blinding of an Athenian soldier named Epizelos, who said he saw a huge hoplite coming at him with a beard so large it covered his shield, but the hoplite passed by and killed the next man. Though he was not hit, Epizelos went blind and remained blind for the rest of his life. Doctors today would say he suffered from conversion disorder or hysterical blindness.[26]

Epizelos appeared in the painting of the battle in the Stoa Poikile, as did a "man of rustic appearance" who killed many enemies with a plough handle. Pausanias says that the anonymous fighter vanished after the battle. When the Athenians inquired of the Delphic oracle, the god Apollo told them to honor the hero Echetlaios (Plough Handle). Though Herodotus doesn't mention Echetlaios, I find this story entirely credible. If a farmer's spear broke, he might well have grabbed a broken plough handle and swung it as a club.[27]

Finally, the Persians and the (Asiatic) Scythians in the center broke the thinner Greek line and pursued the Greeks toward the *mesogaia*. This word is usually translated "inland," which made good sense when the Persians were imagined as facing the Vrana valley with their backs to the sea. If the Persians were perpendicular to the coast, as most scholars now believe, the phrase doesn't tell us much, since just about any direction back from the point of engagement led toward some pass out of the Marathon plain. Today Mesogaia is the name of the plain in which the new Athenian airport lies, separated from the city plain by Mount Hymettos. If Herodotus meant that the Athenians fled toward that plain, he meant that they retreated toward their camp and the southwest exit along the coast.

On both wings the Greeks won. Instead of pursuing the enemy, they "brought together" the wings and fought the Persians and Scythians who had broken through in the center. Scholars have understood this phase of the battle in various ways. On one interpretation, the men on the wings formed a single phalanx and attacked the Persian center from the rear. On another interpretation, the wings re-formed separately and executed a tactical double envelopment. Supporters of both ideas tend to agree that Miltiades planned the whole thing, as evidenced by the Greeks' deployment with a thinner center between deeper wings. Some Miltiades fans have even suggested that he lured the Persians into a trap by ordering his center to fall back.[28]

I do not believe that untrained and inexperienced Athenian and Plataean hoplites—very different from Spartan warriors—could have executed such maneuvers in the middle of a battle. As far as we know, the Athenians had not fought a pitched battle since 506. Hans van Wees even doubts the story altogether, dismissing it as "a story of ideal hoplite behavior pushed to heroic extremes." But we can take "brought together" as "rallied" or "regrouped" rather than "brought together into a tight phalanx formation." The Greeks on the wings stopped, regrouped, and turned to help their center. Meanwhile the Persians and Scythians, realizing they had lost on both wings, turned back, perhaps in a panic. As they made for the ships, fighting the Greeks on their flanks, the other Persian infantry and the cavalry had time to board.[29]

The Greeks later boasted that they cut down the Persians "until they came to the sea." The Stoa Poikile painting showed many Persians losing their way in the marshy lake. The painting's original sea blue might have aged to a confusing green that Pausanias misinterpreted as the marsh he could see in his own day. That would fit Richard Dunn's reconstruction of the topography. The Greeks pursued toward the water. The Persians were pushing and shoving and falling in shallow water as they tried to reach their ships. Herodotus' use of the Homeric verb *kopto* (cut or smite) lends an epic quality to the narrative, as does the scene at the ships where the Greeks call for fire, as the Trojans had in the *Iliad*. Aristophanes, on the other hand, recalls Aeschylus' *Persians* when he says the Greeks were "spearing them like tuna through their baggy trousers." In desperate fighting at the water's edge, the polemarchos Kallimachos died—later legend said that so many spears pierced his body that his corpse remained up-right—together with "many other famous Athenians," including one of the generals, Stesilaos son of Thrasylaos. Aeschylus' brother Kynegeiros died when he grabbed a Persian ship and a sailor chopped off his arm. (Justin later embellished this story: Kynegeiros lost first his right arm, then his left, and died holding on to the ship with his teeth!) In the end, almost all Persian ships escaped. The Athenians captured seven.[30]

How Did the Greeks Win?

Dedications after the battle show that the Athenians credited the gods and heroes for the victory. Most historians—Pritchett is an exception—have credited Miltiades. Miltiades does deserve recognition. Without his prodding, the Athenians might have stayed in Athens. Without his per-suasiveness, the generals might have continued to wait for the Spartans. Without his bold plan to cross the plain before Persian horsemen could enter it, and without his order to run when it seemed they might not get across in time, the Athenians might never have closed for hand-to-hand fighting with the infantry.

Part of the explanation must be the difference in equipment. The Persians may have had some hoplites—they had picked up some Greeks on their way across the Aegean, and the Athenian soldier Epizelos reported seeing that huge hoplite coming at him—but they relied primarily on archers and cavalry. The Athenians' thrusting spears gave them an ad-vantage in hand-to-hand fighting. The Greeks also had better defensive equipment, especially stronger helmets and sturdier shields. On the other hand, the difference in equipment did not stop the Persians from break-ing the Athenian ranks in the center. The Persians were probably better trained and better disciplined. They fought bravely. The conscripts on their wings may have been less well trained, less well equipped, and less committed. But evidently the battle was no foregone conclusion even af-ter the Greeks charged through the hail of arrows.

Perhaps it is fair to say that Miltiades put the Greeks in a position where they could win. But praise should also go to the Athenians who elected him, who voted to take the field, who made the run, who fought to defend their land, their families, and their freedom. Plutarch tells a story that is certainly *ben trovato*. When Miltiades asked the Athenian assembly for a crown of olives, Sophanes retorted, "When you have fought and defeated the barbarians by yourself, Miltiades, then you may ask to be honored by yourself."[31]

CHAPTER 8

After the Fighting

The Shield Signal

After the battle, the Persian ships pulled away from the shore. "At Athens," Herodotus reports, "the Alkmeonids were later blamed for having contrived a scheme whereby a shield would be displayed to send a signal to the Persians aboard their ships." A few paragraphs later Herodotus vigorously defends the Alkmeonids, the family of Kleisthenes, against the charge of medism. No family opposed tyranny more consistently. It is inconceivable, he says, that the Alkmeonids collaborated with the Persians. Someone did raise a shield. But it was not the Alkmeonids.[1]

What are we to make of this story? Was holding up a shield really a big deal? Some scholars have dismissed the shield signal as an invention of the Alkmeonids' political opponents, perhaps Themistokles, or an embellishment of something that happened but did not have the significance the story attached to it. Lionel Scott, for example, suggests that the tale grew after someone raised his shield to taunt the losers. Such attempts to dismiss the story stem partly from the speculations it has prompted.

Here are some of the speculations. John B. Bury turned the story on its head. Instead of a signal shown by a Greek after the battle, he suggested, the shield was a signal shown *before* the battle by a detachment of

Persians sent to take control of the route to Athens via Stamata. Sending troops to cut off the Athenians from the city makes some sense. But it is not credible that a Persian contingent reached Mount Pentelikon, flashed a signal, and somehow escaped after the Greek victory. Where did it go? This sort of tale is not history.

Harris Gary Hudson admitted that a Greek gave the signal but suggested that it was intended for Miltiades, not the Persians. A lookout, seeing that the Persians had partially reembarked, signaled Miltiades that the time was right for an attack. This too is a nice story, but not history.

G. B. Grundy acknowledged that a Greek used a shield to signal the Persians, but he altered the chronology. The signal was given before the battle, he suggested, and prompted the Persians to divide their forces. But as we have seen, there's no good evidence that the Persians divided their forces.

Asserting that a raised shield could signal nothing more than yes or no, P. K. Baillie Reynolds wondered why it was necessary if the direct communication needed to agree on the yes or no question was possible. He answered that the Persians planned to be in their ships. The message was that the conspiracy at Athens had failed. But if that was it, why did the Persians sail to Phaleron? They already had all the evidence they needed to tell the king that Hippias did not have as many friends in Athens as he had suggested. Perhaps thinking along these lines, Fritz Schachermeyr suggested that the shield was raised at Phaleron, not Marathon. But again this is not what Herodotus says.

Recently A. Trevor Hodge has shown that the curved surface of a hoplite shield would have diffused sunlight too much for it to be used to flash a signal. As if to anticipate this objection, Hammond suggested that the signaler used a signaling disk rather than an actual shield. But Herodotus uses the word *aspis*, the standard word for a hoplite shield. In fact Herodotus does not say anything about the shield reflecting sunlight. The verb he uses means simply "to show by lifting up." The notion of a heliograph goes back at least to Colonel Leake, but not to an ancient source. It is a modern myth.

Where then was the signaler? For the Persians on board ship to see the signal, the signaler must have stood somewhere near the coast. How would the Persians have distinguished the signal shield from all the other shields being waved about by jubilant soldiers? Presumably the signaler held it above arm's length. If a soldier on the battlefield had raised his shield on a stick, he would have been identified. Most likely, then, the signaler stood somewhere else, perhaps on a roof in the village of Marathon.

It is true that a shield could only be shown or not shown, but that does not mean the signaler could only indicate yes or no. The signaler might have agreed with the Persians on a set of items, each meaning something different. For instance, a white flag if the collaborators had taken over the city, a red cloak if the Spartans had reached Attica, a shield if the city was still defended. Datis would want to know what he was going to find.

If Herodotus could not discover the full story of the shield signal, we certainly are not likely to stumble on the truth by guesswork 25 centuries later. But we should not deny the signal just because Herodotus could not identify the signaler. It shows that Athenians suspected they had potential collaborators among them. It confirms Miltiades' argument to Kallimachos that the Athenians needed to fight or risk dissension leading to surrender.

The potential collaborators might have been the Alkmeonids, in spite of Herodotus' protests. Granting his point that the Alkmeonids opposed tyranny, they might have been willing to take the Persians' side if Datis guaranteed the survival of the democracy. After the great victory at Marathon, they could not have expected to persuade a majority in the assembly to vote for submission, but if the Persians reached Athens before the Athenian army, there would have been no need for a vote. Eretria had shown another way.

A Message for Athens

Of all the tales told about Marathon, the most famous one relates that Thersippos (or was it Eukles or Philippides or Phidippides?) ran (in full armor, in one version) to Athens after the battle, shouted, "Rejoice, we have won!" and dropped dead. This story appears first in Plutarch, who credits it to an author who wrote much earlier, but still 150 years after the battle. It is not found in Herodotus and probably is not historical, though not because the feat was impossible. In the annual Bataan Memorial Death March held at White Sands, New Mexico, soldiers in the Male Military Heavy division carry a rucksack weighing a minimum of 35 pounds for 26.2 miles. The 2008 winner, 21-year-old Jack Glojek, finished in 5:15:27, an impressive pace of 12:02 minutes per mile. A 40-year-old in the Civilian Male Heavy division named David Pokorny did even better, finishing in 4:02:29. The real reason to doubt the story, as Frank Frost once remarked, is that someone would have jumped on a horse.

The same thought occurred to patriotic Greeks in the nineteenth century. The modern Greek folktale version of Phidippides' fatal run to Athens connected Marathon explicitly to the fight for liberation from the Turks. According to the story, a big battle took place at Marathon when many Turks (not Persians, Turks) came to enslave Marathon and then Athens. So much blood flowed that it became a river and turned the sea red. After the Greeks won, two messengers went to Athens. One mounted a horse and followed the coast road. The other, still wearing his armor, took the shorter but more difficult route over the hills. As he passed through a village, women who wanted to know what happened shouted *"Stamata!"* (Stop!). Pausing only briefly to catch his breath, he beat the messenger on horseback to Athens. He called out "We won!" and collapsed. The story lives on today. While walking from Marathon to Stamata in May 2006, I found myself on Marathonodromou Pheidippidou (Street of the Marathon-runner Phidippides).

The Persians' Voyage to Phaleron

After seeing the shield signal, the Persians picked up their Eretrian prisoners from the tiny island of Aigilia and sailed round Cape Sounion. Most scholars imagine Persian ships racing tired Athenian hoplites to Phaleron, the Athenian harbor in 490. Hammond's scenario has both ships and soldiers arriving eight to nine hours after the battle. As Herodotus says, the Athenians went "as fast as their feet would carry them." They moved from one Herakleion at Marathon to another Herakleion at Kynosarges, a gymnasium sometimes used for military training, on the banks of the

Ilissos River not far from the city. When the Persians reached Phaleron, they anchored offshore. They eventually sailed off to Asia without trying to land.[2]

A realistic assessment of fleet speed rules out a dramatic race for the city. The sea voyage from Marathon to Phaleron is 70 miles or more around Cape Sounion, much longer than by land. Under favorable conditions, a single trireme rowed at seven to eight knots might have made it in nine to ten hours. But because of the U-shaped course, a wind that favored the Persian fleet for the first leg would have hindered it for the second and vice versa. Moreover, a fleet moves at the speed of its slowest ship, and ancient sailing vessels moved at two to three knots. The entire Persian fleet, moving at the speed of its transport ships, would have taken 30 to 45 hours for the journey. If the Persians divided their forces, a "flying squadron" could have traveled more quickly. Although such a tactic is possible, Herodotus mentions no division of the Persian fleet. Almost certainly the fleet anchored off Phaleron the day after the battle.

The same-day march is no more plausible than the same-day sail. Before starting their return to Athens, the Athenians had advanced from the Herakleion to Kynosoura and returned to the Herakleion, perhaps ten miles in all, jogging for nearly a mile and fighting hand-to-hand for a long time under the hot summer sun. The Athenians would have been in no condition to march back to Athens the same day—and there was no need for them to try.

Plutarch says in his *Aristeides* that the Athenians got back on the same day: "When the Athenians had routed the barbarians, driven them aboard their ships, and saw that they were sailing away, not toward the islands, but into the gulf toward Attica under compulsion of wind and wave, then they were afraid that the enemy would find Athens empty of defenders. So they hurried to the city with nine tribes and reached the city on the same day." Does "on the same day" mean on the same day as the battle? The same author says in his *Moralia* either that "Miltiades, having joined battle at Marathon on the next day, returned to the city victorious with his army" or that "Miltiades, having joined battle at Marathon, on the next day returned to the city victorious with his army."[3] The uncertainty is whether to take "on the next day" with the participle or the main verb.

If we take it with the participle, Plutarch contradicts Herodotus in deny-ing a delay before the battle. If we take it with the main verb, Plutarch contradicts himself, unless we take "on the same day" in the *Aristeides* passage as meaning "on the same day they set out for Athens." I think it is preferable to interpret Plutarch charitably so that he contradicts neither Herodotus nor himself. The Athenians hurried all the way back to the city on the day after the battle.

The Athenians spent the rest of the day of the battle celebrating their victory, collecting their corpses, looting the enemy dead, erecting a tro-phy of captured arms and armor, and securing the Persian camp. Then they rested for the night. The next morning, leaving Aristeides and his tribe at Marathon, they hurried back to Athens as fast as they could man-age, arriving in time to take up a position in Kynosarges before the Per-sians arrived.

The Persians put down their anchors but did not try to land. Perhaps the Athenians marched down to the shore and demonstrated their inten-tion to contest a landing, but Herodotus does not say so. Perhaps the Persians sent a few scouts to see what was going on. Perhaps they looked for another signal that did not come. In any event, they set off for home.

The Persians Return to Susa

On their way back to Asia, the Persians again made their way through the Cyclades islands. At Mykonos, Herodotus says, Datis had a dream that prompted him to search his ships. On one of the Phoenician ships, he found a gilded statue of Apollo that had been looted from Delion on the mainland opposite Chalcis. One would like to know more about the cir-cumstances in which this statue was taken. Most likely, men looking for provisions took the statue during the siege of Eretria. But Datis consid-ered the theft regrettable and deposited the statue in Apollo's sanctuary on Delos, instructing the Delians to take it back to Delion. (They didn't, but 20 years later the Thebans came and got it themselves.)

The rest of the trip passed without incident. Though Darius had a bitter grudge against the Eretrians, when he saw them as prisoners he did them no further harm. He settled them 210 stadia (about 26 miles) from

Susa near a well that produced bitumen (a tarlike form of petroleum), water, and oil. In 1836 Major (later Colonel) Henry Rawlinson identified a likely site at Kir-Ab, about 40 miles northeast of Susa, where he found bitumen still being collected.

When the philosopher Apollonios of Tyana visited the place in the first century AD, he learned that the Persians took 780 Eretrian captives— men, women, even some children—to Ionia by ship. The Eretrians had to walk the rest of the way. Only 400 men and 10 women survived the trek. Apollonios supposedly saw the Eretrians' tombs, with the names of the deceased and their fathers written in Greek, accompanied by carvings of ships. One tomb had this touching epitaph:

> We once left the deep-sounding Aegean waves,
> who lie here in the middle of the plain of Ecbatana
> Farewell, famous Eretria, our former home; farewell, Athens,
> neighbor of Euboea; farewell, dear sea.[4]

Apollonios' visit may be fictitious. Elsewhere the epigram is attributed to Plato, and it may be an even later composition. It certainly has the geography wrong, for Ecbatana is 186 miles north of Susa. But let it stand as a reminder that however gloriously the campaign ended for Athens, for Eretria it was a disaster from which the city never recovered.

Dio Chrysostom, a Greek orator from Asia Minor who also lived in the first century AD, says that he heard "a Mede declare that the Persians concede none of the claims made by the Greeks, but maintain that Darius sent Datis and Artaphernes against Naxos and Eretria, and that after capturing these cities they returned to the king. However, while they were lying at anchor off Euboea, a few of their ships, not more than 20, were driven on to the Attic coast and their crews had some kind of an engagement with the inhabitants of that place." Dio comments that the account is false, but it contains considerable truth. Darius must have been pleased that his forces had taken Naxos, the rest of the Cyclades, and Eretria. His commanders no doubt reported that they had ravaged some Athenian territory and killed many Athenians, but that Hippias' promised supporters had failed to materialize. Datis had indubitably expanded the Persian Empire, and a conqueror such as Darius was accustomed to taking some casualties in order to expand.[5]

Datis then disappears from history. One Persian tradition said that he died fighting at Marathon; when the Persians asked for his body, the Greeks refused to give it back. This version contradicts Herodotus' evidence that Datis survived at least as far as Delos, and I suspect that if the Greeks had killed him they would have boasted about it. More likely, Datis survived the campaign. There is no hint that the king punished him. As for Artaphrenes, the Great King's nephew, he commanded the Lydians and Mysians on his cousin Xerxes' invasion of Greece ten years later.

The Athenians Bury the Dead

When the Athenians marched for Athens, they left Aristeides and the men of his tribe, Antiochis, together with the Plataeans, to guard the captives and the booty. No source specifies the number of captives. Given their high casualties, probably few invaders survived unless they got away by ship. As for the booty, Plutarch speaks of silver and gold lying in heaps, all kinds of clothing, unspeakable wealth in the tents, and captured utensils. Since Herodotus does not mention booty at Marathon, skeptical scholars have supposed that Plutarch had no evidence and simply drew on what Herodotus says about the camp and the booty captured after the battle of Plataea in 479. But the list of dedications made after the battle leaves no doubt that the profits were large indeed.[6]

Plutarch tells an anecdote about Kallias, whose descendants were called *lakkoploutoi* ("pit rich"). A barbarian begged Kallias for mercy and showed him a mass of gold in a pit. Kallias took the gold, but killed the man so no one would learn what he had done. This story has been challenged too: A more mundane explanation of the family nickname would be that they made their money in mining. Yet since Herodotus attests that the locals found hoards of gold and silver hidden in the area after Plataea, it is plausible that the Persians buried gold and silver at Marathon.[7]

The seven captured ships would have had their share of wealth, similar to the gold and silver cups and other treasures that washed ashore after a storm wrecked Persian ships in 480. The 6,400 Persian corpses may not have had much armor to interest the Greeks, but the Persians went into battle wearing gold bracelets and necklaces. Gold attachments decorated their embroidered clothing, and they carried gilded daggers.[8]

Attention must soon have turned from shiny gold to decomposing corpses. Greek funerals normally took place on the second day after death. As most of the Athenians marched back to Athens, Aristeides and his men must have prepared for the cremation of the dead. They began by collecting all the Athenian corpses. They apparently planned from the start to erect a funeral mound over the remains, for they began by marking out the location of the Soros with a layer of sand and greenish earth. Directly on top of the sand they built a brick-lined cremation tray, about 3 feet wide and at least 16 feet long, on which the pyre was laid. Homer gives a vivid description of the process when he tells of Patroklos' funeral:[9]

> Now powerful Agamemnon
> gave order for men and mules to assemble from all the shelters
> and bring in timber, and a great man led them in motion,
> Meriones, the henchman of courtly Idomeneus. These then
> went out and in their hands carried axes to cut wood
> and ropes firmly woven, and their mules went on ahead of them.
> They went many ways, uphill, downhill, sidehill and slantwise;
> but when they came to the spurs of Ida with all her well springs,
> they set to hewing with the thin edge of bronze and leaning
> their weight to the strokes on towering-leafed oak trees that toppled
> with huge crashing; then the Achaians splitting the timbers
> fastened them to the mules and these with their feet tore up
> the ground as they pulled through the dense undergrowth to the flat
>   land.
> All the woodcutters carried logs themselves; such was the order
> of Meriones, the henchman of courtly Idomeneus. These then
> threw down their burdens in order along the beach, where Achilleus
> had chosen place for a huge grave mound, for himself and Patroklos.

Then the body is brought, a prayer said, and most people depart. The poet resumes:

> The close mourners stayed by the place and piled up the timber,
> and built a pyre a hundred feet long this way and that way,
> and on the peak of the pyre they laid the body, sorrowful
> at heart; and in front of it skinned and set in order numbers

of fat sheep and shambling horn-curved cattle; and from all
great-hearted Achilleus took the fat and wrapped the corpse in it
from head to foot, and piled up the skinned bodies above it.

Achilleus kills and adds to the pyre four horses, nine dogs, and a dozen young Trojans. When the pyre would not light, he prays to the winds, and

> They came with a sudden blast upon the sea, and the waves rose
> under the whistling wind. They came to the generous Troad
> and hit the pyre, and a huge inhuman blaze rose, roaring.
> Nightlong they piled the flames on the funeral pyre together
> and blew with a screaming blast, and nightlong swift-footed Achilleus
> from a golden mixing-bowl, with a two-handled goblet in his hand,
> drew the wine and poured it on the ground and drenched the ground
>   with it,
> and called upon the soul of unhappy Patroklos. And as
> a father mourns as he burns the bones of a son, who was married
> only now, and died to grieve his unhappy parents,
> so Achilleus was mourning as he burned his companion's
> bones, and dragged himself by the fire in close lamentation.

Achilleus finally sleeps, and in the morning,

> First with gleaming wine they put out the pyre that was burning,
> As much as was still aflame, and the ashes dropped deep from it.

Then they collect Patroklos' bones and save them for later, after Achilleus' death, when they will raise a burial mound over them both.

With a few minor adjustments—the Athenians did not sacrifice horses, dogs, and humans at Marathon—this description gives a good sense of what happened in 490. Beside the cremation tray, the excavator Staes found early black-figure lekythoi—that is, pots frequently used at funerals, but ones made about a century before the battle. Evidently the relatives of the dead used family heirlooms for a funeral meal and left the tableware at the tomb. Immediately thereafter, for hardly any later pottery was found, the Athenians raised the large mound that has been such a prominent feature ever since, rising at least 39 feet above the plain.

That was not all. The Athenians made a second brick-lined tray on the outer face of the mound, where the residents of Marathon still made offerings to the heroized dead 600 years later in the time of Pausanias.[10] Staes found this tray three feet below the surface of the mound, where it had been covered by eroded soil.

And finally, the Athenians had the names of their 192 casualties, organized by tribe as they had fought, inscribed on tombstones placed on top of the mound, where Pausanias saw them.[11] Greek archaeologist Theodoros Spyropoulos announced in 2000 that he had found one of these inscriptions at Herodes Atticus' villa in the Peloponnese. Originally from Marathon, Herodes might have moved these famous stones, or had them copied. The potentially spectacular find remains unpublished, but the inscription is said to have an epigram followed by a casualty list including 25 names cut in letters that look late Archaic.

The Marathon burial revived an aristocratic form—cremation, mound, offering trench, marker—that had gone out of fashion in the previous century. To heroize the Marathon fighters, as they were called, the young Athenian democracy collectivized the form of burial once used for individual aristocratic warriors.

The Plataeans and the slaves, the non-Athenians who fought in the battle, were buried separately, with a separate mound raised over their remains.

Persian corpses were treated altogether differently. Stripped and left to rot in the blazing sun until the Spartans arrived and inspected them the day after the battle, they were tossed into a trench. Kallimachos' vow to sacrifice a goat for every Persian casualty meant that the bodies were counted, at least approximately. The ratio of dead Persians (6,400) to dead Athenians (192) works out to 100 Persians for every 3 Athenians.

CHAPTER 9

What If?

T
he "What if?" game goes back to Herodotus. In a famous passage,
the Father of History considers what would have happened in 480
if the Athenians had abandoned their country or surrendered to
Xerxes. Either the Persian fleet would have taken the Greek cities one by
one, he says, leaving the Spartans to fight and die, or the Spartans would
have bowed to the inevitable and come to terms with Xerxes. "In either
case," Herodotus opines, "Greece would have come under Persian rule."[1]

As a way to think about Marathon's importance, I'll suggest my own
"What ifs." What if the battle of Marathon had turned out differently?
What if the Athenians had deployed more slowly and the Persians more
quickly? The story might have ended like this:

Miltiades shaded his eyes as he looked to the east. The morning sun
was already well up, since deploying the troops had taken longer than he
had hoped. The slaves, unused to serving as hoplites, had slowed everything down. Still, the generals had prodded everyone to hurry. They had
now reached the middle of the plain.

Miltiades could see Persian horses. He had hoped that they would
reach the plain no more quickly than they had on previous days, but as
soon as scouts reported movement out of the Greek camp, Datis had recognized what Miltiades was trying to do. He ordered his troops to deploy
as quickly as possible. "The Greeks must not be allowed to escape," he

told his officers. "Let's catch them in the middle of the plain and make them pay for all that they have done to us." Full of confidence and excited at the prospect of finally getting to fight, Datis' men carried out their orders. Artaphrenes began to lead the cavalry into the plain.

The Greeks began their charge at Miltiades' order, but it was too late. As they jogged, they saw hundreds of mounted archers riding into the space between the two infantry lines. The Greeks hesitated. When the Persian archers came within bowshot and began shooting, the Greek advance came to a halt as men took cover behind their shields.

Meanwhile Datis, on horseback, led the Persian infantry in their own charge. The commanders of the other contingents, as soon as they saw Datis advance, raised their standards—the signal to charge—and rushed forward, shouting their battle cry. They had always intimidated Greeks in the past and they expected to do so now.

As their infantry approached, the Persian cavalry rode off to the flank, where they could attack the Plataeans. Meanwhile the front line of Persian infantry set up a barricade of wicker shields. Though shaken by the first cavalry charge, the Athenians resumed their advance through the hail of arrows. Many of them fell, including the polemarchos Kallimachos, who was riddled with arrows. Many more were wounded; those who lacked good shields were especially vulnerable. They began to hang back. Some turned and ran the other way (Figure 31).

When the depleted Greek ranks reached the Persian shield wall, hand-to-hand fighting began. The Persians dropped their bows and fought with spears and swords. Though they lacked the good helmets and solid shields used by the Greeks, they had similar chest protection. The Persians in the center were better trained in hand-to-hand fighting than the Greeks, and even managed to snatch and break some of the Greek spears. One stout farmer who lost his spear grabbed a broken plough handle someone had left in the field and began to swing it as a club. He was no Herakles, however, and was soon cut down. The Plataeans on the left broke and ran first, which freed some of the Persian cavalry to attack the Athenians next to the Plataeans. Like a wave, the Greek retreat grew from left to right. On the Athenian right, the Greek allies of the Persians fought better and better as they sensed what was happening. One bearded Parian, a tall

31. Interior of an Athenian red-figure cup, showing a warrior fleeing from arrows
(Staatliche Museen, Berlin, 2304; from Eduard Gerhard, *Trinkschalen und Gefässe
des Königlichen Museums zu Berlin und Anderer Sammlungen* [Berlin: Reimer, 1848]
pl. VI–VII, no. 5)

man with an unusually robust physique, so terrified an Athenian named
Epizelos that he went blind. He was an easy mark for the next Parian. The
playwright Aeschylus fell, mortally wounded, but his brother Kynegeiros
managed to escape.

Finally, all the Greeks fled. The Persians rushed after them, killing
many and capturing not a few, including the general Miltiades. He was
brought to Datis, who killed him on the spot, afraid that if Miltiades
reached Darius, the Great King would have pity on him, remembering
his previous service. The prisoners were put on board the ships. Pick-
ing up the Eretrian prisoners along the way, the fleet sailed around to
Phaleron. They disembarked without opposition. As they set up camp

outside the city of Athens, a delegation arrived offering earth and water to the king. Datis accepted the offer, installed Hippias as dictator, and erected a victory monument carved from a large block of Parian marble. He then sailed back to Asia, leaving a garrison behind to keep the peace. Several hundred Athenians from distinguished families were resettled with the Eretrian prisoners near Susa. Miltiades' son Kimon received a grant of land near the estate previously given to his brother.

When Hippias died of old age less than a year later, Darius chose Xanthippos, a member of the Alkmeonid family, to succeed him. Xanthippos joined the campaign of Artaphrenes two years after Marathon. Artaphrenes' fleet sailed around the Peloponnese, accepting earth and water wherever it went. Sparta was the last holdout, but after the liberation of Messenia, Spartan soldiers accepted an offer to become mercenaries for a Persian campaign in Egypt. The survivors came home rich men and retired to a life of ease. Athens, too, prospered under Persian rule. Xanthippos' brilliant son, Pericles, succeeded him as tyrant.

Had the Athenians submitted without fighting, or run away, or defended their walls against a siege, the eventual outcome would not have been much different. The only other realistic scenario to ponder is this: What if the Athenians had waited for the Spartan 2,000 to arrive? Datis would then have expected them to fight and would not have allowed them to cross the plain virtually untouched. He might have withdrawn, setting up the next, larger campaign. He might have defeated the Greeks in the open plain. If he lost—if the Athenians won with Spartan help—the myth of Marathon would have taken on a quite different tone. In their collective memory, the Athenians could not have brushed the Spartans aside as easily as they did the Plataeans. Without the boost to their egos that their "single-handed" victory gave, would the Athenians have dared to assert their claim to the leadership of the Greeks?

When he made Marathon the first of his 15 *Decisive Battles,* Creasy did not forget that the Persians invaded again ten years later with more ships and more men. Marathon did not end Persian hopes of conquering Greece. Plataea did that, and without Salamis there would have been no Plataea. What Creasy realized is that Marathon "broke forever the spell of Persian invincibility, which had previously paralyzed men's minds."[2] Marathon made Salamis conceivable and Plataea possible.

Appendix A
Important Ancient Sources on Marathon

Aeschylus (c. 525/4–456/5), the Athenian tragic poet, refers to Marathon three times in his *Persians,* produced 18 years after the battle (231–245, 286–289, and 472–476).

Aristophanes (c. 447–386), the Athenian comic poet, calls the *Marathonomachai,* the Marathon fighters, "hard as holm-oak, men of maple" (*Acharnians* 180–181). In *Wasps* 1078–1088, he describes the battle of Marathon, though not by name. He lifts some details from the stories of Xerxes' invasion ten years later, but not inappropriately. Datis' men probably did burn Athenian land and shoot many arrows. The Athenians probably did spear the Persians like tuna as they scrambled to their ships. *Knights* 1333, *Wasps* 711, and a quotation from the *Holkades* (Athenaios 3.111) provide the earliest references to "the trophy at Marathon."

The *Athenian Constitution,* written by the philosopher Aristotle (384–322) or one of his students, describes the constitutional position of the generals at the time of the battle. In his *Rhetoric,* Aristotle mentions Miltiades' motion calling for the Athenians to march to Marathon.

In one of his speeches, Demosthenes (384–322) quotes Miltiades' motion calling for the Athenians to go out and meet the Persians.

Unfortunately the Marathon section of the *Universal History* written by Diodoros of Sicily (first century BC) is almost entirely lost. A fragment describing an exchange of messages between Datis and Miltiades does survive.

Herodotus of Halicarnassus (c. 484–c. 425) wrote the earliest extant narrative of the battle in his *Histories.* His great commentator, Reginald Walter Macan, called him "the prince of story-tellers," and his account of Marathon lives up to that accolade. Herodotus was indefatigably curious. No doubt he talked to many veterans. Though it is unlikely that he talked to any of the generals, he could have spoken with their descendants. A century ago scholars often took a hypercritical attitude toward Herodotus and his sources, but his reputation has improved more recently. Most historians today take him at his word that he wrote down what he heard people say (2.123.1, 4.195.2, and 7.152.3), though those people were more likely ordinary people he met on his travels than truly learned individuals. And most historians today believe that Herodotus went where he says he went. He certainly visited Athens, where he gave public readings of his work.

Justin (second, third, or fourth century AD) wrote a condensed version of Pompeius Trogus' *Philippic Histories,* originally composed during the reign of the emperor Augustus. His brief battle narrative is perhaps most memorable for the line that the Greeks fought as men, the barbarians as sheep. It offers little to the historian.

Ktesias (late fifth century BC), a Greek doctor who worked at the court of Artaxerxes, wrote a history of Persia that survives only in fragments. A description of Marathon is not among them, other than a paragraph saying that Datis died in the battle.

Lysias (?459/8–380) includes in his *Funeral Oration* a highly rhetorical version of the battle, showing such a "reckless disregard of tradition and of probabilities" (Macan) that it is of no use whatsoever for reconstructing what happened.

Cornelius Nepos (c. 100–24), born in northern Italy, includes the battle in his brief biography of Miltiades. The story here differs considerably from that in Herodotus, but Nepos has had his champions, from George Grote in the nineteenth century to Johan Henrik Schreiner in the twenty-first. Some bits of other late writers match parts of Nepos' account. His defenders argue that an alternative tradition derives from Ephoros of Cyme, a historian of the fourth century BC. Hammond championed instead an Atthidographer (a local historian of Attica) who wrote after the death of Demetrios of Phaleron in 307, perhaps Demon, whose work survives only in quotations.

Among the works of the philosopher Plato (c. 429–347) is a dialogue known as the *Menexenos* that contains a funeral oration in which Marathon figures prominently. Scholars have questioned the authorship and the seriousness of the dialogue; in it Socrates credits the speech to Pericles' partner Aspasia. Two passages in the *Laws* overlap somewhat with the *Menexenos,* but contain some new material as well.

Pausanias, an early travel writer, describes what he saw in Greece in the second century AD. He was little interested in contemporary buildings and events, but fascinated by the heritage of Classical Greece. He gives an important description of the plain of Marathon as it looked in his day. He also describes the famous painting of the battle in the Stoa Poikile (Painted Stoa) in Athens, an original work from the 460s that would be our earliest source for the battle had it survived.

Plutarch (c. AD 46–120), the prolific writer from Chaironeia, unfortunately did not include Miltiades in his series of parallel *Lives* of famous Greeks and Romans. His lives of Theseus, Aristeides, and Kimon have some relevant material, as do his treatises *On the Glory of the Athenians* and *On the Malice of Herodotus.*

Two or three epigrams relating to Marathon are attributed to Simonides of Keos (c. 556–466), who had more to say about Xerxes' invasion.

A ninth- or tenth-century Byzantine encyclopedia known as the *Suda* contains several relevant entries, including one under the heading *choris hippeis* (the cavalry are apart), which some scholars have made the foundation for an ingenious reconstruction. A group of scholars is now translating the *Suda* and making it available online at http://www.stoa.org/sol/.

Thucydides (born 460–455, died after 404), the great Athenian historian of the Peloponnesian War, refers to Marathon a half dozen times.

Xenophon (c. 430–c. 355) has a lot to say about Persia, especially in his *Anabasis, Education of Cyrus,* and *Hellenica.* He provides the earliest evidence for Kallimachos' vow to Artemis.

Appendix B
The Date of the Battle

The Year

As if to prove that nothing about Marathon is beyond challenge, J. A. R. Munro put the battle in 491. He maintained that Herodotus, Thucydides, and Aristotle's *Athenian Constitution,* "simply and naturally interpreted," all put the battle a year earlier than 490. I cannot explain how he reached this conclusion. Aristotle puts the battle in the archonship of Phainippos (490/89). Thucydides says that the Persians invaded Greece again in the tenth year after Marathon. He refers to Xerxes' campaign of 480, which therefore began in 481/80, the tenth year after 490/89, counting inclusively in the Greek way. The series of dates offered by Herodotus is internally consistent and fits with Aristotle and Thucydides. After Marathon, Asia was in commotion for three years preparing warships, horses, and so on: 490/89, 489/8, and 488/7. In the fourth year, 487/6, Egypt revolted. In the next year, 486/5, Darius died. In the second year, 485/4 counting inclusively, Xerxes recovered Egypt, and he then prepared for four full years (485/4, 484/3, 483/2, 482/1) for the invasion of Greece, which began in the fifth year after the recovery of Egypt, 481/80 counting inclusively. All the evidence hangs together: The battle of Marathon took place in 490.[1]

The Month and the Day

The following evidence pertains to the month and the day:

- According to Herodotus, the Spartans told Philippides that they wanted to help but could not do so immediately without violating

their law, "for it was the ninth day of the month, and it was not permissible to set out [on the ninth] unless the moon was full."
- Herodotus also says that "after the full moon, 2,000 Spartans marched to Athens in such great haste that they arrived in Attica on the third day out of Sparta. They were too late to engage in battle, but nevertheless wished to see the Medes, which they did when they reached Marathon."
- Plato says that the Spartans arrived one day too late for the battle.
- According to Plutarch, the battle occurred on Boedromion 6, and the Athenians later commemorated it annually on that day.[2]

In 1855 August Boeckh combined this evidence with modern astronomical calculations to put the battle on September 12. Since Herodotus' evidence about the moon cannot be reconciled with Plutarch's date of Boedromion 6, he reasoned, Plutarch must have confused the date of the victory celebration with the date of the battle. The battle occurred shortly after the full moon in the preceding month, Metageitnion, the second month in the Athenian lunar year. The Athenian lunar year began with the first new moon after the summer solstice, which in 490 fell on June 29. Metageitnion would have begun on August 25, and the next full moon fell on September 9. If the Spartans marched on September 10, they reached Attica on September 12 and Marathon on September 13, the day after the battle. Boeckh's chronology has dominated the field, though some scholars put the battle one day earlier by supposing that the Spartans went to Marathon the same day they reached Attica, making the impressive speed of their march even more remarkable.

In 1962 Burn revived an alternative date for the battle favored by Georg Busolt, a distinguished German historian of the late nineteenth century. In 490 a new moon occurred on June 27, very close to the summer solstice of June 29. If the new moon was not observed until after the solstice, the first full moon of the new year would have fallen in July and the second in August rather than September, putting the battle a month earlier than on Boeckh's chronology. Burn thought an earlier date advantageous because it made the Persian advance less leisurely, and when the Persians ravaged the Karystians' land, they might have destroyed grain standing in the field before the harvest in June.

In 2004 Donald W. Olson, Russell L. Doescher, and Marilynn S. Olson put a new twist on Burn's argument. We must look to the Spartan calendar, they argued, rather than the Athenian. Though Herodotus does not mention the Spartan month, they assume it was Karneios, in which the Spartans celebrated the Karneia, a nine-day festival of Apollo that culminated with the full moon. Earlier scholars made Karneios the eleventh month in the

Spartan calendar, which they believed started after the autumnal equinox. The eleventh full moon after the equinox of September 29, 491, occurred on August 10. So Olson, Doescher, and Olson put the battle in August. This argument is not conclusive because the Spartan calendar is so uncertain. Catherine Trümpy's 1997 study of the ancient Greek months puts the start of the Spartan year in the summer and makes Karneios the third month of the year. So Olson, Doescher, and Olson have not settled the issue.

Hammond began the year in June, but kept the battle in September by reversing the usual interpretation of the battle and the celebration. He suggested that Kallimachos made his vow on behalf of Athens at the festival of Artemis Agrotera on Boedromion 6. The battle took place eleven days later, after the full moon of Boedromion, the third month of the year, rather than Metageitnion. This scenario seems unlikely. Kallimachos probably made his vow on the day of the battle when he sacrificed before the Athenians deployed.

Francis M. Dunn is the only scholar to defend Boedromion 6, the only explicit date given by an ancient source. He shows that Greek calendars were not astronomically precise. A month began not with the astronomical conjunction—the moment when the moon crosses a line between the earth and the sun—but when the crescent first became visible. On an observational calendar at Athens, the full moon could fall anywhere from the ninth to the sixteenth of the month, or even (less commonly) on the eighth. Therefore—I'm oversimplifying somewhat—what Herodotus says about the Spartan calendar is credible. The full moon did not necessarily occur on the fifteenth, as commonly assumed. It could have occurred on the eighth or on any day in the week that followed. Boedromion 6 would fall at least two days before a full moon, so Dunn suggested that the Athenians added days to the calendar so that the campaign would not interfere with the celebration of the Eleusinian Mysteries that began on Boedromion 13. In other words, the archon may have called multiple days Boedromion 6. On this reasoning, the battle took place in September or even October. But all those Boedromion 6s do sound a bit like Harpo Marx playing one ace of spades after another in *Animal Crackers*.

Whether or not Dunn is correct to defend Boedromion 6, he makes an important point relative to the stalemate at Marathon. It might have lasted anywhere from three to nine days, so it is impossible to name a specific day in our calendar. The battle occurred about the time of the full moon in either August and September. I lean toward August.

Notes

Abbreviations

Asheri 2007   Asheri, David, Alan Lloyd, and Aldo Corcella. 2007. *A Commentary on Herodotus Books I-IV*. Oxford: Oxford University Press.

Briant 2002   Briant, Pierre. 2002. *From Cyrus to Alexander: A History of the Persian Empire*. Winona Lake, Ind.: Eisenbraun.

Burn 1984   Burn, Andrew Robert. 1984. *Persia and the Greeks: The Defence of the West, c. 546–478 BC*. 2nd ed. Stanford: Stanford University Press.

CAH 4(2)   *Cambridge Ancient History*, vol. 4, 2nd ed., ed. John Boardman, Nicholas G. L. Hammond, David M. Lewis, and Martin Ostwald. Cambridge: Cambridge University Press, 1988.

Cawkwell 2005   Cawkwell, George. 2005. *The Greek Wars: The Failure of Persia*. New York: Oxford University Press.

Clarke 1818   Clarke, Edward D. 1818. *Travels in Various Countries of Europe, Asia, and Africa*, 4th ed. London: Cadell and Davies.

Delbrück 1887   Delbrück, Hans. 1887. *Die Perserkriege und die Burgunderkriege*. Berlin: Walther and Apolant.

Delbrück 1975   Delbrück, Hans. 1975. *History of the Art of War within the Framework of Political History*, vol. 1. Trans. of the third (1920) German edition by Walter J. Renfroe, Jr. Westport, Conn: Greenwood.

Evans 2006   Evans, James Allan Stewart. 2006. *The Beginnings of History: Herodotus and the Persian Wars*. Campbellville, Ont: Edgar Kent.

FGrHist   *Die Fragmente der Griechischen Historiker*, ed. Felix Jacoby. Leiden: Brill, 1923–1958.

Hammond 1973   Hammond, Nicholas Geoffrey Lemprière. 1973. *Studies in Greek History.* Oxford: Clarendon.
IG   *Inscriptiones Graecae.*
Kuhrt 2007   Kuhrt, Amélie. 2007. *The Persian Empire: A Corpus of Sources from the Achaemenid Period.* 2 vols. London: Routledge.
Lazenby 1993   Lazenby, John F. 1993. *The Defence of Greece, 490–479 B.C.* Warminster: Aris and Phillips.
Leake 1835   Leake, William Martin. 1835. *Travels in Northern Greece.* London: Rodwell.
Leake 1841   Leake, William Martin. 1841. *The Topography of Athens.* 2 vols. London: Rodwell.
Macan 1895   Macan, Reginald Walter. 1895. *Herodotus: The Fourth, Fifth, and Sixth Books.* London: Macmillan.
ML   Meiggs, Russell, and David M. Lewis. 1988. *A Selection of Greek Historical Inscriptions to the End of the Fifth Century B.C.* Oxford: Clarendon.
Munro 1899   Munro, John Arthur Ruskin. 1899. "Some Observations on the Persian Wars, I. The Campaign of Marathon," *Journal of Hellenic Studies* 19: 185–197.
Petrakos 1996   Petrakos, Vasileios Ch. 1996. *Marathon.* Athens: [The Archaeological Society at Athens].
Pritchett 1971–1991 Pritchett, W. Kendrick. 1971–1991. *The Greek State at War.* 5 vols. Berkeley: University of California Press.
Schachermeyr 1951   Schachermeyr, Fritz. 1951. "Marathon und die Persische Politik." *Historische Zeitschrift* 172: 1–35.
Scott 2005   Scott, Lionel. 2005. *Historical Commentary on Herodotus Book 6.* Leiden: Brill.
Sekunda 2002   Sekunda, Nicholas. 2002. *Marathon 490 BC: The First Persian Invasion of Greece.* Oxford: Osprey.

Introduction

1. "Rush at them," attributed to Miltiades by a scholiast (anonymous commentator) on Aelius Aristeides (ed. Dindorf III 566).

2. Homer, *Iliad* 3.2–6, trans. Lattimore.

3. *IG* 2(2).1006 lines 26–27.

4. Thirlwall, *A History of Greece* (New York: Harper, 1845) 1.247; They had stood alone, Thucydides 1.73.2; Plato, *Menexenos* 240c; Plato, *Laws* 4.707c; Aeschylus' epitaph, *Life of Aeschylus* 11; Pausanias 1.14.5.

5. Johnson, *Journey to the Western Isles of Scotland,* "Inch Kenneth," available from the 1775 edition at http://ebooks.adelaide.edu.au/j/johnson/samuel/western/chapter30 .html; Byron, *Don Juan,* 3rd Canto 86, "The Isles of Greece" 13–18. Byron was not the only man to mistake the Soros for the burial of the Persians; for another example, see chapter 6.

6. Barrett, letter to R. H. Horne, 5 October 1843, quoted in *The Complete Poetical Works of Elizabeth Barrett Browning* (Boston: Houghton Mifflin, 1900) 485, where it is followed by the complete text of the poem.

7. Finlay, "On the Battle of Marathon," *Transactions of the Royal Society of Literature of the United Kingdom* 3 (1839): 392; Mill, review of George Grote, *History of Greece*, in his *Essays on Philosophy and the Classics,* ed. John M. Robson (Collected Works of John Stuart Mill, 11) (Toronto: University of Toronto Press, 1963) 273, originally in *Edinburgh Review* 84 (1846) 343–377; Bulwer-Lytton, *Athens: Its Rise and Fall* (New York: Harper, 1856 [orig. 1837]) 274–275; Creasy, *The 15 Decisive Battles of the World: From Marathon to Waterloo* (New York: Harper & Brothers, 1851) 13.

8. Browning, *The Complete Works of Robert Browning,* ed. Charlotte Porter and Helen A. Clarke (New York: Crowell, 1898) 123 lines 106–112.

9. Fuller, *A Military History of the Western World* (New York: Funk and Wagnalls, 1954) 25; Toynbee, *The Greeks and Their Heritage* (Oxford: Oxford University Press, 1981) 65.

10. Cartledge, *Thermopylae: The Battle That Changed the World* (New York: Vintage, 2006); Strauss, *The Battle of Salamis: The Naval Encounter That Saved Greece—and Western Civilization* (New York: Simon and Schuster, 2004).

11. Cicero, *Laws* 1.5; Theopompos, *FGrHist* 115 F 153 = Theon, *Progymnasmata* 2.

12. Whatley 1964: 124.

13. Whatley 1964: 128.

14. Gomme, "Herodotos and Marathon," *Phoenix* 6 (1952): 77. See Macan 1895: 151–169 for his six cruces.

15. Kagan, *The Outbreak of the Peloponnesian War* (Ithaca: Cornell University Press, 1969) x; Lazenby 1993: 15.

Chapter 1. Athens' Alliance with Darius

1. Herodotus 5.63.1.

2. Herodotus 5.66.2; Aristotle, *Athenian Constitution* 22.1.

3. Herodotus 7.61.1. This description is consistent with the pitch Aristagoras the Milesian makes when trying to get help from the Spartans. He says that the Persians carry bows and short spears, and wear trousers and turbans. When trying to get help from the Athenians, Aristagoras says the Persians do not carry round shields or long spears (Herodotus 5.49). The one place where Herodotus seems inconsistent is in his description of the battle of Plataea in 479, where he says the Persians did not have armor (9.62–63). Sekunda 2002: 22 has photographs of the two later *gerra* found at Dura-Europos.

4. Herodotus 1.192.3, 7.196.

5. DNb 2h, translated in Kuhrt 2007: 2.505; Strabo 15.3.18, expanding on Herodotus' statement that "The Persians teach their sons, between the ages of five and twenty, only three things: to ride, use a bow, and speak the truth" (1.136.2); Xenophon, *Education of Cyrus* 1.2.8–9, 13 (length of service), 1.2.15 (access limited to wealthy), 8.6.10 (provincial education modeled on the homeland).

6. In their study of the military capabilities of ancient armies, Richard A. Gabriel and Karen S. Metz conclude that the combination of armor and shield meant that "unless a lucky shot struck a particularly inattentive or poorly trained soldier, the infantry formations of ancient armies had little to fear from archery fire" (*From Sumer to Rome: The Military Capabilities of Ancient Armies* [Westport, Conn: Greenwood, 1991] 72). This conclusion seems valid even if some of their facts about ancient armies are inaccurate for Greeks (for example, Greeks did not carry two-by-four-foot shields).

7. Kaptan, *The Daskyleion Bullae: Seal Images from the Western Achaemenid Empire* (Leiden: Nederlands Instituut voor het Nabije Oosten, 2002) 2.107. See 1.80 n. 315 for the explanation of bashlyk I include in brackets, and 1.80–81 for the pilos-like helmet with a flowing crest.

8. Mellink, "Excavations at Karatas-Semayük and Elmalı, Lycia, 1971," *American Journal of Archaeology* 76 (1972): 268.

9. For Herodotus' catalogue, see 7.60–86.

10. "Compare small things with great" comes from Herodotus 2.10, but it also appears in numerous other classical authors, including Thucydides, Cicero, Vergil, Ovid, and Statius.

11. Herodotus 5.2.2.

12. Herodotus 5.27.

13. Herodotus 3.11.3; for the Carians and Ionian mercenaries, see Herodotus 2.163.1, 169.1.

14. DB II.32, trans. Kuhrt 2007: 145–146.

15. Herodotus 5.73.1.

16. Aeschylus, *Persians* 41.

Chapter 2. Athens' Victories over the Boeotians and Chalcidians

1. Herodotus 5.74.1, where the root of the word Herodotus uses is *hubris*.

2. Plutarch, *Pericles* 23.1.

3. Herodotus 6.108.5.

4. Xenophon, *Hellenika* 2.2.20.

5. Xenophon, *Hellenika* 5.1.31.

6. For ship districts (*naukrariai*), see Photios, *Lexicon, s.v.* "naukraria" (= Kleidemos, *FGrHist* 323 F 8); Pollux, *Onomastikon* 8.108; Bekker, *Anecdota Graeca* I 283.20f (all translated in Charles W. Fornara, *Archaic Times to the End of the Peloponnesian War* [Baltimore: Johns Hopkins University Press, 1977] no. 22).

7. Tyrtaios F 12.10–22 and F 11.27–34 West, trans. Lattimore.

8. Delbrück 1887: 56 n. 1 cites Rüstow and Köchly, *Geschichte des Griechischen Kriegswesens von der Ältesten Zeit bis auf Pyrrhos* (Aarau: Verlags-Comptoir, 1852) 44. In 1920 Delbrück repeated the estimate, conceding that Rüstow and Köchly lacked evidence, but asserting that the fact that hoplites were heavily armed cannot be denied (1920: 71 = 1975: 86). That he did not question the Rüstow-Köchly figure is not surprising when one considers the weight soldiers carried in his day: Austrians and French 61.2 pounds, English 62.4, Germans 63.9, Italians 67.2, Russians 69.0, Swiss 69.2 (1887: 56 n.1).

9. Bergk, review of W. Rüstow and H. Köchly, *Geschichte des Griechischen Kriegswesens,* in *Zeitschrift für die Alterthumswissenschaft* 5 (1853): 434; Droysen, *Heerwesen und Kriegführung der Griechen* (Freiburg: Mohr, 1889) 3 n. 2.

10. See the description of the painting at [Demosthenes] 59.94.

11. Crapper, personal email dated September 11, 2007.

12. In his *Argivische Schilde* (Berlin: de Gruyter, 1989), Peter Bol catalogues 279 bronze outer fittings found at Olympia. He estimates the diameters for 78 of these (his catalogue does not give a diameter for his A278, perhaps because it is so large—47.2 inches—that it was probably intended for ceremonial or display use). The 78 diameters range from 30.3 to 43.3 inches. The mean is 35.4 inches, and the middle 50 percent fall between 34.6 and 36.2 inches.

13. Pliny, *Natural History* 16.209. Aristophanes (fr. 65) and Euripides (*Cyclops* 7, *Heraclidae* 376, *Suppliants* 695, *Trojan Women* 1193) mention shields made of willow.

14. For Manning Imperial's online catalogue, go to http://www.manningimperial .com/index.php. For the pine shield, item no. 117, see http://www.manningimperial.com/ item.php?item_id=117&g_id=2&c_id=10. Cherilyn Fuhlbohm and Craig Sitch supplied additional information in a personal email dated April 17, 2008. For the poplar, item no. 486, see http://www.manningimperial.com/item.php?item_id=486&g_id=2&c_id=10. All these shields have a bowl about 3.9 inches deep. For details from the Hoplite Association, go to http://www.4hoplites.com/Aspis.htm, accessed on April 11, 2008. The Hoplite Association prefers a deeper bowl of 6.3 inches.

15. Homer, *Odyssey* 18.376–380; Plutarch, *Moralia* 220A; Aristophanes, *Wasps* 1081; Homer, *Iliad* 14.370–383.

16. For Marshall's recommendation, see *The Soldier's Load and the Mobility of a Nation* (Washington: Combat Forces Press, 1950).

17. Thucydides 5.71; Herodotus 7.9; Thucydides 5.70.

18. Homer, *Iliad* 16.212–217, 259–267.

19. Lissarrague, *L'Autre Guerrier: Archers, Peltastes, Cavaliers dans l'Imagerie Attique* (Paris: La Découverte, 1990) 14. The following vases show a group of hoplites standing in a line: Boston (Mass.), Museum of Fine Arts 21.21; London, British Museum 1836.2–24.218; Munich, Antikensammlungen 244 and 1436; Paris, Musee du Louvre E876 and E855; Würzburg, Martin von Wagner Museum 251 and 255. The following vases show a group of hoplites advancing: Bologna, Museo Civico Archeologico PU191; Kurashiki, Ninagawa XXXX302758; Naples, Museo Archeologico Nazionale 132615. The following vases show a group of hoplites running: Brussels, Musées Royaux A715; Göttingen, Georg-August-Universität: XXXX350353; London, British Museum 1836.2–24.218; Munich, Antikensammlungen 1510; New York, Metropolitan Museum of Art 91.1.463; Taranto, Museo Archeologico Nazionale 20129. The first two look like races in armor, though the contestants are not known ever to have carried spears.

20. Herodotus 7.225.1, 9.62.2; Thucydides 4.96.2. For the othismos of words, see Herodotus 8.78, 9.26.

21. Macan 1908: 730, commenting on 9.62.

22. Delbrück 1975: 53 and 54, a translation of the 1920 third edition; the first edition was published in 1900.

23. Grundy, *Thucydides and the History of His Age* (London: Murray, 1911) 268 (the passage is unchanged in the 1948 second edition) and 268–269.

24. Woodhouse, *King Agis of Sparta and His Campaign in Arkadia in 418 B.C.: A Chapter in the History of the Art of War among the Greeks* (Oxford: Clarendon, 1933) 78–79.

25. Gomme, *Essays in Greek History and Literature* (Oxford: Blackwell, 1937) 135.

26. Herodotus 6.37.1, 8.3.2, 9.25.

27. Pritchett 1971–1991: 4.29.

28. Homer, *Iliad* 13.145–148, trans. Lattimore (slightly modified).

29. Xenophon, *Hellenika* 4.3.19; Homer, *Iliad* 4.446–451 = 8.60–65, trans. Lattimore (slightly modified); Xenophon, *Agesilaos* 2.12–14; Homer, *Iliad* 8.66–67.

30. Diodoros 15.85.4.

31. Keegan, *The Face of Battle* (New York: Viking, 1976) 100.

32. Tyrtaios F 11.35–38; Homer, *Iliad* 8.266–272, 11.377, 507, 582, and 13.714–722.

33. Homer, *Iliad* 4.391; see Strabo 10.448 for the inscription.

34. Aristotle, *Politics* 8.3.4, 1338b, trans. Barker; Hanson, *The Other Greeks: The Family Farm and the Agrarian Roots of Western Civilization,* 2nd ed. (Berkeley: University of California Press, 1999) 262.

35. On Spartan maneuvers, see Xenophon, *Lacedaemonian Constitution* 11.8.

36. Herodotus 5.77.2.

37. Simonides 2 (Denys L. Page, *Epigrammata Graeca* [Oxford: Clarendon, 1975] 9).

38. Herodotus 5.78. Herodotus saw the monument and copied the epigram (5.77). Not one but two stone bases inscribed with this text were found on the Acropolis, one in Archaic letters and one with later letter forms. The inscriptions have lines 1 and 3 reversed. Herodotus quotes the later version. Most likely the Persians destroyed the original monument in 480 and the Athenians replaced it. I quote Fornara's translation of the earlier inscription (*Archaic Times* no. 42). For the Greek texts and a succinct discussion, see ML no. 15 (= *IG* 1[2] 394). The Archaic inscription is heavily but reliably restored on the basis of Herodotus' text and the other inscription.

39. Thucydides 6.59.3; Herodotus 5.96.1, 2.

Chapter 3. The Ionian Revolt

1. Herodotus 5.97.3; Brosius, *The Persians* (London: Routledge, 2006) 23.

2. Herodotus 5.30.1.

3. Herodotus 5.30.4.

4. Herodotus 5.35.2; Cawkwell 2005: 69–70.

5. For the earliest mention of a trireme, see Hipponax F 28 West.

6. For Xerxes' navy, see Herodotus 7.184.

7. Polykrates, Herodotus 3.39, 44; Corinthians at Salamis, Herodotus 8.1, 43; Aeginetans, Herodotus 8.46; Athenians, Herodotus 8.44.1; Gelon of Syracuse in Sicily, the second-largest city in the Greek world after Athens, claimed to have 200 triremes ready to go (Herodotus 7.158.4), but he did not send them. Nor did the Corcyreans fight at Salamis with their 60 triremes (Herodotus 7.168), preferring to wait and side with the winner. Athenian purchase of Corinthian ships, Herodotus 6.89. Herodotus describes them with the generic word for ships, and some scholars have supposed them to be triremes; it seems to me more likely that the Corinthians sold the Athenians 20 of their outmoded penteconters. Miltiades' triremes, Herodotus 6.39, 41.

8. Herodotus 5.37.1.

9. Herodotus 5.103.2.

10. Herodotus 6.42.1, 2.

11. Herodotus 5.105.

12. Herodotus 6.1.2.

13. Herodotus 6.139.4.

14. Herodotus 6.33.1.

15. Herodotus 5.103.2.

Chapter 4. Darius and the Greeks of Europe

1. Herodotus 7.133; for Miltiades, see Pausanias 3.12.7; for Themistocles, Plutarch, *Themistocles* 6.2, Aelius Aristides, *On the Four* 184, and *Panathenaicus* 99.

2. Herodotus 6.50.3.

3. Herodotus 6.63. For Demaratus' property in Asia, see Xenophon, *Hellenika* 3.1.6, crediting the gift to Xerxes, who might have extended the award.

4. Herodotus 6.75.3.

5. Herodotus 6.45.2, 6.94.2, and 6.44.1.

6. Herodotus 6.44.1, 7.9a2 (repeated in b2), and 7.108.1.

7. Herodotus 7.120.

8. Ktesias, *FGrHist* 688 F 13 (22), translated Kuhrt 2007: 1.236 no. 58; Persepolis Fortification Tablet no. 1809, translated Kuhrt 2007: 1.224.

9. Other sources giving Persian numbers include Simonides F 90 Bergk; Lysias 2.2; Plato, *Menexenos* 240a; Nepos, *Miltiades* 4.1, 5.6; Justin 2.9; Pausanias 4.25.4.

10. Herodotus 9.27.5.

11. Pliny, *Natural History* 18.43.

12. Homer, 4.601–608 from *The Odyssey of Homer, Translated and with an Introduction by Richmond Lattimore,* copyright © 1965, 1967 by Richmond Lattimore; reprinted by permission of HarperCollins Publishers.

13. Plato, *Menexenos* 240b. In the *Laws,* Plato said simply that the penalty for failure would be death (698c).

14. Herodotus 6.96; Plutarch, *Moralia* 869B.

15. Thucydides 3.104.

16. Herodotus 6.97.2.

17. *IG* 11.2.154A.51–52 (restored), 153.7 (restored), 161B.96 (which specifies that the torque lay against the wall), 164A.34, 199B.24.

18. For the inscribed column from Thebes, see Vassilis L. Aravantinos, "A New Inscribed *Kioniskos* from Thebes," *Annual of the British School at Athens* 101 (2006): 369–377. Aravantinos takes "loosening" as referring to the ransoming of captives after the 506 battle, which means the Thebans commemorated a loss. I prefer Kurt Raaflaub's suggestion that it refers to the liberation of Chalcis, not mentioned in Herodotus; *The Discovery of Freedom in Ancient Greece* (Chicago: University of Chicago Press, 2004) 117.

19. Herodotus 6.101.2.

20. Euripides, *Phoenician Women* 1179–1186, trans. W. P. Childs. Herodotus 6.101.2. For the Eretrians' reward, see Plutarch, *Moralia* 510B. By "the only Eretrian to medize" (*Anabasis* 7.8.8 and *Hellenika* 3.1.6), Xenophon might refer to some otherwise unattested action in 480, but it would be odd for an Athenian to have forgotten those who betrayed Eretria in 490.

21. Philostratus, *Life of Apollonius* 1.24.

Chapter 5. The Armies Arrive at Marathon

1. Plato, *Laws* 698d. Another version, found in the first-century historian Diodoros 10.27, says that Datis demanded the return of what was rightfully his, for the Athenians had driven out their king Medos, who had migrated to Asia and founded the Median people. If the Athenians surrendered, Datis said, he would forgive them; but if they resisted, they would suffer a worse fate than the Eretrians had. In its present form, this story is anachronistic, for the tradition of an Athenian named Medos, son of Medea and Aigeus, is not attested until later. The earlier version connecting the Medes to Medea, reflected in Herodotus 7.62, says nothing about this son, and only has her coming to Athens for

protection after she killed her sons and left Corinth, where her lover Jason had abandoned her for a chance to marry the Corinthian king's daughter (see Euripides, *Medea*).

2. Plato, *Laws* 698d.

3. Athenian numbers according to late sources: Not more than 9,000, including the old and the slaves, Pausanias 10.20.2; 9,000, Nepos, *Miltiades* 5 and *Suda*, s.v. *Hippias* (I); 10,000, Justin 2.9. For the Athenians at Plataea, Herodotus 9.28.6–29.

4. Aristotle, *Rhetoric* 1411 a 9–10; Demosthenes 19.303; Plutarch, *Moralia* 628E; schol. Aristeides 2.219.

5. Herodotus 6.107.4.

6. Plutarch, *Aristeides* 5; Herodotus 9.80.1–2, 83.

7. Mitford, *The History of Greece*, 3rd ed. (London: Cadell, 1795) 2.97.

8. P. J. Rhodes and Robin Osborne, *Greek Historical Inscriptions: 404–323 BC* (Oxford: Oxford University Press, 2003) no. 88 lines 39–46.

9. Green, *The Greco-Persian Wars* (Berkeley: University of California Press, 1996) 32 n.

10. Xenophon, *Education of Cyrus* 6.2.32.

11. Xenophon, *Memorabilia* 4.3.10.

12. Herodotus 6.105.2. According to Pausanias 8.54.6, Pan promised to go to Marathon and fight. Since Herodotus does not mention this specific promise, it was probably added to the story later.

13. Herodotus 6.106.2.

14. Plato, *Laws* 692d, 698e.

Chapter 6. The Plain of Marathon

1. Chandler, *Travels in Greece* (Oxford: Clarendon, 1776) 162; Clarke 1818: 7.37–38.

2. Leake 1841: 86; Dodwell, *A Classical and Topographical Tour through Greece, during the Years 1801, 1805, and 1806* (London: Rodwell and Martin, 1819) 163.

3. Pritchett, "Marathon Revisited," in *Studies in Ancient Greek Topography*, vol. 1 (Berkeley: University of California Press, 1965) 84.

4. Personal email from Boris Rankov, February 12, 2008.

5. Pausanias 1.32.3–7.

6. Pindar, *Pythian* 8.79.

7. Lucian, *Assembly of the Gods* 7; Strabo, *Geography* 8.377.

8. The inscription is *IG* 1(3) 3 (the regulations for the Herakleia), trans. Vanderpool.

9. E. V. Vanderpool, "Regulations for the Herakleian Games at Marathon," in *Studies Presented to Sterling Dow on his Eightieth Birthday*, ed. Alan L. Boegehold (Durham, N.C.: Duke University, 1984) 296.

10. Pritchett 1965: 88.

11. Marinatos, "Further Discoveries at Marathon," *Archaiologika Analekta ex Athenon/Athens Annals of Archaeology* 3 (1970): 349.

12. Clarke 1818: 7.18; Byron, *The Works of Lord Byron* (London: Murray, 1821) 154; Legrand, "Biographie de Louis-François-Sebastian Fauvel, Antiquaire et Consul (1753–1838)," *Revue Archeologique* 3rd ser. 30 (1897): 56.

13. Mary Nisbet Ferguson and John Patrick Nisbet Hamilton Grant, *The Letters of Mary Nisbet of Dirleton, Countess of Elgin* (London: Murray, 1926) 204.

14. Finlay, "On the Battle of Marathon," *Transactions of the Royal Society of Literature of the United Kingdom* 3 (1839): 365; Neroulos, translated in Petrakos 1996: 186 n. 43.

15. Pausanias 1.29.4.

16. Clarke 1818: 7.23.

17. Dodwell, *Classical and Topographical Tour* 2.159 and 160.

18. Gell, *The Itinerary of Greece; Containing One Hundred Routes in Attica, Boeotia, Phocis, Locris, and Thessaly* (London: Rodwell and Martin, 1819) 59.

19. Hammond 1973: 176–177; Leake 1941: 2.80 (repeated from the first edition published in 1929); Leake 1835: 2.431–432.

20. Forsdyke, "Some Arrow-Heads from the Battlefield of Marathon," *Proceedings of the Society of Antiquaries of London* 32 (1919–1920): 147; Hammond 1973: 177 n.2.

21. Leake 1841: 2.101.

22. Hauptmann von Eschenburg, *Topographische, Archaeologische, und Militärische Betrachtungen auf dem Schlachtfelde von Marathon* (Berlin: Reichsdruckerei, 1886) 10.

23. Strabo 8.377; Leake 1941: 2.96; Clarke 1818: 7.36; Frazer, *Pausanias's Description of Greece* (London: Macmillan, 1898) 2.432.

24. Leake 1841: 2.96; Frazer, *Pausanias's Description* 2.432.

25. Susan Hyman, ed., *Edward Lear in the Levant: Travels in Albania, Greece, and Turkey in Europe, 1848–1849* (London: Murray, 1988) 47.

26. Pindar, *Olympian* 13.110; Kallimachos F 90–91 Kapp; Nonnos, *Dionysiaka* 13.184; Chandler, *Travels in Greece* 163; Nepos, *Miltiades* 5.3.

Chapter 7. When Marathon Became a Magic Word

1. The chapter title comes from Byron, *Childe Harold's Pilgrimage* 2.89.7 (*The Works of Lord Byron* [London: Murray, 1821] 113); Herodotus 6.109.2–6.

2. Bury and Meiggs, *A History of Greece to the Death of Alexander the Great*, 4th ed. (New York: St. Martin's, 1975) 159.

3. Herodotus 6.112.3.

4. Mikalson, *Herodotus and Religion in the Persian Wars* (Chapel Hill: University of North Carolina Press, 2003) 29–30.

5. Munro, "Marathon," in *Cambridge Ancient History*, ed. J. B. Bury, S. A. Cook, and F. E. Adcock (Cambridge: Cambridge University Press, 1926) 4.245–246; Plutarch, *Aristeides* 5.1.

6. Hignett, *Xerxes' Invasion of Greece* (Oxford: Clarendon, 1963) 71.

7. Herodotus 6.116.1.

8. Macan, *Herodotus: The Fourth, Fifth, and Sixth Books* (London: Macmillan, 1895) 230; Evans, *The Beginnings of History: Herodotus and the Persian Wars* (Campbellville, Ont: Edgar Kent, 2006) 182.

9. Pausanias 1.32.3; Aristeides, *Panathenaikos* 106–108.

10. Burn 1984: 247.

11. Xenophon, *Anabasis* 3.4.35.

12. Herodotus 6.112; [Demosthenes] 59.94 and Pausanias 1.15.3; Aristophanes, *Wasps* 1081; Morris, *Daidalos and the Origins of Greek Art* (Princeton: Princeton University Press, 1992) 303.

13. Delbrück 1975: 74.

14. Donlan and Thompson, "The Charge at Marathon," *Classical Journal* 71 (1976): 340 and "The Charge at Marathon Again," *Classical World* 72 (1979): 420.

15. Schute, "The First Battalion," *Royal Green Jackets Chronicle* 38 (2003): 43–47.

16. For Caesar's charge at Pharsalus, see Caesar, *Civil War* 3.92–93, cited by Delbrück 1975: 86; for the Spanish parallel, see Caesar, *Civil War* 1.82.4.

17. The standard Greek-English dictionary is H. G. Liddell, R. Scott, H. S. Jones, and Roderick McKenzie, *A Greek-English Lexicon*, 9th ed., revised and augmented (Oxford: Clarendon, 1996). The parallels I cite are Pindar, *Nemean* 1.51 and Thucydides 3.24.1.

18. Aristophanes, *Knights* 781. The verb *diexiphiso* derives from *xiphos* (sword). See also the Suda entry for *diexiphiso*.

19. Aristophanes, *Wasps* 1083–1086 mentions both the drink and the owl.

20. Herodotus 6.111.1. For the point that Herodotus always uses the verb "count" (*arithmeo*) to refer to a numerical count, see W. K. Pritchett, *Marathon* (Berkeley: University of California Press, 1960) 147. Herodotus is not referring to the order of the tribes.

21. Herodotus 6.112.2.

22. Jameson, "Sacrifice before Battle," in *Hoplites: The Classical Greek Battle Experience*, ed. Victor D. Hanson (London: Routledge, 1991) 221.

23. In the event, the Athenians could not find 6,400 goats to sacrifice, so they decided to sacrifice 500 each year instead (Xenophon, *Anabasis* 3.1.12, followed by Plutarch, *Moralia* 862 B). Aristophanes parodies the vow at *Knights* 660–661, where the Sausage-Seller vows to sacrifice 1,000 female goats to Agrotera if the price of anchovies stays low until the next day. Late sources have some curious variations: A scholiast to the Aristophanes passage says that Kallimachos vowed oxen, but goats were substituted; Aelian says that the Athenians sacrificed 300 goats in fulfillment of Miltiades' vow (*Varia Historia* 2.25). An argument can be made for either Kallimachos or Miltiades. The polemarchos was responsible for this sacrifice (Aristotle, *Athenian Constitution* 58.1), which could have led the scholiast to credit the original vow to Kallimachos; alternatively, someone might have credited Miltiades with the vow as he was the leading general. Another uncertainty is when the vow was made. Some scholars think the sight of the temple of Artemis Agrotera, near the Lykeion, might have prompted the vow before the Athenians marched to Marathon. Pritchett's collection of Greek military vows (1979: 230–239) does not contain enough Archaic and Classical historical examples to help. To my mind, such an extraordinary vow fits best in the tense moment immediately before the charge.

For Artemis' statue with a bow, see Pausanias 1.19.6.

24. Aristophanes, *Wasps* 1084. He comes close to plagiarizing a tale about the Spartan Dienekes, who when told at Thermopylae that Persian arrows hid the sun, replied simply, "Then we'll fight in the shade" (Herodotus 7.226.2).

25. Herodotus 6.113.1; Aristophanes, *Wasps* 1085; Aristophanes, *Wasps* 1081–1083.

26. For the cloud and woman at the battle of Salamis, see Herodotus 8.65, 84.2. Plutarch does assert that "not a few" Athenians saw an apparition of Theseus, armed, leading their charge (*Theseus* 35), but this is the only evidence for an epiphany of Theseus on the battlefield. The Stoa Poikile painting showed Theseus emerging out of the ground, not charging into battle. It also included the hero Marathon, Athena, and Herakles. As far as we know no one claimed to have seen them on the battlefield.

27. Pausanias 1.15.3, 32.5.

28. Herodotus 6.113.2.

29. Van Wees, *Greek Warfare: Myths and Realities* (London: Duckworth, 2004) 180.

30. Herodotus 6.113.2, 114; Aristophanes, *Wasps* 1087 (compare Aeschylus, *Persians* 424–426). For *koptontes*, see *Iliad* 11.146 and *Odyssey* 8.528. For the attempt to burn the ships, see *Iliad* 15.718–720. On Kynegeiros' death, see Justin 9.2.17–18.

31. Plutarch, *Kimon* 8.1.

Chapter 8. After the Fighting

1. Herodotus 6.115.
2. Herodotus 6.116.
3. Plutarch, *Aristeides* 5.5; Plutarch, *Moralia* 350E.
4. Philostratos, *Life of Apollonios* 1.24.
5. Dio Chrysostom, *Discourses* 11.148.
6. Plutarch, *Aristeides* 5.5.
7. Herodotus 9.83.1.
8. Herodotus 7.190.
9. Homer, *Iliad* 23.110–127, 163–169, 214–225, 250–251.
10. *IG* 2(2) 1006 lines 26–27, 69–70; Pausanias 1.32.4.
11. Pausanias 1.32.3.

Chapter 9. What If?

1. Herodotus 7.139.4.
2. Creasy, *The 15 Decisive Battles of the World: From Marathon to Waterloo* (New York: Harper & Brothers, 1851) 14.

Appendix B. The Date of the Battle

1. Munro, "Marathon," in *Cambridge Ancient History,* vol. 4, ed. J. B. Bury, S. A. Cook, and F. E. Adcock (Cambridge: Cambridge University Press, 1926) 233.
2. Herodotus 6.106–107, 120; Plato, *Menexenos* 240c and *Laws* 698d; Plutarch, *Moralia* 861E-862A (compare *Camillus* 19.3 and *Moralia* 349F).

Bibliographical Notes

Chronology

I follow P. J. Rhodes, "Herodotean Chronology Revisited," in *Herodotus and His World*, ed. P. Derow and R. Parker (Oxford: Oxford University Press, 2003) 58–72 on when Darius' heralds visited mainland Greece and when the sequence of events in Aegina began. Scott 2005: 546–552 reviews a variety of different proposals, preferring to put the fighting of Herodotus 6.88–93 after the battle of Marathon.

Introduction

The Significance of the Battle

Michael Jung, *Marathon und Plataia: Zwei Perserschlachten als "Lieux de Mémoire" im Antiken Griechenland* (Göttingen: Vandenhoeck and Ruprecht, 2006) 27–224, describes the cults, dedications, and monuments with references to earlier bibliography. H. R. Goette and T. M. Weber, *Marathon: Siedlungskammer und Schlachtfeld—Sommerfrische und Olympische Wettkampfstätte* (Mainz: Von Zabern, 2004) 78–94, has color photographs and reconstruction drawings of burial mounds, monuments, and statues. To the items discussed by Jung, add an Athenian dedication at Olympia deduced by Holger Baitinger from the findspots of two helmets, arrowheads, and pieces of a bronze bow-case ("Waffen und Bewaffnung aus der Perserbeute in Olympia," *Archaeologischer Anzeiger* [1999]: 125–139). In *The Invention of*

Athens: The Funeral Oration in the Classical City (Cambridge: Harvard University Press, 1986), Nicole Loraux probes how speakers used Marathon in the annual ceremonies honoring Athenian war dead.

Full publication details on the books listing decisive battles: Richard A. Gabriel and Donald W. Boose, Jr., *Great Battles of Antiquity: A Strategic and Tactical Guide to Great Battles That Shaped the Development of War* (Westport, Conn.: Greenwood, 1994); Paul K. Davis, *100 Decisive Battles: From Ancient Times to the Present* (Santa Barbara, Calif.: ABC-CLIO, 1999); William Weir, *50 Battles That Changed the World: The Conflicts That Most Influenced the Course of History* (Franklin Lakes, N.J.: Career, 2001); Michael Lee Lanning, *The Battle 100: The Stories behind History's Most Influential Battles* (Naperville, Ill.: Sourcebooks, 2003).

On the Possibility of Reconstructing Marathon

Anyone interested in Marathon should run, not walk, to consult Herodotus. Robert B. Strassler's *The Landmark Herodotus: The Histories* (New York: Pantheon, 2007) offers a wealth of helpful material, especially maps, in addition to a modern translation by Andrea L. Purvis. Lighter and more portable are John M. Marincola's revision of Aubrey de Sélincourt's Penguin translation (Harmondsworth: Penguin, 1996) or Robin Waterfield's version in the Oxford World's Classics series (Oxford: Oxford University Press, 1998). Both contain notes and a few maps.

Noah Whatley's paper, "On the Possibility of Reconstructing Marathon and Other Ancient Battles" (*Journal of Hellenic Studies* 84 [1964]: 119–139), blisters what he calls the "excessive ingenuity" of Oxford scholars. He had in mind above all J. A. R. Munro, whose speculative ideas in "Some Observations on the Persian Wars, I. The Campaign of Marathon," *Journal of Hellenic Studies* 19 (1899): 185–197, continue to influence popular conceptions of what happened at Marathon. Munro also wrote the Marathon chapter in volume 4 of the *Cambridge Ancient History,* ed. J. B. Bury, S. A. Cook, and F. E. Adcock (Cambridge: Cambridge University Press, 1926) 229–267.

A team of scholars has published the first volume of a welcome new commentary on Herodotus (Asheri 2007) designed to replace W. W. How and J. Wells, *A Commentary on Herodotus* (Oxford: Clarendon, 1912), which was never adequate. For book 6, the Marathon book, Scott 2005 provides a full commentary, though Macan 1895 remains worth reading. Two recent collections of essays give a good idea of current approaches to Herodotus: Egbert J. Bakker, Hans van Wees, and Irene J. F. de Jong, *Brill's Companion to Herodotus* (Leiden: Brill, 2002) and Carolyn Dewald and John Marincola,

The Cambridge Companion to Herodotus (Cambridge: Cambridge University Press, 2006).

W. Kendrick Pritchett, *The Liar School of Herodotos* (Amsterdam: Gieben, 1993), takes aim particularly at Detlev Fehling, *Herodotus and His "Sources": Citation, Invention, and Narrative Art* (Leeds, Great Britain: Francis Cairns, 1990), and O. Kimball Armayor's two books, *Herodotus' Autopsy of the Fayoum: Lake Moeris and the Labyrinth of Egypt* (Amsterdam: Gieben, 1985) and *Herodotus' Great Army and Satrapy Lists of the Persian Empire* (Amsterdam: Gieben, 1986).

Macan 1895: 2.174–233 surveys the other literary sources. Important recent books on Pausanias include Susan E. Alcock, John F. Cherry, and Jas Elsner, *Pausanias: Travel and Memory in Roman Greece* (New York: Oxford University Press, 2001) and William Hutton, *Describing Greece: Landscape and Literature in the Periegesis of Pausanias* (Cambridge: Cambridge University Press, 2005). In "The South Frieze of the Nike Temple and the Marathon Painting in the Painted Stoa," *American Journal of Archaeology* 76 (1972): 353–378, Evelyn B. Harrison collects the sources for the battle painting in the Stoa Poikile. Vin Massaro, "Herodotos' Account of the Battle of Marathon and the Picture in the Stoa Poikile," *L'Antiquité Classique* 47 (1978): 458–475, suggests that the colors of the painting may have changed over time (possibly during a restoration), misleading Pausanias.

Chapter 1. Athens' Alliance with Darius

A Desperate Situation

For Sparta's policy of expelling tyrants and restoring aristocracies, see Herodotus 5.92a.1 and Thucydides 1.18.1, defended by George Cawkwell, "Sparta and Her Allies in the Sixth Century," *Classical Quarterly* 43 (1993): 364–376, against doubters such as Paul Cartledge, who refers to the "myth of Sparta's principled opposition to tyranny" (*Sparta and Lakonia: A Regional History, 1300–362 B.C.,* 2nd ed. [New York: Routledge, 2002] 127).

On the end of the tyranny in Athens, see W. G. Forrest, "The Tradition of Hippias' Expulsion from Athens," *Greek, Roman, and Byzantine Studies* 10 (1969): 277–286, which argues that Herodotus is the best available source.

The 2,500th anniversary of Kleisthenes' reforms in 508/7 prompted a number of reassessments of this enigmatic Athenian politician. A good starting point is Ian Morris, Kurt A. Raaflaub, and David Castriota, eds. *Democracy*

2500?: Questions and Challenges (Dubuque, Iowa: Kendall/Hunt, 1998). See also the interesting study in Greg Anderson, *The Athenian Experiment: Building an Imagined Political Community in Ancient Attica, 508–490 B.C.* (Ann Arbor: University of Michigan Press, 2004).

The Persian Army

The Achaemenid Persian Empire has become a scholarly field in itself. On all aspects, see Briant 2002 and his rich Web site, http://www.achemenet.com/. Less intimidating are Josef Wiesehöfer, *Ancient Persia: From 550 BC to 650 AD* (London: Tauris, 1996) and Maria Brosius, *The Persians: An Introduction* (London: Routledge, 2006). Amélie Kuhrt has now published an indispensable collection of sources from seven different languages translated into English: *The Persian Empire: A Corpus of Sources from the Achaemenid Period* (London: Routledge, 2007).

Though Briant's survey is almost 1,200 pages long, it says very little about the Persian military, nor does Kuhrt's collection of sources include a chapter on the subject; she describes the evidence for Persian armies and warfare as "bitty" (Kuhrt 2007: xxix). Despite enormous interest in the Achaemenid Empire, no detailed study of its army has appeared. For now, see Duncan Head, *Achaemenid Persian Army* (Stockport: Montvert, 1992); Nicholas Sekunda, *The Persian Army 560–330 BC* (Oxford: Osprey, 2003); and the brief chapter by Briant, "The Achaemenid Empire," in *War and Society in the Ancient and Medieval Worlds,* ed. Kurt Raaflaub and Nathan Rosenstein (Washington, D.C.: Center for Hellenic Studies, 1999) 105–128.

For images of Greeks and Persians fighting, see A. Bovon, "La Représentation des Guerriers Perses et la Notion de Barbare dans la Première Moitié du Ve Siècle," *Bulletin de Correspondance Hellénique* 87 (1963): 579–602.

On Persian horses, see Ahmed Afshar and Judith Lerner, "The Horses of the Ancient Persian Empire at Persepolis," *Antiquity* 53 (1979): 44–47, summarized in Evans 2006: 204.

On the distance Persian archers could shoot, see W. McLeod, "The Range of the Ancient Bow," *Phoenix* 19 (1965): 1–14, supported by P. H. Blyth, "The Effectiveness of Greek Armour against Arrows in the Persian War (490–479 B.C.): An Interdisciplinary Enquiry" (Diss. University of Reading, 1977), an important study that remains unpublished. Hammond 1973: 177 n. 3, by contrast, settles on 164 yards as the maximum effective range. McLeod rebuts in "The Bowshot at Marathon," *Journal of Hellenic Studies* 90 (1970): 197–198 and "The Range of the Ancient Bow. Addenda," *Phoenix* 26 (1972): 78–82.

The painted Lycian tomb known as Karaburun II will be published by Stella Miller-Collett. For now, see the preliminary reports of Machteld J. Mellink, "Excavations at Karatas-Semayük and Elmalı, Lycia, 1970," *American Journal of Archaeology* 75 (1971): 249–255, "Excavations at Karatas-Semayük and Elmalı, Lycia, 1971," *American Journal of Archaeology* 76 (1972): 263–269, "Excavations at Karatas-Semayük and Elmalı, Lycia, 1972," *American Journal of Archaeology* 77 (1973): 297–301, and "Excavations at Karatas-Semayük and Elmalı, Lycia, 1973," *American Journal of Archaeology* 78 (1974): 355–359. Mellink identifies the tomb's occupant as a local ruler who lived under Persian auspices. Bruno Jacobs, *Griechische und Persische Elemente in der Grabkunst Lykiens zur Zeit der Achämenidenherrschaft* (Jonsered: Åström, 1987) 29–33, argues that he was actually a Persian.

The best studies of the painted wooden beam from Tatarlı are Lâtife Summerer, "Imaging a Tomb Chamber: Pictures, Choices, and Identities on the Wall Paintings of Tatarli," in *Ancient Greece and Ancient Iran: Cross-Cultural Encounters*, ed. Seyed Mohammad Reza Darbandi and Antigoni Zournatzi (Athens: National Hellenic Research Foundation, 2008) 265–298, and "Picturing Persian Victory: The Painted Battle Scene on the Munich Wood," in *Achaemenid Culture and Local Traditions in Anatolia, Southern Caucasus, and Iran: New Discoveries*, ed. Askold Ivantchik and Vakhtang Licheli (Leiden: Brill, 2007) 3–30. I agree with Summerer against P. Calmeyer, "Zwei mit Historischen Szenen Bemalte Balken der Achaemenidenzeit," *Münchener Jahrbücher* 43 (1993): 7–18, that the scene need not represent any particular battle.

Darius, the Great King, King of Kings

Jack M. Balcer, *A Prosopographical Study of the Ancient Persians Royal and Noble, c. 550–450 B.C.* (Lewiston, N.Y.: Mellen, 1993), sets out what is known about high-ranking Persians.

For the documents relating to the royal centers, see Kuhrt 2007: 488–490 (Persepolis, including a plan), 491–497 (Susa, with plans), 497–501 (Ecbatana). On Pasargadae, see David Stronach, *Pasargadae* (Oxford: Oxford University Press, 1978).

The Athenian Embassy in 507/6

For Achaemenid Sardis, see Elspeth R. M. Dusinberre, *Aspects of Empire in Achaemenid Sardis* (Cambridge: Cambridge University Press, 2003). Hasan

Dedeoğlu, *The Lydians and Sardis* (Istanbul: A Turizm Yayınaı, 2003) has excellent color photographs.

Louis L. Orlin finds the significance of earth and water in their functions in Zoroastrian thought ("Athens and Persia ca. 507 B.C.: A Neglected Perspective," in *Michigan Oriental Studies in Honor of George G. Cameron*, ed. George Glenn Cameron and Louis L. Orlin [Ann Arbor: Department of Near Eastern Studies, University of Michigan, 1976] 255–266). Amélie Kuhrt suggests that earth and water formed part of an oath-taking ritual ("Earth and Water," in *Method and Theory: Proceedings of the London 1985 Achaemenid History Workshop*, ed. Amélie Kuhrt and Heleen Sancisi-Weerdenburg [Leiden: Nederlands Instituut voor het Nabije Oosten, 1988] 87–99). Mark H. Munn finds a symbolic significance tied to a concept of kingship (*The Mother of the Gods, Athens, and the Tyranny of Asia: A Study of Sovereignty in Ancient Religion* [Berkeley: University of California Press, 2006] 222–225).

On the treaty between Athens and Persia, I find myself in almost total agreement with Fritz Schachermeyr, "Athen als Stadt des Grosskönigs," *Gräzer Beitrage* 1 (1973): 211–220.

Chapter 2. Athens' Victories over the Boeotians and Chalcidians

Kleomenes' Big Invasion

Hans van Wees argues that Athens required only those in the top three income classes to fight, but allowed anyone who had the equipment to participate. In van Wees' view, many in the lowest (fourth) class must have fought as hoplites, for the top three classes comprised no more than 20 percent of the population ("The Myth of the Middle-Class Army: Military and Social Status in Ancient Athens," in *War as a Cultural and Social Force: Essays on Warfare in Antiquity*, ed. Tonnes Bekker-Nielsen and Lise Hannestad [Copenhagen: Det Kongelige Danske Videnskabernes Selskab, 2001] 45–71, and "Mass and Elite in Solon's Athens," in *Solon of Athens: New Historical and Philological Approaches*, ed. Josine H. Block and André P. M. H. Lardinois [Leiden: Brill, 2006] 351–389). Victor Davis Hanson paints a more traditional view of Athenian hoplites as middling farmers in *The Other Greeks: The Family Farm and the Agrarian Roots of Western Civilization*, 2nd ed. (Berkeley: University of California Press, 1999).

G. E. M. de Ste. Croix, *The Origins of the Peloponnesian War* (Ithaca, N.Y.: Cornell University Press, 1972), champions the common view of the Peloponnesian League as a tightly organized body with a constitution and a standard oath. Donald Kagan, *The Outbreak of the Peloponnesian War* (Ithaca, N.Y.: Cornell University Press, 1969), represents the minority view that the alliance was loosely organized and intended primarily for defense, with a common oath that was not well enforced. Recently some scholars have suggested that the oath did not apply to all allies, or even that it did not exist until the fifth century; it is first attested in 404/3. See Sarah Bolmarcich, "The Date of the 'Oath of the Peloponnesian League,' " *Historia* 57 (2008): 65–79.

In "The Athenian Treaty in Theopompos F 153," forthcoming in *Phoenix*, I argue that Theopompos, *FGrHist* 115 F 153, refers to the 507 treaty between Persia and Athens.

Greek Warfare

Victor Davis Hanson brilliantly evokes the experience of Archaic battle according to the conventional interpretation, particularly in *The Western Way of War: Infantry Battle in Classical Greece,* 2nd ed. (Berkeley: University of California Press, 2000) and in his best book, *The Other Greeks* (1999). Hanson relies, as we all do, on the wide-ranging studies of Pritchett 1971–1991. Hans van Wees, *Greek Warfare: Myths and Realities* (London: Duckworth, 2004), and Louis Rawlings, *The Ancient Greeks at War* (Manchester: Manchester University Press, 2007), provide an alternative to Hanson along the lines I am suggesting.

Anthony M. Snodgrass' two books on Greek military equipment have not yet been replaced: *Early Greek Armour and Weapons, from the End of the Bronze Age to 600 B.C.* (Edinburgh: Edinburgh University Press, 1964) and *Arms and Armor of the Greeks,* 2nd ed. (Baltimore: Johns Hopkins University Press, 1999). Important monographs on the finds at Olympia have appeared in German: Emil Kunze, *Archaische Schildbänder: Ein Beitrag zur Frühgriechischen Bildgeschichte und Sagenüberlieferung* (Berlin: de Gruyter, 1950); Peter Bol, *Argivische Schilde* (Berlin: de Gruyter, 1989); Emil Kunze, *Beinschienen* (Berlin: de Gruyter, 1991); Holger Baitinger, *Die Angriffswaffen aus Olympia* (Berlin: de Gruyter, 2001); and Hanna Philipp and Hermann Born, *Archaische Silhouettenbleche und Schildzeichen in Olympia* (Berlin: de Gruyter, 2004).

On the weight of Greek armor and weapons, see Eero Jarva, *Archaiologia on Archaic Greek Body Armour* (Rovaniemi, Finland: Pohjois-Suomen Historiallinen Yhdistys, 1995), and Johann Peter Franz, *Krieger, Bauern, Bürger: Untersuchungen zu den Hopliten der Archaischen und Klassischen Zeit* (Frankfurt am Main: Lang, 2002). Important reenactors include the Hoplite

Association in London (http://www.hoplites.org/index.htm), the Sydney Ancients (http://sydneyancients.5u.com/), and the Hoplitikon of Melbourne (http://hoplitikon.com/Mission.htm). For Craig Sitch's reproductions, go to http://www.manningimperial.com/.

On helmets, see P. H. Blyth and A. G. Atkins, "Stabbing of Metal Sheets by a Triangular Knife: An Archaeological Investigation," *International Journal of Impact Engineering* 27 (2002): 459–473. On the spear, see Minor M. Markle, III, "The Macedonian Sarissa, Spear, and Related Armor," *American Journal of Archaeology* 81 (1977): 323–339.

For the three shields with identifiable wood, see (1) G. Seiterle, "Techniken zur Herstellung der Einzelteile (Exkurs zum Schild Nr. 217)," in *Antike Kunstwerke aus der Sammlung Ludwig, II. Terrakotten und Bronze,* ed. Ernst Berger (Mainz: von Zabern, 1982) 250–263, and David Cahn, *Waffen und Zaumzeug* (Basel: Antikenmuseum Basel und Sammlung Ludwig, 1989) 15–17; (2) P. H. Blyth, "The Structure of a Hoplite Shield in the Museo Gregoriano Etrusco," *Bolletino dei Monumenti, Musei e Gallerie Pontificie* 3 (1982): 5–21; (3) Bol, *Argivische Schilde* (1989) 3. For the shield found at Olynthos, see David M. Robinson, *Excavations at Olynthus, X: Metal and Minor Miscellaneous Finds* (Baltimore: Johns Hopkins University Press, 1941) 443–444.

On the earliest vases that apparently represent hoplites in close formation, see Hans van Wees, "The Development of the Hoplite Phalanx: Iconography and Reality in the Seventh Century," in *War and Violence in Ancient Greece,* ed. Hans van Wees (London: Duckworth and the Classical Press of Wales, 2000) 125–166, to which add a Proto-Corinthian fragment, painted by the Macmillan or Chigi Painter, found at Erythrai: Meral Akurgal, "Eine Protokorinthische Oinochoe aus Erythrai," *Istanbuler Mitteilungen* 42 (1992): 83–96. François Lissarrague, *L'Autre Guerrier: Archers, Peltastes, Cavaliers dans l'Imagerie Attique* (Paris: Découverte, 1990) 14–15, lists two dozen or so more from the late seventh through the early fifth centuries. The Beazley Archive Pottery Database can be searched at http://www.beazley.ox.ac.uk/databases/pottery.htm. Wolf-Dietrich Niemeier reports on the painting at Kalapodi in the *Jahresberichte des Deutschen Archäologischen Instituts* for 2006, available online at http://www.dainst.org/index_74507e76bb1f14a153620017f0000011_en.html. In 2007 he did not find further fragments of the battle scene.

For the debate on othismos, see Robert D. Luginbill, "Othismos: The Importance of the Mass-Shove in Hoplite Warfare," *Phoenix* 48 (1994): 51–61, defending the literalist view, and Adrian K. Goldsworthy, "The *Othismos,* Myths and Heresies: The Nature of Hoplite Battle," *War in History* 4 (1997): 1–26, arguing for the figurative interpretation.

On Greek cavalry, see Glenn Richard Bugh, *The Horsemen of Athens* (Princeton: Princeton University Press, 1989); I. G. Spence, *The Cavalry of Classical Greece: A Social and Military History with Particular Reference to Athens* (Oxford: Clarendon, 1993); Leslie J. Worley, *Hippeis: The Cavalry of Ancient Greece* (Boulder: Westview, 1994).

Everett Wheeler questions the authenticity of the inscription Strabo saw at Eretria, suggesting that Strabo depended on Ephorus, who might have invented the treaty to provide a precedent for a ban on missile fire ("Ephorus and the Prohibition of Missiles," *Transactions of the American Philological Association* 117 (1987): 157–182.

Recently Mario Rausch suggested that a competition in the war dance in armor was added to the Athenian Panathenaia festival in the late sixth century due to the Peloponnesian threat (*Isonomia in Athen: Veränderungen des Öffentlichen Lebens vom Sturz der Tyrannis bis zur Zweiten Perserabwehr* [Frankfurt: Franz Steiner, 1999] 175–177, 257–258). He may be right (the evidence is far from conclusive), but his suggestion only underlines the lack of communal training in general. See J. K. Anderson, *Military Theory and Practice in the Age of Xenophon* (Berkeley: University of California Press, 1970) 84–110; Pritchett 1971–1991: 2.208–231; van Wees 2004: 89–93.

For the earliest Athenian casualty list, see the list of names found on Lemnos, with early-fifth-century Attic letter forms (*IG* 1[3].1477). It contains the name of the tribe Hippothontis, suggesting that it is a casualty list organized according to the ten Kleisthenic tribes, as was the normal practice later. It has been plausibly connected to Miltiades' conquest of Lemnos.

On the organization of the Athenian army, van Wees (2004: 96) cites Herodotus 5.71.2 as support for his view that the *prutaneis* (presidents) of the *naukraroi* (ship captains) were responsible for mobilizing troops and ships in the 48 *naukrariai* (ship districts). The naukraroi are obscure and the prutaneis even more shadowy, but this passage does not say that the naukraroi raised troops.

The Battles of the Euripos

Keith G. Walker makes the case for Eretrian involvement in the double battle in *Archaic Eretria: A Political and Social History from the Earliest Times to 490 BC* (London: Routledge, 2004) 257–262.

For figures on ransom of prisoners of war, see Pritchett 1971–1991: 5.245–312.

On the epigram for the battle dead and the thank-offering dedicated on the Acropolis, see Greg Anderson, *The Athenian Experiment: Building an*

Imagined Political Community in Ancient Attica, 508–490 B.C. (Ann Arbor: University of Michigan Press, 2003) 151–157.

For doubts about the story that Artaphrenes told the Athenians to take Hippias back, see Amélie Kuhrt, "Earth and Water," in *Method and Theory: Proceedings of the London 1985 Achaemenid History Workshop,* ed. Amélie Kuhrt and Heleen Sancisi-Weerdenburg (Leiden: Nederlands Instituut voor het Nabije Oosten, 1988) 93.

Chapter 3. The Ionian Revolt

The Outbreak of the Revolt

The causes of the revolt have prompted a large bibliography. For a rebuttal to the claim that "the western expansion of Persia was disastrous for the Greek mercantile cities of Ionia" (Oswyn Murray in *CAH* 4[2].477), see Pericles B. Georges, "Persian Ionia under Darius: The Revolt Reconsidered," *Historia* 49 (2000): 1–39. Cawkwell 2005: 61–86 takes a much more positive view of Histiaios and Aristagoras than Herodotus does. Cawkwell sees Aristagoras as a real hero of the fight for Greek freedom, whereas Herodotus portrays him as a coward who escaped to Thrace when the revolt began to fail (5.50.2, 97.2, and 124.1). It is difficult to decide between these views, since it is unclear to what extent Aristagoras dictated the actions of the rebels, and since Herodotus has him make the boldest statement of his ambitions in a private conversation with Kleomenes of Sparta, about which Herodotus is unlikely to have been well informed.

For democracies outside Athens, see Eric W. Robinson, *The First Democracies: Early Popular Government outside Athens* (Stuttgart: Franz Steiner, 1997).

Archaic Navies

For the Persian Wars Shipwreck Survey Project, go to http://nautarch.tamu .edu/pwss/homepage/.

The best place to start on how a trireme was built is J. S. Morrison, J. F. Coates, and N. B. Rankov, *The Athenian Trireme: The History and Reconstruction of an Ancient Greek Warship* (New York: Cambridge University Press, 2000). They survey the history of the problem, report on the construction and performance of *Olympias,* and suggest possible improvements. Using a cubit about two inches longer (attested on a recently discovered Archaic metrological relief) and canting the seats by an angle of 18.4 degrees, they believe, would increase the maximum stroke length by 25 percent. Using the longer cubit would make the ship almost 130 feet long; they would also like to widen it about seven inches.

Alec Tilley continues to champion an alternative reconstruction, in which each horizontal cross-section has three rather than six rowers (*Seafaring on the Ancient Mediterranean: New Thoughts on Triremes and Other Ancient Ships* [Oxford: Hedges, 2004]; "Rowing Ancient Warships: Evidence from a Newly-Published Ship-Model," *International Journal of Nautical Archaeology* 36 [2007]: 293–299). I find his arguments attractive and his proposed oar system sounds workable to this landlubber, but I do not see how the attested number of rowers can be squeezed into a boat of his design. For the time being I prefer to stick with the majority view. But the case is not closed, especially since archaeologists have discovered shipsheds at Naxos in Sicily that are shorter and narrower than those at Peiraieus. Triremes might have come in a variety of sizes.

On the introduction of the trireme and the construction of a Persian fleet, see H. T. Wallinga, *Ships and Sea-Power before the Great Persian War: The Ancestry of the Ancient Trireme* (Leiden: Brill, 1993). Wallinga rejects as anachronistic Herodotus' ascription (2.159.1) of triremes to the Egyptian pharaoh Necho (610–595) on the grounds that if triremes had existed at the time of the battle of Alalia (540), the Carthaginians would have had them (104). There is no explicit evidence for Wallinga's conjectures that Cambyses built a royal navy with a base in Cilicia prior to his invasion of Egypt in 525, or that Darius expanded this navy before 513 and added a second base on the Aegean coast. Alternatively, and I think more likely, the king had no standing navy, but called on his subjects to contribute ships as well as their rowers (Cawkwell 2005: 255–259 defends this view). For example, when Herodotus says that Otanes took ships from Lesbos and conquered Lemnos and Imbros (5.26), or when Thucydides says that Darius used the Phoenician fleet to conquer the islands (1.16), we should understand that the Persians used Lesbian and Phoenician ships, not merely Lesbian and Phoenician rowers. Van Wees' attempted compromise (2004: 206)—the Persian king directed and paid for the Greeks' shipbuilding, but allowed them to keep the ships— seems to me conceivable but unlikely.

Most scholars have regarded the numbers Herodotus gives for the Persian fleet as patriotic exaggerations or round numbers meaning only "a large fleet" (Cawkwell 2005: 260–267 is a good recent example). Alternatively, H. T. Wallinga proposes that the triremes were not fully manned (*Xerxes' Greek Adventure: The Naval Perspective* [Leiden: Brill, 2005] 32–46).

The Course of the Revolt

For the theory that the Greeks intended to overthrow Kybebe (Kybele) and upset the Lydian ideology of the good ruler, see Mark Munn, *The Mother of the Gods, Athens, and the Tyranny of Asia* (Berkeley: University of California Press, 2006). Not all scholars agree with the identification of Kybebe with Kybele; for an opposing view, see Lynn E. Roller, *In Search of God the Mother: The Cult of Anatolian Cybele* (Berkeley: University of California Press, 1999).

Clive Foss has identified two ancient roads, with paving still extant in part, between Hypaipa and Sardis ("Explorations in Mount Tmolus," *California Studies in Classical Antiquity* 11 [1979]: 27–37 with a map on 29). He suggests that the Ephesians led the Greeks along the less common route, which reaches the Paktolos River about five minutes' walk south of the Temple of Artemis. He gives the distance from Ephesos to Sardis via Hypaipa as 100 miles. Rose Lou Bengisu, "Lydian Mount Karios," in *Cybele, Attis, and Related Cults*, ed. E. N. Lane (Leiden: Brill, 1996) 23, also shows an ancient road from Hypaipa to Sardis; it looks slightly different from either of Foss's, but the precise course must be conjectural where paving does not survive. The route via Hypaipa was presumably the sacred route used for processions from the Temple of Artemis at Ephesos to the Temple of Artemis at Sardis, which leads Munn, *Mother of the Gods* 246–247, to suggest that the guides were reenacting a religious procession rather than taking the Greeks along an unusual route in order to surprise Sardis (as Oswyn Murray suggested in *CAH* 4[2].143).

Fritz Schachermeyr suggested that Eretrians continued fighting in Ionia after the Athenians went home ("Marathon und die Persische Politik," *Historische Zeitschrift* 172 [1951]: 6). Keith G. Walker believes that Eretria kept up its support until the fall of Miletus in 494 (*Archaic Eretria: A Political and Social History from the Earliest Times to 490 BC* [London: Routledge, 2004] 278), though Herodotus does not list Eretrians among the naval forces at the battle of Lade in 494.

For the Persian siege mound at Paphos, see Elisabeth Erdmann, *Nordosttor und Persische Belagerungsrampe in Alt-Paphos* (Konstanz: Universitätsverlag, 1977), summarized by Murray in *CAH* 4(2).484.

W. Kendrick Pritchett collected a dozen examples of delays of three days or more before battles, not including this one (1971–1991: 2.154).

Two Enigmatic Figures: Histiaios and Miltiades

On Miltiades, see Helmut Berve, *Miltiades: Studien zur Geschichte des Mannes und seiner Zeit* (Berlin: Weidmann, 1937); H. T. Wade-Gery, "Miltiades," *Journal of Hellenic Studies* 71 (1951): 212–221; Konrad Kinzl, *Miltiades-Forschungen* (Wien: Verlag Notring, 1968). Scott 2005: 507–512 doubts Herodotus' story of Miltiades and the Dolonci. Miltiades' archonship is known from ML no. 6, an inscribed fragment of an archon list.

The chronology of Miltiades' career is disputed. It takes Scott almost a dozen pages to unravel the problems in Herodotus 6.40, which is textually corrupt (2005: 522–532). I agree with his analysis, which avoids adding "before" in 6.40.1 (Andrea Purvis in the *Landmark Herodotus*, John Marincola in the revised Penguin, and Robin Waterfield in the Oxford World's Classics edition all accept the addition of "before").

When did Miltiades conquer Lemnos? Herodotus tells this story in connection with Miltiades' trial in 489, without any chronological indicators. Some scholars place the conquest before the Scythian expedition (N. G. L. Hammond, "The Philaids and the Chersonese," *Classical Quarterly* 50 [1956]: 122–127, 129). Others put it about 510 (Scott 2005: 453). The unsettled conditions of the Ionian Revolt seem the most likely context to me (David Lewis, *CAH* 4[2].298).

Chapter 4. Darius and the Greeks of Europe

Events in Greece

For the story of Darius' heralds, see the sensible article by Raphael Sealey, "The Pit and the Well: The Persian Heralds of 491 B.C.," *Classical Journal* 77 (1976): 13–20, countering the once popular view that this story is a doublet of the heralds sent in 481. Mark Munn, *The Mother of the Gods, Athens, and the Tyranny of Asia* (Berkeley: University of California Press, 2006), has reconstructed an expanded story based on a combination of scattered, late sources (the earliest being the Roman emperor Julian in the fourth century AD). A priest of the Mother of the Gods, Kybele, came to Athens to address the burning of the shrine at Ephesos. He spoke to the Athenian Council of 500, which normally received foreign embassies, and demanded that the Athenians revere the Mother of the Gods and the Great King whom she supported. The Athenians threw him into the pit. Later, on the advice of an oracle, they dedicated their Council House to the Mother of the Gods, and used it as an archives building. In her review of Munn's book, Lynn Roller pinpoints the weakness of the idea: "Why would the Persians require submission to a deity who was not Persian?" (*Classical Philology* 103 [2008]: 199).

Ernst Badian, the caustic Harvard historian best known for his work on Alexander the Great and the late Roman Republic, once remarked of Athenian internal history before the Persian Wars that there are "practically

no facts known," with the result that scholars' "ingenuity and imagination
have been limited only by what the audience has been willing to believe." He
added that "these limits have traditionally been generous" ("Archons and
Strategoi," *Antichthon* 5 [1971]: 1). For lucidly written contrasting views see
M. F. McGregor, "The Pro-Persian Party at Athens from 510 to 480 B.C.,"
Athenian Studies Presented to William Scott Ferguson (Cambridge: Harvard
University Press, 1940) 71–95, arguing that no strong pro-Persian group ex-
isted at Athens, and C. A. Robinson, Jr., "Athenian Politics, 510–486 B.C.,"
American Journal of Philology 66 (1945): 243–254, identifying three major
political factions (anti-Spartan and anti-Persian democrats, pro-Spartan
and pro-Persian aristocrats, and pro-Spartan and pro-Persian tyrannists).
Michael Arnush provides an updated bibliography—there was a burst of interest in the 1970s and 1980s—in "The Career of Peisistratos Son of Hippias,"
Hesperia (1995) 64: 135–162. Arnush dates the altar dedicated by Peisistratos,
son of Hippias and grandson of the tyrant (*IG* 1[3] 948), to the 490s, providing additional support for the view that Hippias' relatives were welcome in
Athens before Marathon.

For the theory that Kleomenes was assassinated, contrast W. P. Wallace,
"Kleomenes, Marathon, the Helots and Arcadia," *Journal of Hellenic Studies* 74 (1954): 32–35, blaming the ephors, with David Harvey, "Leonidas the
Regicide? Speculations on the Death of Kleomenes I," in *Arktouros: Hellenic
Studies Presented to Bernard M. W. Knox on the Occasion of His 65th Birthday*,
ed. Glen W. Bowersock, Walter Burkert, and Michael C. J. Putnam (Berlin:
de Gruyter, 1979) 253–260, ruling out the ephors on the grounds that Plutarch says Agis IV was the first Spartan king to die at their hands. Harvey is
also skeptical that the obvious beneficiary Leonidas could have had anything
to do with Kleomenes' death since Herodotus heard not a hint of such a
scandal.

Mardonios

See Michael Zahrnt, "Der Mardonioszug des Jahres 492 v. Chr. und Seine
Historische Einordnung," *Chiron* 22 (1992): 237–280. For preliminary reports on the attempt to locate the Athos canal, go to http://www.gein.noa.gr/
xerxes_canal/ENG_XERX/ENGWEB.htm.

Datis and Artaphrenes

For the identification of Datis the Mede with the Datiya mentioned on Persepolis Fortification Tablet no. 1809, see David Lewis, "Datis the Mede,"
Journal of Hellenic Studies 100 (1980): 194–195.

The Expedition Departs

Scholars have varied quite widely on how many fighting troops Datis had. On the high end, Ernst Curtius gave the Persians 100,000 (*The History of Greece* [New York: Scribner, Armstrong, 1876] 2.235), while Georg Busolt favored half that (*Griechische Geschichte Bis zur Schlacht bei Chaeroneia* [Gotha: Perthes, 1893–1904] 2.575). On the low end, Delbrück (who paid little attention to the numbers in any source) put Datis' forces at only 10,000 to 15,000 (1887: 161). Hammond (1973: 222) and Cawkwell (2005: 88) give 25,000 at a minimum and up to 30,000 respectively, based on the size of the potential opposition forces, if other Greeks rallied to support Athens. Munro (1899: 189) thought that 20,000 Persians fought, on the grounds that one-third of them died (he believed that Datis started with 40,000, but divided his forces). Lazenby (1993: 46) and Sekunda (2002: 23) reason as I do based on the attested figures for soldiers on triremes, arriving at 18,000 to 24,000 (30 to 40 soldiers on each of 600 triremes). Frederick Maurice used the estimated water supply to arrive at 16,000 ("The Campaign of Marathon," *Journal of Hellenic Studies* 52 [1932]: 20).

Few scholars accept Nepos' figure of 10,000 for the number of Persian horsemen; for one who does, see Curtius, *History of Greece* 2.235. At the other extreme, Maurice ("Campaign" 16–17) followed Karl Julius Beloch in doubting that cavalry participated in the campaign at all. Evans, who devotes the most attention to the problem, sets the minimum at 200 horsemen (2006: 208), while Hammond estimates at least 1,000 (1973: 222). These figures represent the likely range.

For the food and drink requirements of horses, see Jonathan P. Roth, *The Logistics of the Roman Army at War (264 B.C.–A.D. 235)* (Leiden: Brill, 1999) 62.

Rhodes

On the inscription that is the only evidence for Datis' siege of Lindos, see Carolyn Higbie, *The Lindian Chronicle and the Greek Creation of Their Past* (Oxford: Oxford University Press, 2003), with a text, translation, and commentary. Michael Heltzer, "The Persepolis Documents, the Lindos Chronicle, and the Book of Judith," *La Parola del Passato* 44 (1989): 81–101, puts Datis at Lindos in 497, near the beginning of the Ionian Revolt. Burn 1984: 210–211 favors 495, as the Persian fleet headed for Lade. Higbie herself seems inclined to think the episode is fictitious, though she also explains the puzzling reference to Mardonios with the suggestion that he might have been sent ahead to transport the horses to Greece as quickly as possible (147).

The Cyclades

On frankincense, see Nigel Groom, *Frankincense and Myrrh: A Study of the Arabian Incense Trade* (London: Longman, 1981).
    For Karystos, see M. Chidiroglou and A. Chatzidimitriou, eds., *Antiquities of Karystia* (Karystos: Kronos, 2006).

The Persian Assault on Eretria

On siege warfare, see the vivid description by Josiah Ober in "Hoplites and Obstacles," in Victor D. Hanson, *Hoplites: The Classical Greek Battle Experience* (London: Routledge, 1991) 176–196, and the book by Paul Bentley Kern, *Ancient Siege Warfare* (Bloomington: Indiana University Press, 1999).

Chapter 5. The Armies Arrive at Marathon

Decisions at Athens

Robert G. A. Weir, "The Lost Archaic Wall around Athens," *Phoenix* 49 (1995): 247–258, accepts its existence, tries to describe it based on contemporary parallels, and explains its total disappearance by suggesting that the Themistoklean wall reused every block of the socle.
    Victor D. Hanson, *Warfare and Agriculture in Classical Greece*, 2nd ed. (Berkeley: University of California Press, 1998), shows how difficult it was to destroy virtually all of a city's crops. Lin Foxhall, "Farming and Fighting," in *War and Society in the Greek World*, ed. John Rich and Graham Shipley (London: Routledge, 1993) 134–145, offers something of a corrective to Hanson's view that invaders hurt farmers' pride more than their property, but she agrees with him that invasions almost never threatened a city's food supply, in either the short or the long term.
    General studies of Miltiades include Helmut Berve, *Miltiades: Studien zur Geschichte des Mannes und Seiner Zeit* (Berlin: Weidmann, 1937), H. T. Wade-Gery, "Miltiades," *Journal of Hellenic Studies* 71 (1951): 212–221, and Konrad Kinzl, "Miltiades-Forschungen" (Diss., University of Vienna, 1968).

The Persians Land at Marathon

For the suggestion that the Persians timed their arrival at Marathon to coincide with the Karneia festival at Sparta, see Schachermeyr 1951: 10–11.

Interpreters have suggested that Hippias understood the tooth as a phallus (J. Glenn, "The Dream of Hippias," *Rivista di Studi Classici* 20 Suppl. [1972]: 5–7), or as a seed (R. Drew Griffith, "Hippias' Missing Tooth [Hdt. 6.107]," *Ancient History Bulletin* 8 [1994]: 121–122). Philip Holt, "Sex, Tyranny, and Hippias' Incest Dream (Herodotos 6.107)," *Greek, Roman, and Byzantine Studies* 39 (1998): 221–241, discusses the dream in the context of typical tyrannical behavior.

The Oath That the Athenians Swore When They Were about to Fight against the Barbarians

These words are the heading (lines 21–22) of an inscribed oath usually identified with the Oath of Plataea (P. J. Rhodes and Robin Osborne, *Greek Historical Inscriptions: 404–323 BC* [Oxford: Oxford University Press, 2003] no. 88). I assume here the correctness of the case I made in 2007: This inscribed oath is instead the "traditional oath" that the orator Lykourgos says (1.80) served as a template for the Oath of Plataea ("The Oath of Marathon, not Plataia?" *Hesperia* 76 [2007]: 731–742). A description of the oath-taking ceremony (lines 46–51) follows the oath (lines 23–46), which is the second oath inscribed on the stele.

For the trumpet (*salpinx*), see Peter Krentz, "The Salpinx in Greek Warfare," in *Hoplites,* ed. Victor Hanson (London: Routledge, 1991) 110–120. To the references there add Homer, *Iliad* 18.219–220 and 21.388.

For the distinction between campaigns carried out by hoplites "in the catalogue" and Athenians "in full force," see Hans van Wees, "The Myth of the Middle-Class Army: Military and Social Status in Ancient Athens," in *War as a Cultural and Social Force: Essays on Warfare in Antiquity,* ed. Tønnes Bekker-Nielsen and Lise Hannestad (Copenhagen: Det Kongelige Danske Videnskabernes Selskab, 2001) 45–71.

"It is highly improbable," G. B. Grundy once observed, "that the Persians outnumbered the Greeks by two to one, and quite possible that the disproportion between the two armies was not very great" (*The Great Persian War and Its Preliminaries: A Study of the Evidence, Literary and Topographical* [London: Murray, 1901] 185). Others who think the later sources underestimate the total number of Athenians include Leake, who gave 10,000 Athenian hoplites an equal number of light-armed (1841: 2.222), as did A. R. Burn ("Thermopylae Revisited and Some Topographical Notes on Marathon and Plataia," in *Greece and the Eastern Mediterranean in Ancient History and Prehistory: Studies Presented to Fritz Schachermeyr on the Occasion of his 80th Birthday,* ed. K. H. Kinzl [Berlin: de Gruyter, 1977] 91); Julius Beloch, who gives the Athenians 6,000–7,000 hoplites plus at least the same number of light-armed (*Griechische Geschichte* [Strassberg: Trübner, 1912] 2.1.21); and J. A. R. Munro, who estimates 15,000 including a few thousand light-armed and slaves (Munro 1899: 189). On the other hand, Hans Delbrück, who calls the figures found in the later sources "completely unverified," thinks that "the Athenians at Marathon had at the very most 8,000 hoplites, and probably only some 5,000, accompanied by the same number of unarmored men" (Delbrück 1975: 37, 64).

For the significance of the oath-taking ritual I follow Christopher A. Faraone, who compares this ritual to sacrifices in Xenophon and Aeschylus in which the blood of sacrificed animals was collected in a shield ("Molten Wax, Spilt Wine, and Mutilated Animals: Sympathetic Magic in Near Eastern and Early Greek Oath Ceremonies," *Journal of Hellenic Studies* 113 [1993] 66–67).

The March to Marathon

Richard M. Berthold, "Which Way to Marathon?" *Revue des Études Anciennes* 78/79 (1976/1977): 85–95, defends the longer but easier route. For Clarke's description of the shorter route, including traces of an ancient road between Stamata and the modern town of Marathona, see Clarke 1818: 12–15. Eugene Vanderpool relocated this road; Josiah Ober published an article about it with maps and photographs ("Edward Clarke's Ancient Road to Marathon, A.D. 1801," *Hesperia* 51 [1982]: 453–458). If Ober is right that the road was not built until the fourth century, it was not used by the Athenians in 490, a point stressed by J. A. G. Van der Veer, "Clarke's Road," *Mnemosyne* 39 (1986): 417–418. Hammond described his day hike in Hammond 1973: 210. An exceptionally vigorous young man, Hammond later served in Greece and Albania during World War II; see his account of those days, *Venture into Greece: With the Guerrillas, 1943–1944* (London: Kimber, 1983).

For my description of what men took on campaign, I draw on my chapter in *The Cambridge History of Greek and Roman Warfare*, ed. Philip Sabin, Hans van Wees, and Michael Whitby (Cambridge: Cambridge University Press, 2007) 1.150–153.

In Cornelius Nepos, the Athenians deploy in a defensive position "at the foot of the mountain in an area with scattered trees," so the Persian cavalry would be hampered by the trees and the Persians could not surround them with greater numbers (*Miltiades* 5). Nevertheless, Datis attacked because he wanted to fight before the Spartans arrived. Johann Henrik Schreiner, *Two*

Battles and Two Bills: Marathon and the Athenian Fleet (Athens: Norwegian Institute at Athens, 2004), combines Nepos with various other late sources to argue for two separate battles at Marathon. No single source records two battles. The Suda entries under the headings *Hippias* (2) and *choris hippeis* come the closest, I suppose, but not very close. Schreiner admits that the Athenians did not win on the same day they marched out, as the *Hippias* entry says. Schreiner also admits that Nepos presents "a host of problems" (29). I lack his confidence in two battles. Schreiner's reasoning reminds me of the sixteenth-century theologian Andreas Osiander, who confronted divergent accounts in Matthew, Mark, and Luke of the raising of Jairus' daughter from the dead by supposing that Jesus raised her from the dead three times.

Philippides

For the growing popularity of barefoot running today, see http://runningbarefoot.org/.

The statistics for the modern race from Athens to Sparta are available at http://www.spartathlon.gr/results.php. Hugh M. Lee, "Modern Ultra-Long Distance Running and Philippides' Run from Athens to Sparta," *Ancient World* 9 (1984): 107–133, argues that such modern performances show that Philippides' run was possible.

On the name of the runner, see Frank J. Frost, "The Dubious Origins of the 'Marathon,'" *American Journal of Ancient History* 4 (1979): 159–163, defending Philippides, against Ernst Badian, "The Name of the Runner," *American Journal of Ancient History* 4 (1977): 163–166, defending Pheidippides.

Pamela-Jane Shaw, "Message to Sparta: The Route of Pheidippides before Marathon," *Geographia Antiqua* 6 (1997) 53–78, reconstructs the route as described in the text. The Spartathlon follows a longer route that avoids the Argive plain, on the grounds that Argos was hostile to Sparta and Athens in the 490s.

On religion in Greek warfare, see especially Pritchett 1971–1991 vol. 3, *Religion*, and Anna Jacquemin, *Guerre et Religion dans le Monde Grec (490–322 av. J.-C.)* ([Paris]: SEDES, 2000).

Paul Cartledge, *Sparta and Lakonia: A Regional History, 1300–362 BC*, 2nd ed. (London: Routledge, 2002) 132–133, succinctly summarizes the evidence for a helot revolt at the time of the battle of Marathon. To his list should be added Strabo's comment that there were four, not three, Messenian Wars (8.4.10, 362). The inscription at Olympia is ML no. 22, with additional bibliography.

Chapter 6. The Plain of Marathon

In this chapter I draw frequently on the fascinating reports of early travelers, including Richard Chandler, *Travels in Greece* (Oxford: Clarendon, 1776); Clarke 1818; Edward Dodwell, *A Classical and Topographical Tour through Greece, During the Years 1801, 1805, and 1806* (London: Rodwell and Martin, 1819); William Gell, *The Itinerary of Greece; Containing One Hundred Routes in Attica, Boeotia, Phocis, Locris, and Thessaly* (London: Rodwell and Martin, 1819); Leake 1835 and 1841. Once found mainly in rare book rooms, these volumes are now easily accessible through Google Books (http://books.google .com/). Dietram Müller, *Topographischer Bildkommentar zu den Historien Herodots: Griechenland, im Umfang des Heutigen Griechischen Staatsgebiet* (Tübingen: Wasmuth, 1987) 655–673, provides a helpful survey with excellent black-and-white photographs. See also J. A. G. Van der Veer, "The Battle of Marathon: A Topographical Survey," *Mnemosyne* 35 (1982): 290–321.

Geography

For the tragic story of the 1870 Dilessi murders, see Josslyn Francis Pennington Muncaster and Crosby Stevens, *Ransom and Murder in Greece: Lord Muncaster's Journal, 1870* (Cambridge: Lutterworth, 1989), including on page 57 a photograph of the severed heads.

W. Kendrick Pritchett returned to Marathon several times, both on the ground and in print: *Marathon* (Berkeley: University of California Press, 1960); "Marathon Revisited," in *Studies in Ancient Greek Topography* (Berkeley: University of California Press, 1965) 1.83–93; "Deme of Marathon: von Eschenburg's Evidence," in *Studies in Ancient Greek Topography* (Berkeley: University of California Press, 1969) 2.1–11.

George Finlay's map of Marathon appears in his article "On the Battle of Marathon," *Transactions of the Royal Society of Literature of the United Kingdom* 3 (1839), following 394. Hauptmann von Eschenburg's map appears in his *Topographische, Archaeologische, und Militärische Betrachtungen auf dem Schlachtfelde von Marathon* (Berlin: Reichsdruckerei, 1886) opposite 18, and as sheets 18–19 of the *Karten von Attika*, accessible in color at http://digi.ub .uni-heidelberg.de/diglit/curtius1895a/0022 and http://digi.ub.uni-heidelberg .de/diglit/curtius1895a/0023.

For geological studies of the northern end of the plain, see Cecile Baeteman, "Late Holocene Geology of the Marathon Plain (Greece)," *Journal of Coastal Research* 1 (1985): 173–185; Richard K. Dunn and Kirsten Olson, "Holocene Epoch Evolution of the Plain of Marathon, Greece, and Its Significance on Regional Archaeology and Paleoclimate Records," *Geological*

Society of America Abstracts with Program 31 no. 7 (1999): 401, abstract no. 51897, available online at http://rock.geosociety.org/absindex/annual/1999/51897.htm; K. Pavlopoulos, P. Karkanas, M. Triantaphyllou, and E. Karymbalis, "Climate and Sea-Level Changes Recorded during Late Holocene in the Coastal Plain of Marathon, Greece," in *The Mediterranean World Environment and History,* ed. Eric Fouache (Mayenne, France: Elsevier, 2003) 453–465; K. Pavlopoulos, P. Karkanas, M. Triantaphyllou, E. Karymbalis, T. Tsourou, and N. Palyvos, "Paleoenvironmental Evolution of the Coastal Plain of Marathon, Greece, during the Late Holocene: Deposition Environment, Climate, and Sea Level Changes," *Journal of Coastal Research* 22 (2006): 424–438. Petros G. Themelis, "Marathon," *Archaiologikon Deltion* 29 (1974): 226–244, anticipated the geologists' conclusion that the coastline has moved.

For the twentieth-century recession of the coastline at the former outlet of the Charadra, see H. Maroukian, A. Zamani, and K. Pavlopoulos, "Coastal Retreat in the Plain of Marathon (East Attica), Greece: Cause and Effects," *Geologica Balcanica* 23 (1993): 67–71.

The Herakleion

For the various suggestions, see H. G. Lolling, "Zur Topographie von Marathon," *Mitteilungen des Deutschen Archaeologischen Instituts* 1 (1876): 67–94; W. W. How and J. Wells, *A Commentary on Herodotus* (Oxford: Clarendon Press, 1912) 2.109; G. Soteriades, "The Campaign of Marathon according to a Recent Critic," *Praktika tis Akademias Athenon* 8 (1933): 377–381; Pritchett, "Marathon Revisited" 83–93 and "Deme of Marathon"; E. V. Vanderpool, "The Deme of Marathon and the Herakleion," *American Journal of Archaeology* 70 (1966): 319–323—which includes a translation of parts of Soteriades' reports—and "Regulations for the Herakleian Games at Marathon," in *Studies Presented to Sterling Dow on his Eightieth Birthday,* ed. Alan L. Boegehold (Durham, N.C.: Duke University, 1984) 295–296. The inscriptions are *IG* 1(3) 3 (the regulations for the Herakleia), 503/504 (the epigrams), and 1015bis (the dedication). The epigrams have their own long bibliography, but see now Angelos P. Matthaiou, "*Athenaioisi Tetagmenoisi en Temenei Herakleos* (Hdt. 6.108.1)," in Peter Derow and Robert Parker, *Herodotus and His World: Essays from a Conference in Memory of George Forrest* (Oxford: Oxford University Press, 2003) 190–202.

The Deme of Marathon

Petrakos 1996 summarizes the finds at both Vrexisa and Plasi. For the latter, see also Eschenburg, *Topographische, Archaeologische, und Militärische*

Betrachtungen, summarized in *Archaeologischer Anzeiger* 1 (1889): 33–39, and Spyridon Marinatos, "Further Discoveries at Marathon," *Archaiologika Analekta ex Athenon / Athens Annals of Archaeology* 3 (1970): 349.

The Grave of the Athenians

For Fauvel's digging in the mound, see Philippe-Ernest Legrand, "Biographie de Louis-François-Sébastian Fauvel, Antiquaire et Consul (1753–1838)," *Revue Archéologique* 3rd ser. 30 (1897): 41–66. We know about Elgin's visit from his wife's letters: Mary Nisbet Ferguson and John Patrick Nisbet Hamilton Grant, *The Letters of Mary Nisbet of Dirleton, Countess of Elgin* (London: Murray, 1926). Heinrich Schliemann reported on his work in a brief article, "Das Sogenannte Grab der 192 Athener in Marathon," *Zeitschrift für Ethnologie* 16 (1884): 85–88. Valerios Staes published several reports, including "Ho Tumbos ton Marathonomachon," *Archaiologikon Deltion* (1890): 123–132, "Anaskaphai en Marathoni," *Archaiologikon Deltion* (1891) 34, 67, 97, and "Ho en Marathoni Tumbos," *Athenische Mitteilungen* 18 (1893): 46–63. Hammond 1973: 173–176 summarizes Schliemann's and Staes' findings in English.

The exception to the rule that scholars accept the mound as the collective burial of the Marathon fighters is Andrea Mersch, "Archäologischer Kommentar zu den 'Grabern der Athener und Plataier' in der Marathonia," *Klio* 77 (1995): 55–64.

Pritchett (1971–1991) 4.125–139 lists eleven excavated collective burials containing war dead. Norman A. Doenges appreciates the point relative to Marathon, for he notes that the location of the Soros "had more to with the road system through the plain than the site of the battle" ("The Campaign and Battle of Marathon," *Historia* 47 [1998]: 13 n. 21). On the Chaironeia burials under the Lion Monument, see now John Ma, "Chaironeia 338: Topographies of Commemoration," *Journal of Hellenic Studies* 128 (2008): 72–91. In the storerooms of the National Museum in Athens, Ma rediscovered some of the bones excavated in 1879–1880 by Panayiotis Stamatakis. In this article, Ma reports physical anthropologist Maria Liston's observations on these bones.

Pritchett quotes George Finlay's 1839 letter to Leake at *Marathon* 140 n. 20. See also Finlay, "On the Battle of Marathon" 392–393.

For the arrowheads in museums said to come from Marathon, see E. J. Forsdyke, "Some Arrow-Heads from the Battlefield of Marathon," *Proceedings of the Society of Antiquaries of London* 32 (1919–1920): 146–157, and Elisabeth Erdmann, "Die sogenannten Marathonpfeilspitzen in Karlsruhe," *Archaeologischer Anzeiger* (1973) 30–58. Spyridon Marinatos describes and illustrates the arrowheads he found at Thermopylae in *Thermopylae: An Historical and Archaeological Guide* (Athens: [Ekdosis Ellenikou Organismou Tourismou], 1951).

The Tomb of the Plataeans?

Marinatos published his work only briefly: "From the Silent Earth," *Archaiologika Analekta ex Athenon / Athens Annals of Archaeology* 3 (1970): 64–66, "Further News of Marathon," *Archaiologika Analekta ex Athenon/ Athens Annals of Archaeology* 3 (1970) 153–166, and "Further Discoveries at Marathon," *Archaiologika Analekta ex Athenon / Athens Annals of Archaeology* 3 (1970): 357–366. Skeptics include Petros G. Themelis, "Marathon," *Archaiologikon Deltion* 29 (1974): 226–244, and Petrakos 1996: 65–67. Mersch, "Archäologischer Kommentar," accepts the identification, despite her skepticism about the Soros.

The Monument of Miltiades

For Vanderpool's opinion, see his "A Monument to the Battle of Marathon," *Hesperia* 35 (1966): 101.

The Trophy

Vanderpool, "Monument," reports on his identification of the remains of the trophy. A sign at the site in 2007 said that Manolis Korres later identified a block of the euthynteria, which now sits next to the column replica. The original capital and column drums have been moved to the museum. Sekunda 2002: 61 points out that a trophy marks the turning point and locates the battle correctly. Pritchett (1971–1991: 2.246–275) collects the references in the Greek historians to trophies.

Chapter 7. When Marathon Became a Magic Word

The Athenian Generals Debate

Critics have accused Herodotus of misrepresenting the polemarchos' constitutional position. The Aristotelian *Athenian Constitution* says that in 501/500 "the Athenians began to choose their generals by tribes, one from each tribe, but the polemarchos was the leader of the whole army" (22.2). A few paragraphs later, Aristotle notes that in 487/6 the Athenians began to choose their archons (one of whom was the polemarchos) by lot (22.5). When this document was first published in 1890, a groundswell of opinion against Herodotus built into a formidable wave, but over the past century the waters have calmed down. Opinion is now as divided as Herodotus says the Athenian generals were. In itself, Herodotus' account makes a coherent story. The ten generals had probably not yet served on a campaign together. They determined strategy as a group, but rotated the field command each day. The later date and uneven historical reliability of the *Athenian Constitution* do not justify favoring it over Herodotus. I accept Ernst Badian's solution: The Athenians first elected nine archons and then held a lottery to determine which of them filled which particular archonship ("Archons and Strategoi," *Antichthon* 5 [1971]: 1–34). For a different view, see P. J. Bicknell, "The Command Structure and Generals of the Marathon Campaign," *L'Antiquité Classique* 39 (1970): 427–442. Bicknell dismisses Herodotus as based on the biased painting in the Stoa Poikile; the polemarchos was the elected commander; the generals were only the commanders of the tribes, though Miltiades might have had more *auctoritas* than the others.

For the suggestion that "if the gods are impartial" might refer to Pan helping the Greeks *not* to panic, see Henry R. Immerwahr, *Form and Thought in Herodotus* (Cleveland: Published for the American Philological Association [Chapel Hill, N.C.] by the Press of Western Reserve University, 1966) 253. Jon D. Mikalson, *Herodotus and Religion in the Persian Wars* (Chapel Hill: University of North Carolina Press, 2003) 29–30, translates "if the gods make it a fair fight."

"The Cavalry Are Apart"

In his *Griechische Geschichte,* originally published in 1857–1867, Ernst Curtius proposed that the cavalry were reembarked; see the English translation of Ernst Curtius and William A. Packard, *The History of Greece,* trans. Adolphus William Ward (New York: Scribner, Armstrong, 1876) 2.250–251. Munro 1899 popularized the idea. For a spirited—and to my mind decisive—rebuttal, see Noah Whatley, "On the Possibility of Reconstructing Marathon and Other Ancient Battles," *Journal of Hellenic Studies* 84 (1964): 119–139, the first publication of a lecture delivered in 1920. The recent video programs are History Channel (television network), Arts and Entertainment Network, and New Video Group, *Decisive Battles: Marathon* (New York: A and E Television Networks, 2004) and *Command Decisions: Battle of Marathon and Battle of Chalons* (New York: A and E Television Networks, 2004).

For the suggestion that the Brescia sarcophagus reproduces part of the Stoa Poikile painting, see Vanderpool, "Monument" 105. E. B. Harrison,

"The South Frieze of the Nike Temple and the Marathon Painting in the Painted Stoa," *American Journal of Archaeology* 76 (1972): 353–378, argues that the south frieze of the Nike Temple also represents the battle. With regard to the latter, Cawkwell (2005: 116 n. 6) comments, "It is absurd to treat the sculpture as a precise record of events forty or fifty years past, and it is a refinement of fancy to suppose that the artist of the temple of Athena Nike was reproducing what he saw in the painting in the Painted Porch." Fair enough. (But who treats the frieze as a "precise record"?) The case for the Brescia sarcophagus is stronger, since it does seem to show a Greek about to have his hand chopped off as he grasps a ship.

Miltiades' Plan

Evans (2006: 190) and Lazenby (1993: 62) both propose that the Persians had sent their cavalry on ahead to secure the road to Athens between Mount Agrieliki and the sea. Vanderpool's location of the Greek camp at Valeria rules out that idea.

Scholars who accept the numbers given by the late sources for the Greeks generally put the Greek frontage at 1,500–1,600 yards: Pritchett 1960: 144; Hammond 1973: 178; Lazenby 1993: 64; Sekunda 2002: 54. Scholars who have envisioned a longer line include Leake 1841: 2.224 (3,500 yards); George Finlay, "On the Battle of Marathon," *Transactions of the Royal Society of Literature of the United Kingdom* 3 (1839): 386 (2,500 yards); Frederick Maurice, "The Campaign of Marathon," *Journal of Hellenic Studies* 52 (1932): 20–23 (2,300 yards); John L. Myres, *Herodotus, Father of History* (Oxford: Clarendon, 1953) 210 (2,750 yards).

In making the case I do for Miltiades' plan, I find myself anticipated to some degree by Leake, who wrote that "the operations of the cavalry were frustrated by the suddenness of the Athenian attack and by the narrowness of the plain, the whole breadth of which appears to have been occupied by the line of Persian regular infantry" (*On the Demi of Attica* [London: Valpy, 1829] 188).

The Run for Eight Stadia

For the length of the Greek stadion, see David G. Romano, *Athletics and Mathematics in Archaic Corinth: The Origins of the Greek Stadion* (Philadelphia: American Philosophical Society, 1993) 17. Romano puts the Corinthian stadion at about 541 feet, slightly shorter than the one at Halieis.

Delbrück 1887: 56 ruled out the feasibility of the run; he defended his view further in Delbrück 1975: 20, 83–86 n. 7. Not quite everyone has agreed with him. For the minority view, see Amédée Hauvette, *Hérodote, Historien des Guerres Médiques* (Paris: Hachette, 1894) 261, and Hammond 1973: 225. Hammond describes Herodotus' claim as "completely unimpeachable," without further argument. Hammond describes the Greeks as attacking "at the double" and claims that they returned to Athens after the battle at an even faster rate (1973: 209)!

For the translation of *dromoi* as "at the quick step," see Leake 1841: 2.212, followed by G. B. Grundy, *The Great Persian War and Its Preliminaries: A Study of the Evidence, Literary and Topographical* (London: Murray, 1901) 188, F. Schachermeyr, "Marathon und die Persische Politik," *Historische Zeitschrift* 172 (1951): 28, and Burn 1984: 249. W. W. How rebuts in "On the Meaning of *BADEN* and *DROMOI* in Greek Historians of the Fifth Century," *Classical Quarterly* 13 (1919): 40–42. But *dromoi* need not conform to either "at the quick step" or "double time." For the speed at which humans switch from a walking to a running gait, see A. Hanna, B. Abernethy, R. J. Neal, and R. Burgess-Limerick, "Triggers for the Transition between Human Walking and Running," in *Energetics of Human Activity*, ed. William Anthony Sparrow (Champaign, Ill.: Human Kinetics, 2007) 124–164. Their research suggests that we all begin to run at about the same pace, no matter how long our legs are.

I have seen Félix Regnault's brief article, "La Marche et le Pas Gymnastique Militaires," *La Nature* 1052 (1893): 129–130, but not his book, *Comment On Marche: Des Divers Modes de Progression de la Supériorité du Mode en Flexion* (Paris: Charles-Lavauzelle, 1898), for which I have to rely on Delbrück's summary. Regnault reports Captain de Raoul's methods.

Rudolph H. Storch, "The Silence Is Deafening: Persian Arrows Did Not Inspire the Greek Charge at Marathon," *Acta Archaeologica Academiae Scientiarum Hungaricae* 41 (2001): 381–394, rightly stresses that Herodotus does not say the Athenians ran to get through the Persian arrows quickly.

A Reconstruction of the Battle

On sacrifices in Greek warfare, see Pritchett 1971–1991: 1.109–115, Michael H. Jameson, "Sacrifice before Battle," in *Hoplites: The Classical Greek Battle Experience*, ed. Victor D. Hanson (London: Routledge, 1991) 197–227, and Robert Parker, "Sacrifice and Battle," in *War and Violence in Ancient Greece*, ed. Hans van Wees (London: Duckworth, 2000) 299–314.

Scholars who maintain that the Persians deployed first include Delbrück 1975: 78–79, Lazenby 1993: 62, Sekunda 2002: 54, Scott 2005: 387, 620, and Evans 2006: 176 ("If the Athenians were able to draw up their battle line to equal the length of the Persian front, they must have been able to gauge its length, which they could not do until they saw it!").

The positioning of the tribes has led to more discussion than its importance merits. Citing a lost elegiac poem written by Aeschylus, who fought in the battle, Plutarch says the tribe of Aiantis was on the right (*Moralia* 628D–E). The locals from Marathon, Oinoë, and Trikorynthos belonged to Aiantis, as did Kallimachos the polemarchos. In *Aristeides* 5.3, Plutarch says that Themistokles son of Neokles of Phrearrhioi and Aristeides son of Lysimachos of Alopeke fought side by side in the battle. They belonged to the tribes of Leontis and Antiochis, respectively. Since these tribes, numbers IV and X in the official order known later, would not be contiguous according to that order, J. A. R. Munro invented a marching scheme that would put them together: The Athenians marched out in two columns, on the right Aiantis (IX) followed by tribes I-IV, on the left tribes V-X ("Marathon," in *Cambridge Ancient History*, vol. 4, ed. J. B. Bury, S. A. Cook, and F. E. Adcock [Cambridge: Cambridge University Press, 1926] 246). When the columns wheeled right and left, tribes IV and X wound up next to each other in the center. This procedure would also explain how Miltiades managed the thinning of the center: Moving from the center outward, the Greeks took up their positions on the wings first and left the final two tribes to close any gap that was left. This procedure is easier to imagine for Greeks coming from a camp at Vrana than at Valaria. It is best to admit that we really do not know how they deployed. The story of Themistokles and Aristeides fighting side by side might be only a tale told to advance the story of their later political rivalry. Or the official order known from later sources might not have been in effect. Several variant lists exist. (Sekunda 2002: 54–58 summarizes the evidence neatly.) Or a lottery might have determined the order.

On the duration of the battle, James P. Holoka, "Marathon and the Myth of the Same-Day March," *Greek, Roman, and Byzantine Studies* 38 (1997): 329–353, challenges earlier views that the battle lasted an hour or so, at most three. Considering the distances covered in the advance, the pursuit, and the return to camp, Holoka puts the minimum at six hours. The urge to compress the time involved comes from the desire to have the Athenians return to Athens on the same day, but there was no need for that, given the time required for the Persian ships to get there. The earlier views include Burn's "minutes rather than hours" (1984: 251), Hammond's "an hour or so" (1973: 196 n. 1, citing the battle of Pydna), Petrakos' "about one hour" (1996: 12), and Peter Green's "the battle and pursuit had taken something under three hours" (*The Greco-Persian Wars* [Berkeley: University of California Press, 1996] 38).

For the view that the Greek wings formed a single phalanx and attacked the Persian center from the rear, see (for example) Hammond, *CAH* 4(2).512 ("Miltiades, having foreseen this development, had ordered his wings in such a contingency to turn back and attack the enemy centre from the rear"), van der Veer 1982: 319 ("both Greek wings . . . drew together into a single unit. They closed in on the Persian centre . . . so as to enclose it as it were in a pincer movement"), and Burn 1984: 250 ("this was an amazing performance, by citizen soldiers in the heat of battle, and must have been premeditated"). For the view that the wings re-formed separately and executed a tactical double envelopment, see (for example) Green, who writes: "The Athenian and Plataean wings about-faced, and hastened back the way they had come. They did not take the Persians in the rear (tempting though this must have been) because to do so might well have meant sacrificing their own hard-pressed centre altogether in the process. Instead, they outflanked the battle in a double-pincer movement, which strengthened the Athenian line with massive reinforcements, and, eventually, brought Artaphernes' advance to a standstill" (*The Greco-Persian Wars* [Berkeley: University of California Press, 1996] 37). For the view that the Athenians in the center withdrew intentionally, see W. Watkiss Lloyd: "It appears certain from the small number of (Athenian) slain that the victorious pursuit by the Persians here was chiefly and at best a driving in of ranks which obeyed instructions and were prepared to give ground rather than expose themselves to be uselessly crushed" ("The Battle of Marathon," *Journal of Hellenic Studies* 2 [1881]: 388). On the other hand, Lazenby 1993: 68–70 expresses the skeptical view that the Greeks lacked the training necessary for such maneuvers.

On what happened to Epizelos, see the interesting comments in Lawrence A. Tritle, "Alexander and the Killing of Cleitus the Black," in *Crossroads of History: The Age of Alexander,* ed. Waldemar Heckel and Lawrence A. Tritle (Claremont, Calif.: Regina, 2003) 127–146, with references to medical literature. On Echetlaios, see Michael H. Jameson, "The Hero Echetlaeus," *Transactions of the American Philological Association* 92 (1951): 49–61.

Chapter 8. After the Fighting

The Shield Signal

Scholars inclined to throw the story out altogether include Scott 2005: 392, following Lazenby 1993: 72–73. The skeptical tradition goes back to Delbrück. Scholars who retell the story in various ways include J. B. Bury, "The Battle of Marathon," *Classical Review* 10 (1896): 95–98; Harris Gary Hudson, "The Shield Signal at Marathon," *American Historical Review* 42 (1937): 443–459; G. B. Grundy, *The Great Persian War and Its Preliminaries: A Study of the Evidence, Literary and Topographical* (London: Murray, 1901) 190–191; P. K.

Baillie Reynolds, "The Shield Signal at the Battle of Marathon," *Journal of Hellenic Studies* 49 (1929): 100–105; and F. Schachermeyr, "Marathon und die Persische Politik," *Historische Zeitschrift* 172 (1951): 30.

The idea that the shield signal was a heliograph appears as early as Leake 1841: 2.207 n. 1. It was disproved by A. Trevor Hodge, "Reflections on the Shield at Marathon," *Annual of the British School at Athens* 96 (2001): 237–259. Hammond, *CAH* 4(2).512, suggests that the signaler used a flat disk rather than a shield, which contradicts Herodotus. Evans 2006: 174 suggests that the signaler was on a roof near the coast.

A Message for Athens

On the legend that led to the modern marathon race, see Frank J. Frost, "The Dubious Origins of the 'Marathon,'" *American Journal of Ancient History* 4 (1976): 159–163, with references to all the ancient sources. For the results in the annual Bataan Memorial Death March, go to http://www .bataanmarch.com/. For the nineteenth-century Greek folktale, see J. T. Kakridis, *Die Alten Hellenen im Neugriechischen Volksglauben* (Munich: Heimeran, 1967) 79–80, translated into German. On April 30, 2008, a version in English could be found on Wikipedia: http://en.wikipedia.org/wiki/Battle_ of_Marathon#Marathon_run.

The Persians' Voyage to Phaleron

For fleet speeds, see J. S. Morrison, J. E. Coates, and N. B. Rankov, *The Athenian Trireme* (Cambridge: Cambridge University Press, 2000): 102–106. On the specific route from Marathon to Phaleron, see A. Trevor Hodge, "Marathon to Phaleron," *Journal of Hellenic Studies* 95 (1975): 169–171. James P. Holoka, "Marathon and the Myth of the Same-Day March," *Greek, Roman, and Byzantine Studies* 38 (1997): 329–353, assesses the length of the battle and the length of the Athenians' march, concluding that they cannot have happened on the same day.

The Persians Return to Susa

For the case against the historicity of Apollonios' visit, see Scott 2005: 400–401.

Silvana Cagnazzi, "Tradizioni su Dati, Comandante Persiano a Maratona," *Chiron* 29 (1999): 371–393, compares the versions of Datis' fate found in Herodotus and Ktesias, *FGrHist* 688 F 13(22).

The Athenians Bury the Dead

On Persian war booty, see Margaret C. Miller, *Athens and Persia in the Fifth Century B.C.: A Study in Cultural Receptivity* (Cambridge: Cambridge University Press, 1997) 30–32.

See *Supplementum Epigraphicum Graecum* 49.370N and 51.425 for the available information about Spyropoulos' discovery of a Marathon casualty list at Herodes' villa in Kynouria. So far we have only newspaper descriptions based on a lecture given by Spyropoulos. On March 13, 2007, the Greek newspaper *Kathimerini* reported that Spyropoulos' son Giorgios will publish the finds: http://www.ekathimerini.com/4dcgi/news/ell_1KathiLev&xml/&aspKath/ell.asp&fdate=13/03/2007. He is quoted describing the Marathon stone as a "supreme monument to the heroized dead, from the grave and not from the mound of the Athenians at Marathon."

For the construction of the mound, see the reports of Staes listed above under chapter 6. James Whitley, "The Monuments That Stood before Marathon: Tomb Cult and Hero Cult in Archaic Attica," *American Journal of Archaeology* 98 (1994): 213–230, reexamines the finds, compares the burial to known contemporary burials, and concludes that the Athenians heroized the dead warriors by burying them in an aristocratic style that had gone out of use.

For doubts about the number of Persian dead, see Harry C. Avery, "The Number of the Persian Dead at Marathon," *Historia* 22 (1973): 757. Avery suggests that the Athenians simply calculated the ratio of Persian to Greek dead at 33.3:1. But why would they pick this peculiar ratio? For the point about Kallimachos' vow requiring a count, see Burn 1984: 251.

Appendix B. The Date of the Battle

See August Boeckh, *Zur Geschichte der Mondcyclen der Hellenen* (Leipzig: Teubner, 1855) 64–73; Sekunda 2002: 37, 50, 93; Burn 1984: 240–241 n. 10; D. W. Olson, R. L. Doescher, and M. S. Olson, "The Moon and the Marathon," *Sky and Telescope* 108 (2004): 34–41; Catherine Trümpy, *Untersuchungen zu den altgriechischen Monatsnamen und Monatsfolgen* (Heidelberg: Winter, 1997) 135–140; Hammond 1973: 215–217; Francis M. Dunn, "Tampering with the Calendar," *Zeitschrift für Papyrologie und Epigraphik* 123 (1998): 213–231. All these scholars have more faith in the evidence than does James P. Holoka, who argues that the Spartans needed at least eight days to reach Marathon ("Marathon and the Myth of the Same-Day March," *Greek, Roman, and Byzantine Studies* 38 [1997]: 350–351).

Index